TOWNSEND MEMORIAL LIBRARY
UNIVERSITY OF MARY HARDIN-BAYLOR
UMHB STATION 8016
900 COLLEGE ST.
BELTON, TEXAS 76513

What's the Good of Education?

What's the Good of Education?

THE ECONOMICS OF EDUCATION IN THE UK

Stephen Machin

Anna Vignoles

Editors

PRINCETON UNIVERSITY PRESS
PRINCETON AND OXFORD

Copyright © 2005 by Princeton University Press

Published by Princeton University Press,
41 William Street, Princeton, New Jersey 08540

In the United Kingdom: Princeton University Press,
3 Market Place, Woodstock, Oxfordshire OX20 1SY

Library of Congress Cataloguing-in-Publication Data

What's the good of education? : the economics of education in the UK / edited by
    Stephen Machin, Anna Vignoles.
        p. cm.
    Includes bibliographical references and index.
    ISBN 0-691-11734-9 (pbk. : alk. paper)
    1. Education—Economic aspects—Great Britain. I. Machin, Stephen. II. Vignoles, Anna.

LC67.G7W43 2005
370′.941—dc22   2004062442

British Library Cataloguing-in-Publication Data

A catalogue record for this book is available from the British Library

This book has been composed in Times

Typeset by T&T Productions Ltd, London

Printed on acid-free paper ⊗

www.pupress.princeton.edu

Printed in the United States of America

10 9 8 7 6 5 4 3 2 1

Contents

Preface

Thousands of books have been written on the subject of education. Most try to tell the reader how we can have both more and better-quality education. It is taken as read that this should be the goal of any sensible society. Yet is there really sufficient evidence to support the commonly held belief that we as individuals, and as a community, should be investing more in education? To answer this crucially important question, we need to turn to an exciting and rapidly advancing field of research, namely the economics of education. The economics of education is about how education is produced, who gets more (or less) education and the economic impact of education on individuals, firms and society as a whole. It is therefore concerned with an incredibly diverse range of issues, and it provides us with an analytical framework to think about questions such as: what is the best way to raise pupil achievement? What should we be paying our teachers? Why do we have a more unequal society today compared with 20 years ago? How many graduates does our society really need? This book aspires to be a definitive text in the economics of education field, providing as it does top-quality empirical evidence and discussion on a diverse set of topics that all go to the heart of this field of research, namely the economic implications of education, and why people choose to invest in education.[1]

So who is likely to want to read this book? Given the authorship of the book, much of the focus is upon the UK education system, offering an assessment of both how education is produced, and its impact on economic outcomes in that setting. Nonetheless, the messages that come out of the discussion are of much wider interest, as the authors tackle key questions in the economics of education, and education policy, which are of general applicability. The book is largely targeted at a readership with some understanding of economic issues. Indeed some of the chapters present research that is on the technical cutting edge of the field. Where possible, however, we have tried to make the book accessible to the informed lay reader and especially to those with a policy, rather than an academic, background. The result is a book

---

[1] By taking the economic approach, we realize some commentators may view the book to be limited in its range. However, we would argue that this picks up many of the key factors involved in valuing education. Nonetheless, we do also acknowledge that others may assess the value of education differently (in approach and in practice).

that varies in technical difficulty from chapter to chapter. We do not apologize for this. Indeed we feel that it represents an attempt to bring together in one volume a genuinely unprecedented breadth of economic evidence on education issues that affect us all. Moreover, we do not shy away from offering policy recommendations where the evidence supports them.

This said, there is a common theme uniting all the chapters in the book, and that is their policy relevance. Each chapter presents or discusses robust empirical evidence from large-scale data sources on individual pupils and schools, to inform the questions posed. This includes work on schools and on how much teachers matter for children's educational attainment. The acquisition of different forms of educational qualifications and the efficiency of the education system in providing these are also assessed. The book considers what payoff people get from acquiring more education when they enter the labour market and how well the education system functions to provide employers with the skills they want. It also looks at how education is transmitted across generations, considering in some detail how an individual's educational attainment is linked to that of his or her parents and to the economic resources available in the households in which he/she grows up. Moreover, rather than focusing entirely on the academic analysis of education decision-making, inputs and processes, the book also contains an investigation of the policies underpinning the UK government's attempts to raise educational standards. It thus contains research relating to a range of educational policies and discusses evidence from economic evaluations of these policies.

The book concludes by gathering together this large body of work and placing it into its appropriate policy context. Some strong policy conclusions follow from the evidence-based research route adopted by all the authors in this book and these are explored in some detail. Policy recommendations on school effectiveness, education financing, individual investment in education, government education initiatives, higher education, labour-market rewards and lifelong learning are presented.

Acknowledgements

Much of the research cited in this book originated in the Centre for the Economics of Education (CEE), which is funded by the UK Department for Education and Skills, and we are grateful for all their support. We would like to thank all the CEE researchers involved in the research programme over the last five years, which provided the inspiration for this book. Above all, we are extremely grateful to Dr Gavan Conlon, who was one of the main instigators of this project when he worked at the CEE and the Department for Education and Skills. His contribution in developing the initial concept and structure of the book was crucially important to the final outcome. He provided invaluable assistance in managing the initial discussions and the work of the various authors. Discussions with him have significantly helped in the formulation of many of the ideas presented in the book. We are also grateful to all the participants at the CEE conference in July 2003 that was arranged to discuss the contents of the book. Special thanks are owed to the numerous discussants at that conference, who invested considerable time giving us feedback on each chapter. Finally, we would like to thank Paul Johnson, Alan Krueger, Richard Layard, Steve Nickell and several anonymous referees for their insights.

Contributors

Jo Blanden is a Research Officer at the Centre for Economic Performance at the London School of Economics.

Richard Blundell is Professor of Economics at University College London and Research Director of the Institute for Fiscal Studies.

Arnaud Chevalier is a Research Fellow at the Institute for the Study of Social Change at University College Dublin.

Damon Clark is a Visiting Scholar in the Center for Labor Economics at the University of California, Berkeley.

Gavan Conlon is a Manager in the Public Services Division at PriceWaterhouse-Coopers.

Lorraine Dearden is Director of the Education, Employment and Evaluation Sector at the Institute for Fiscal Studies.

Peter Dolton is Professor of Economics at the University of Newcastle and a Research Fellow at the Centre for Economic Performance at the London School of Economics.

Carl Emmerson is Director of the pensions and public-spending research sector at the Institute for Fiscal Studies.

Fernando Galindo-Rueda is a Research Officer at the Centre for Economic Performance at the London School of Economics.

Paul Gregg is Reader in Economics at the University of Bristol and a member of Her Majesty's Treasury Council of Economic Advisers.

Kirstine Hansen is a Lecturer in Social Policy at the London School of Economics and a Research Officer at the Institute of Education.

Andrew Jenkins is a Research Officer at the Institute of Education.

Ros Levacic is a Professor of Economics and Finance of Education at the Institute of Education.

Stephen Machin is Professor of Economics at University College London, Research Director of the Centre for Economic Performance at the London School of Economics and Director of the Centre for the Economics of Education.

Steven McIntosh is a Research Fellow at the Centre for Economic Performance at the London School of Economics.

Sandra McNally is a Research Officer at the Centre for Economic Performance at the London School of Economics.

Costas Meghir is Professor of Economics at University College London and Deputy Research Director of the Institute for Fiscal Studies.

Barbara Sianesi is a Senior Research Economist in the Education, Employment and Evaluation Sector at the Institute for Fiscal Studies.

Anna Vignoles is a Senior Lecturer at the Institute of Education.

Alison Wolf is Professor of Management and Professional Development at King's College London.

All authors are members of the Centre for the Economics of Education (CEE).

A (Advanced) levels: the examinations taken at age 17/18, in the two years after the compulsory school-leaving age, that are used to determine entry to university.

CSE: Certificate of Secondary Education, lower-level examination (i.e. below O (Ordinary) level) taken in the last year of compulsory schooling at age 15/16, replaced in 1988 by GCSE.

CV: curriculum vitae or résumé.

DfES: Department for Education and Skills.

EMA: Education Maintenance Allowance, an allowance paid to 16/17 year olds to encourage them to remain in full-time education after the compulsory school-leaving age.

FEFC: Further Education and Funding Council.

FSM: free school meals, an indicator of the socioeconomic status of pupils and schools. Poorer pupils receive free school meals. Schools in poorer catchments have higher proportions of pupils entitled to free school meals.

GCSE: General Certificate of Secondary Education, the examinations taken in the last year of compulsory schooling at age 15/16, introduced in 1988 to replace O levels and CSEs.

GNVQ: General National Vocational Qualification, classroom-based vocational qualifications taken alongside or as an alternative to A levels.

Grammar: selective secondary schools that admit high-ability pupils on the basis of an ability/aptitude test at age 11.

GTC: General Teaching Council.

Key Stages: the stages of the primary and secondary schooling years: Key Stages 1 and 2 cover the primary years, with national tests taken at age 7 (the end of Key Stage 1) and 11 (Key Stage 2); Key Stages 3 and 4 cover the secondary school years, with tests taken at ages 14 (Key Stage 3) and 16 (Key Stage 4, or GCSE).

ISCED: International Standard Classification of Education.

LEA: Local Education Authority.

LSC: Learning and Skills Council.

National Curriculum: in 1988 a standardized national curriculum was introduced for pupils aged between 7 and 16. The purpose of the national curriculum was to raise standards by ensuring that all students study to a minimum level up to the age of 16.

NEET: Not in Education, Employment or Training, acronym describing young people not in work, education or training upon leaving school.

NVQ: National Vocational Qualification.

O (Ordinary) levels: the examinations that used to be taken at age 15/16 prior to the introduction of the GCSE.

OECD: Organisation for Economic Co-operation and Development.

OFSTED: Office for Standards in Education, the administrative body with responsibility for inspecting every state-funded school in England at least once every four years.

Polytechnic: vocationally oriented higher-education institution. In 1992, all polytechnics gained full university status.

QTS: Qualified Teacher Status, teachers that have the necessary credentials to be certified teachers. Such credentials include the Postgraduate Certificate of Education (PGCE), which is the main route into teaching.

PART 1
Introduction

Overview

This book seeks to provide the reader with an understanding of the key issues in the economics of education. Much of the focus is placed upon empirical research applied to various areas within the economics of education field. But a useful starting point comes from providing the book's readership with some knowledge of historical developments within the economics of education, and some understanding of the main theoretical concepts underpinning the research findings reported in the book.

The economics of education certainly has a long and distinguished history. Adam Smith (1776) alludes to the idea that one might invest in education to increase the productive capacity of society. However, it is Gary Becker who is generally considered the founding father of the economics of education as a distinct research field. In his treatise *Human Capital* (1964), he presents an analytical framework to explain why individuals invest in education and training in a manner analogous to investments in physical capital. The resulting human-capital theory is still the basis of most research in the economics of education field today, and it is certainly the theoretical framework used, or at least the starting point, for most of the discussions in this text. Human-capital theory (HCT) has of course been challenged and amended, sometimes in quite substantial ways (Spence 1973; Arrow 1973; Blaug 1976; Mincer 1974), but it remains the dominant paradigm today. It is also the case that some of the origins of what is presented in the book can be traced back to these ideas and to some of the classic writings from the 1960s and 1970s on the economics of education (like Blaug 1972, 1976; Freeman 1976; Layard and Psacharopoulos 1974; Psachoropoulos 1973; and Schultz 1961, 1963). Indeed much of the progress that has been made in the economics of education field since the pioneering days of the 1960s and 1970s, and this certainly applies to its recent rejuvenation amongst economists, has been in terms of the quality of the empirical evidence available (and the techniques used to obtain that evidence) rather than in terms of theoretical developments.

Although we do not set out a formal model of human-capital theory here (see Becker (1964) for the original statement of this), we do rehearse the basic tenets of the theory, given its importance for the economics of education. HCT represented a distinct break from the past, in that previously education was largely considered to be a consumption good. The wealthy were assumed to consume more non-compulsory education than the less well off, just as they consumed more of other goods. Education was also classified as a status good, consumed by the middle and upper classes to signal higher social standing. Human-capital theory suggested that in fact education should be seen primarily as an investment good. Individuals invest in human capital, such as schooling, because human capital makes a person more productive and this gain in productivity is reflected in higher wages. Thus it is argued that individuals primarily make investments in schooling and other forms of human capital to earn a return, i.e. to increase their income in the future. This book is an attempt to answer, in a number of different contexts, the natural question that arises from this theoretical perspective: namely, what is the economic value of educational investments made by individuals, firms and the state?

This essentially simple theory is particularly powerful because it provides a tool to analyse such a diverse range of phenomena. Firstly, there are numerous forms of human capital, ranging from formal education through to on-the-job learning or firm-provided training. Thus human-capital theory can be used to explain investments in schooling, the provision of training by firms, the acquisition of vocational qualifications, the benefits of informal on-the-job learning and the like. Furthermore, it provides a framework for analysing any policy interventions that result in investments in education and other forms of human capital. Thus when the state invests in programmes such as a youth training scheme or a smaller-class-size initiative, we can analyse the likely impact of these programmes and their expected social and private rates of return using HCT. Of course, the chapters in this book do draw on other theories that are used in the economics of education. For example, Part II draws on models from both the education production function literature and school-effectiveness research, discussing as it does the production of education in schools. Furthermore, some authors challenge aspects of human-capital theory. Chapter 8, for example, is rooted in signalling and screening theory (Spence 1974; Arrow 1973), focusing on how employers use education generally, and qualifications in particular, as potential signals of individuals' innate ability. However, human-capital theory remains the mainstay of this text and indeed of the economics of education field as a whole and we direct the reader to Becker's original work (1964).

The book is structured into four parts: "Introduction"; "Who Gets More Education?"; "Economic Outcomes and Education"; and "What Can Policy Do?". A brief editorial introduction to each of these parts is presented in the following sections.

1.1 INTRODUCTION

This part of the book contains this overview and the first substantive chapter of the book (by Kirstine Hansen and Anna Vignoles), which places the UK educational system into comparative context by highlighting features specific to the UK education system that make it of considerable interest to scholars interested in the economics of education.

1.2 WHO GETS MORE EDUCATION?

This part of the book looks at different phases of the education process. It begins with an assessment of schools and their effectiveness, offering a judgment on the extent to which schools and teachers matter for educational attainment. Chapter 3 (by Arnaud Chevalier, Peter Dolton and Ros Levacic) concludes that the school a pupil attends does matter and that the allocation of resources to schools can have potentially important effects on pupil attainment. Similarly, the chapter shows that the quality of teachers matters in determining school quality. Thus the labour market for teachers provides the subject matter of Chapter 4 (by Arnaud Chevalier and Peter Dolton). Chapter 5 (by Damon Clark, Gavan Conlon and Fernando Galindo-Rueda) moves to the post-compulsory phase of education, looking at what has happened to UK higher education in recent years, particularly its expansion over time. Chapter 6 (by Jo Blanden, Paul Gregg and Stephen Machin) then looks at educational inequality, focusing on the impact of parental education and resources on educational attainment, demonstrating strong links that persist across generations.

All over the world, people leave the education system with very different levels of education. This is certainly the case in the UK. This partly reflects different levels of attainment achieved during the years of compulsory schooling, and partly reflects decisions made by individuals on whether or not to invest in further education after the compulsory school-leaving age. An additional factor shaping why education levels at a point in time vary is adult learning, namely whether one engages in further education or training once out of the formal education system. This part of the book is concerned with who gets how much and what type of education, and the factors that determine this. From a theoretical perspective, taking account of the educational choices made by different types of individual is crucial for our understanding of the role of education in the labour market overall and of course its impact on productivity and wages. Whilst early work in the economics of education focused quite specifically on the problems of estimating the impact of schooling on wages, taking into account the fact that more-able individuals tended to acquire more education, the current research agenda is concerned with broader issues to do with schooling choices. Thus this part of the book is concerned with the education production itself, as well as the role of other factors, such as family background, neighbourhood and the like, that may influence an individual's schooling path. Before engaging with the detailed analyses of these important issues, we highlight some interesting facts about the progression of children through the UK education system.

Table 1.1. Percentage of children achieving government Key Stage targets in 2003.

	Reading	Writing	Mathematics
Key Stage 1: % achieving level 2 or better	84	81	90
Key Stage 2: % achieving level 4 or better	81	60	73
Key Stage 3: % achieving level 5 or better	68	65	70

The UK is one of the very few countries that externally monitor the attainment of children throughout the education system. Since the mid 1990s, every schoolchild in the UK has been assessed from the age of 7 onwards. There are national examinations at ages 7 and 11 in primary school and at ages 14 and 16 in secondary school. Furthermore, since 1995 the government has published school league tables of the results of these examinations, providing information on the achievement of all pupils in all schools at these ages (referred to as Key Stages 1, 2, 3 and 4, respectively). This provides a unique opportunity, in the context of the UK education system, to analyse how children progress through an education system, to identify factors that may improve that progression and to look at inequality in attainment at different stages of the education system. This provides the bulk of the analyses in Chapters 3–6.

Certainly, throughout the school years there are variations in pupil attainment. The percentage of children achieving the government's Key Stage 1, 2 and 3 targets in 2003 is given in Table 1.1.[1] At Key Stage 4 the most-focused-upon statistic is the percentage of children achieving five or more "good" GCSEs (i.e. grades A*–C). In 2003, 52% of children obtained five or more A*–C GCSEs.

There is also clear evidence that higher achievement is negatively associated with economic and social disadvantage. As Table 1.2 shows, breaking down Key Stage test scores by three indicators – ethnicity, whether the pupil's first language is English, and whether or not the pupil gets free school meals – reveals sizeable gaps in pupil attainment across ethnic groups, both for boys and girls, and shows worse levels for the English as an additional language pupils and especially for those on free school meals. Moreover, these gaps tend to widen out and are more marked at the later Key Stage levels (especially by free school meal status).

It is perhaps more interesting to consider how achievement varies as a child moves through the school system, as illustrated by looking at progression between Key Stages. Table 1.3 shows that achieving a target at one level by no means guarantees reaching the next target. Several progressions are given in Table 1.3. As an example consider the final row. This reports that, of those children who achieved level 4 or better on average at Key Stage 3, just over half (51%) went on to obtain five good-grade GCSEs.

---

[1]The source for all the tables in this section is the DfES.

Table 1.2. Key Stage attainment and pupil characteristics, 2003.

	Ethnicity						Free school meals		English as additional language	
	White	Mixed	Asian	Black	Chinese	Other	Yes	No	Yes	No
Boys										
KS1, English	79	79	75	71	85	69	60	82	72	79
KS1, Maths	90	90	85	82	95	85	79	92	84	90
KS2, English	70	72	64	61	77	59	48	74	62	70
KS2, Maths	74	73	68	60	88	68	54	77	66	73
KS3, English	63	62	59	47	74	53	36	67	54	63
KS3, Maths	71	67	65	51	89	64	46	74	62	70
GCSE 5+ A*–C	46	43	47	29	71	41	20	50	43	46
Girls										
KS1, English	88	88	81	82	93	77	74	91	81	88
KS1, Maths	92	92	87	85	96	86	82	94	84	86
KS2, English	81	82	75	74	87	68	61	84	72	81
KS2, Maths	72	72	65	61	89	66	52	76	64	72
KS3, English	77	76	73	65	86	65	52	80	68	77
KS3, Maths	73	71	66	57	90	65	47	76	63	73
GCSE 5+ A*–C	57	55	59	43	79	51	29	61	54	56

Table 1.3. Percentage of children who achieved a target who achieve the next target.

Progression	Subject	Time Period	Percentage of those who achieved earlier target who achieve the next target
KS1 to KS2	English	1998–2002	68
KS1 to KS2	Mathematics	1998–2002	65
KS2 to KS3	English	1999–2002	78
KS2 to KS3	Mathematics	1999–2002	83
KS3 to KS4	5+ A*–C GCSEs	2000–2002	51

This illustrates that children's attainment and progression is altered as the child experiences different phases of the schooling system, as he or she attends different schools and is taught by different teachers. The first two chapters of this part of the book focus on two themes that matter most for pupil attainment and progression. Chapter 3 considers school and teacher effectiveness and how it impacts upon pupil attainment, whilst Chapter 4 considers the crucially important labour market for teachers.

Moving to the post-compulsory schooling phase discussed in Chapter 5, it has already been shown that there has been a sharp expansion in the numbers of UK children who stay on in the schooling system after the compulsory school-leaving age (Chapter 2). Whilst arguably still low relative to participation rates in other advanced countries, around 70% of children in the UK now stay on past the age of 16 and around half of these go on to higher education at age 18/19. Chapter 5 looks in detail at patterns of change in participation in post-compulsory education and at qualification attainment. Here we are interested not just in the quantity of education acquired, but also the type of education. A particular focus is placed upon the economic mechanisms that underpin the large changes in the level and type of post-16 participation that have occurred. Similarly, the role played by education policy is prominent in the discussion.

The other notable observation is that this sharp expansion of post-compulsory education does not seem to have been equally distributed across socioeconomic groups, as it has been concentrated upon children from higher social classes, or from families with higher incomes. This is contrary to views held by some, namely that education, or access to education, acts as a great leveller in society. In Chapter 6 the changing links between education participation and family income are considered. Strong evidence is presented showing that, during the period of higher-education expansion in the UK, links between education and parental income actually strengthened, revealing a significant rise in educational inequality. Rather than education reducing inequality, this then has resulted in a rise in inequality across generations as children from more-educated (and higher-income) parents have increasingly colonized the upper echelons of the education system.

1.3 ECONOMIC OUTCOMES AND EDUCATION

This part of the book contains three chapters on the economic impact of education. It begins with Chapter 7 (by Richard Blundell, Lorraine Dearden and Barbara Sianesi), which considers a very important subject in the economics of education, namely what are the best methods of evaluating the value of education. They provide a careful and detailed discussion of the economic benefits relative to the costs of investment in education, and of how one can best measure such returns. Chapter 8 (by Andrew Jenkins and Alison Wolf) considers what employers want in terms of education. This is important given what has happened to the labour market in recent years, where employers' demand for workers with educational qualifications has risen. The chapter studies the reasons why this may be so. Chapter 9 (by Steven McIntosh) concludes this part with an assessment of how well the education system meets the needs of the labour market.

It has long been established that education yields economic benefits and, as Part II of the book makes clear, one of the reasons why people undertake education is that they perceive there to be a rate of return associated with their investment. But how does the market for education result in such returns, particularly if many more people now possess more and higher-quality qualifications than in the past? This is the subject matter of this part of the book, in which the various chapters look at the wage returns from education, the way that employers view qualifications, and the extent to which the education system is able to meet the needs of the labour market.

It is evident that the labour force is today more educated – in terms of formal educational qualifications – than in the past. Consider Table 1.4, which shows how the distribution of educational qualifications has changed over time in the UK.

The table confirms that there has been rapid upgrading of the educational status of the workforce since 1975. The percentage of men with a postsecondary degree rose from 5.8% in 1975 to 16.3% in 1998. Similarly, the share of men with a higher vocational qualification went up rapidly from 4.7% to 12.1%. But most striking is the falling proportion of men with no qualifications, which goes down from just over half (at 50.2%) in 1975 to less than 20% (18.9%) in 1998.

The patterns for women are even more marked. The percentage with a postsecondary degree rises over fivefold from a very low initial level of 2.2% in 1975 up to 12.5% in 1998. Interestingly there is much less of a shift into higher vocational qualifications compared with men as only 2.7% of working women possess such qualifications in 1998. Again, there is a sharp fall in the percentage with no qualifications, which plummets from 58.3% in 1975 to 23.3% in 1998.

Table 1.4. Employment shares (per cent) by education, 1975–1998.

	1975	1980	1985	1990	1995	1998
Men						
Postsecondary degree or higher	5.8	8.2	12.1	12.5	15.5	16.3
Higher vocational	4.7	6.8	10.5	11.4	11.7	12.1
Teaching and nursing	1.2	1.3	1.4	1.2	1.3	2.0
Intermediate	38.3	41.2	40.7	47.9	50.7	50.7
No qualifications	50.2	42.6	35.4	27.1	20.7	18.9
Women						
Postsecondary degree or higher	2.2	3.6	6.2	7.5	10.8	12.5
Higher vocational	0.7	1.3	2.0	2.9	3.8	2.7
Teaching and nursing	5.8	6.8	8.4	7.9	7.4	7.7
Intermediate	33.1	39.6	46.5	52.1	54.3	53.7
No qualifications	58.3	48.8	36.8	29.6	23.6	23.3

Notes. Calculated from successive General Household Surveys. For 1975–1995, statistics are based on three pooled years with the central year reported in the table. Source: updated from Machin (2003).

Given these large changes a natural assumption would be that this sharp increase in the supply of more-educated workers should depress wage gaps between more highly qualified and less qualified workers and thus lower the wage return to education. The logic here is simple, namely that because there are now more workers with higher education, employers have more of them to choose amongst and this increased competition for higher-education jobs should lower their relative wages. But this simply has not happened. Consider Table 1.5, which (now lumping men and women together) shows that, in both the UK and the US, at the same time as graduate employment shares rose so significantly the wage differentials between graduates and non-graduates did not fall and in fact rose. The table shows that the relative wages of graduates versus non-graduates for full-time workers (after standardizing for age and gender from a statistical regression) rose between 1980 and 2000. The increase is very sharp in the US, going from 1.36 to 1.66, whilst the UK increase is less marked but still shows a rise from 1.48 to 1.64.

It is by now fairly well established that these patterns are due to relative demand growing faster than relative supply. Hence it seems that increased education supply has not resulted in falling wage differentials between more- and less-educated people. A plausible, and attractive, way of thinking about this is in terms of an economic model where the wages and employment of skilled and unskilled workers are the outcomes of a race between supply and demand. In this context, to have generated simultaneously higher wages and employment for the skilled, relative demand must have increased by more than relative supply. Put alternatively, demand must have won the race between demand and supply so that employers are prepared to pay

Table 1.5. Aggregate trends in graduate/non-graduate employment and relative wages, UK and US 1980–2000.

	UK Labor Force Survey/ General Household Survey		US Current Population Survey	
	% graduate share of employment	Relative weekly wage (full-time)	% graduate share of employment	Relative weekly wage (full-time)
1980	5.0	1.48	19.3	1.36
1985	9.8	1.50	22.0	1.47
1990	10.2	1.60	23.8	1.55
1995	14.0	1.60	25.5	1.61
2000	17.2	1.64	27.5	1.66
1980–2000	12.2	0.12	8.2	0.30
1980–1990	5.2	0.08	4.5	0.19
1990–2000	7.0	0.04	3.7	0.11

Notes. Source: Machin (2003).

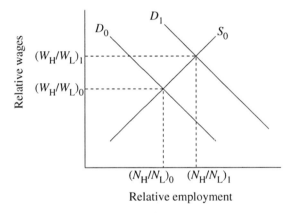

Figure 1.1. Shifts in relative supply and demand.

workers with appropriate skills and education more than less-educated workers, despite there being many more of them supplying their labour.

One straightforward way to rationalize this is to think of the changes in the context of a simple relative demand and supply framework as in Figure 1.1. The figure shows a labour market with two skill types: highly educated (denoted by an "H" subscript) and less educated (denoted by an "L" subscript). The initial equilibrium in the model is given by the intersection of the relative labour demand and supply curves given by D_0 and S_0 in the figure, with a relative wage of $(W_H/W_L)_0$ and relative employment of $(N_H/N_L)_0$.

In terms of the UK and US experience what seems to have happened is that the ratio of high- to low-education wages has gone up at the same time as the ratio of high- to low-education employment. It becomes evident that, to get such an outcome, there has to have been an outward shift in the relative demand curve. Suppose the demand curve shifts out to D_1 (and hold supply fixed for expositional purposes[2]). One then ends up with simultaneously higher relative wages and employment for the skilled at $(W_H/W_L)_1$ and $(N_H/N_L)_1$.

This feature of modern education and labour markets is by now well known. But we need to know more about the magnitude of wage returns, and why employers increasingly demand graduates in such large numbers to offset the rapidly rising supply. This is the subject matter covered in detail by the three chapters in this part of the book.

1.4 WHAT CAN POLICY DO?

This part of the book offers an assessment of where we stand on education, its economic impact and education policy. It starts with an important subject for policy by offering a chapter (by Carl Emmerson, Sandra McNally and Costas Meghir) on how one can best evaluate education policies. The chapter discusses methodological issues, and provides examples from recent education initiatives. Chapter 11 (written by Stephen Machin and Anna Vignoles) is a final concluding chapter that spells out the lessons from the rest of the book that are relevant for the design of education policy. It offers a discussion of what seems to work best and how this links up with theoretical considerations on the key questions in the economics of education field.

---

[2]One can easily move the supply curve as well, but as long as relative supply has shifted to a lesser extent, one will still see higher relative wages and employment for skilled workers.

The United Kingdom Education System in a Comparative Context

By Kirstine Hansen and Anna Vignoles

2.1 INTRODUCTION

This chapter describes the key features of the UK's education system[1] and places the system in an international comparative context. We identify areas of strength and weakness in the system, relative to other countries, and raise and introduce a host of key questions and issues that are addressed in more detail in later chapters. Of course, to do this we have to select certain aspects of the UK education system to analyse, and we also have to identify a group of countries against which to make comparisons. Although the comparator countries are largely determined by data availability, one is open to the accusation that there is subjectivity in the selection of both the educational indicators we use and the choice of comparator countries. For example, we do not include some important Asian economies in our analysis (Ashton *et al.* 1999). We merely note this as the main methodological difficulty inherent in international comparisons of this nature.

The structure of the chapter is as follows. It begins by discussing the main features of the UK education system, including recent major reforms and resource-allocation issues. It then goes on to analyse how the outputs from the UK education system compare with the outputs from the education systems of other countries. In particular, there is a discussion of the relative effectiveness of the outputs from the system, in terms of cost effectiveness and value in the labour market. Lastly, some conclusions, with a mind to what follows in the remainder of the book, are offered.

2.2 MAIN FEATURES OF THE UK EDUCATION SYSTEM

To understand how effective the UK education system is, relative to other countries, it is important to have some idea of the institutional setting in the UK, and the

---

[1] Where possible we discuss the UK. Readers should be aware that the education system in Scotland is quite distinct from in the rest of the UK and much of the discussion applies to England and Wales.

changes that the system has experienced in recent years. Throughout the post-war period, there have been many attempts to reform the UK education system and make it more productive. The list of reforms that have been attempted over the last 50 years is quite extensive, and recently the UK (and in particular England and Wales) has introduced many innovative market-oriented reforms to its education system, in an attempt to raise standards.

The UK spends relatively little on education compared with other OECD countries (4.9% of GDP (gross domestic product) in 2002, compared with an OECD mean of 5.7%). However, the reform experience of the UK education system is of broader interest to policy makers and researchers from other countries. For example, as in many other countries there has been a push to expand post-compulsory participation in education, especially in terms of increasing participation in higher education. However, perhaps the most striking recent reform (in England and Wales in particular) is that parents have increasingly been given much more choice in terms of the school attended by their children, and schools have been forced to be more accountable. Both these trends are discussed, before moving on to consider other facets of the UK education system, such as the role of the private sector, the provision of vocational education and adult learning.

2.2.1 Widening Access and Educational Inequality

Many twentieth century reforms to the UK education system have been designed to widen access to what has historically been thought of as an extremely elitist system. We start with a discussion about state-funded education only; later we discuss the important issue of private schooling in the UK.[2]

School fees for elementary students were abolished in 1918, although the vast majority of students continued to leave school at 14 (the compulsory school-leaving age at that time). Post-war, in response to the need for a more educated workforce, the school-leaving age was raised, in 1947, to age 15 and eventually, in 1973, to the age of 16. Despite these developments, the UK system remained fundamentally elitist, with only around 12% of students staying on past the compulsory school-leaving age in 1960.

During the 1960s and 1970s, UK secondary schools underwent a period of radical change, in a further attempt to widen access. Prior to this period, students of differing abilities were sent to different types of school, receiving very different types of education. "Clever" students (i.e. the relatively small proportion who passed an age 11 entry exam) were sent to state-sponsored academically orientated schools called "grammar schools". These students were considerably more likely to

---

[2] See Green (2003) for a discussion of the political economy of the UK education system, and the role of the privately educated elite.

go on to higher education (HE). Most other students attended "secondary modern schools", undertaking a range of vocationally orientated subjects, and eventually leaving the educational system at the age of 15 (or 16 after 1973). During the 1960s, however, there was a growing movement in favour of mixed-ability or "comprehensive" schooling. This sparked off an ideological battle that was to rage for the next 20 years or more, between those who favoured the old selective grammar-school system and those who wanted comprehensive schooling. Today in the UK most secondary-school pupils are taught in mixed-ability schools. However, many of today's mixed-ability schools "stream" their pupils, that is they allocate them to classes according to their ability. This is discussed in more detail in Chapter 3 on school and teacher effectiveness.

In the 1980s another quite distinctive feature of the English, Welsh and Northern Irish education systems was also subject to major reform, namely the system of national public examinations (Scotland has a somewhat different system). Since the 1950s, secondary-school students who were academically inclined (grammar students) took O (ordinary) level (age 16) and A (advanced) level (age 18) examinations.[3] O and A levels were an essential requirement to enter higher education. Less-academic pupils could take Certificates of Secondary Education (CSE) at 16 before they left school. In 1988 the O level and CSE exams were combined into GCSEs (General Certificates of Secondary Education), still taken at age 16. This was not just a change of name. It marked a turning point in the measured achievement of 16 year olds in the UK. The fact that all students at 16 now take the same examination in each subject means that they no longer have to decide whether to go for the lower-level CSE option or the more difficult O level examination. This may have encouraged those who are academically on the borderline between CSE and O level to aim for a higher level of attainment. Certainly, GCSEs have proved more accessible than O levels and considerably more students now leave school with at least some GCSE qualifications. Furthermore, the drop-out rate is much reduced. In the late 1980s just 35% of 16–18 year olds in England and Wales were in full-time education. By the late 1990s this had increased to 55%. These issues are taken further in Chapter 5 on post-compulsory schooling and qualifications and Chapter 6 on intergenerational mobility.

In the 1990s, the focus shifted to higher education. Prior to 1992, there were two types of higher-education institutions, polytechnics and universities. Polytechnics tended to focus on more vocationally oriented higher education. Universities were more academically focused. In 1992 these institutions were merged and all called universities. This, along with the rising staying-on rate and increased achievement

---

[3] These are national public examinations marked by independent assessors.

at 16–18, led to a marked expansion of the HE participation rate.[4] In the late 1980s around 20% of the age cohort participated in HE in the UK. This had risen to more than one-third in the early 2000s. This expansion is all the more remarkable given the steady erosion of state subsidy of students in higher education (e.g. the abolition of student grants) and, as is discussed further in Chapter 5, the introduction of tuition fees in 1998.

Despite the various policies introduced to widen access, what remains quite distinctive about the UK is the extent to which educational attainment is still related to socioeconomic background, and in particular parental education and income (this is analysed in depth in Chapter 6). It is difficult to make international comparisons on this issue because data on the relationship between family background and educational achievement *across different countries* is remarkably sparse. The limited international data that are available also suggest that the UK is somewhat more unequal than other countries in terms of access to HE in particular. For example, the International Adult Literacy Survey (IALS) suggests that, across all the countries surveyed[5], having a father with a postsecondary degree means an individual is 42% more likely to have a postsecondary degree. In the UK this probability increases to 47%. By contrast, in Sweden this probability is 35%. The IALS data used for this analysis only include a limited number of countries, however.

More-recent OECD data cover a larger sample of countries but confirm the basic finding that educational attainment is more strongly linked to socioeconomic background in the UK, compared with many other countries. For example, Figure 2.1 shows that a larger proportion of the variation in children's educational outcomes is attributable to their socioeconomic background in the UK compared with most other European countries.

We also know that in the UK the gap in participation between rich and poor has been present for a long time, as shown in Figure 2.2. Currently in the UK 48% of young people from professional, managerial and skilled non-manual backgrounds enter university, whilst only 18% from a skilled manual or unskilled background do so.

2.2.2 Market Reforms

In addition to concerns about widening access and educational inequality, in the 1980s there emerged widespread fears about poor and falling standards in UK education. Successive Conservative governments in the 1980s and 1990s increased the

---

[4]The "higher-education participation rate" is calculated by the DfES and is designed to give a reasonably constant definition of higher education over time; specifically, it is the number of students entering higher education as a proportion of the relevant cohort.

[5]Switzerland, Sweden, Canada, the US, Ireland, Germany, Netherlands, Poland, Sweden, New Zealand, Northern Ireland and Belgium.

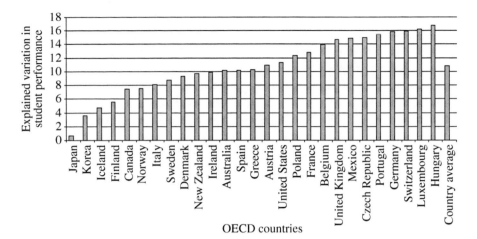

Figure 2.1. Variation in student performance attributable to International Socioeconomic Index (ISEI) of occupational status. (Source: Programme for International Student Assessment 2000.)

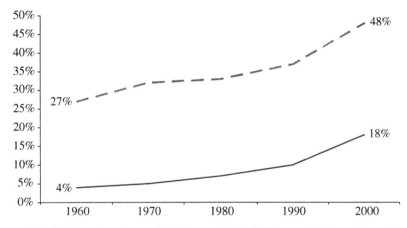

Figure 2.2. Higher-education participation rate in the UK by social class. (Notes. The top three social classes (dashed line) are professional, managerial, skilled non-manual. The bottom three social classes (solid line), IIM, IV, V, are unskilled non-manual, skilled manual, unskilled manual. Source: DfES age participation index.)

pace of reform and introduced so called "market mechanisms" into the UK education system, in an attempt to force schools to raise standards.

The market-oriented reforms aimed to increase parental choice and thereby improve the accountability of state schools. Parents could, at least theoretically, choose which school their child attended and could also have representation on school governing bodies. School funding became more closely linked to student

17

enrolment numbers, giving schools the incentive to attract and admit more students. Some schools were allowed to take control of their own budgets and be financed directly from central government (as opposed to being under local-government control). Alongside greater parental choice, policy makers also endeavoured to improve the information available to parents about the effectiveness of schools, by way of publicly available test-score information. There are, however, limits to the operation of so-called quasi-market in the UK education system. Schools are generally not allowed to go "bankrupt", i.e. exit from the market, and many parents still lack full information on the quality of schools. This weakens the incentive for schools to improve.

Some reforms have gone in the other direction, increasing centralization and reducing school autonomy and their ability to respond to consumer demand. For example, in the late 1980s a standardized National Curriculum was introduced for pupils aged between 7 and 16. The purpose of the national curriculum was to raise standards by ensuring that all students study to a minimum level up to the age of 16. Later, in 1998, literacy and numeracy hours were added to the primary-school curriculum, with the content of these daily lessons tightly prescribed by central government. Students' understanding of the curriculum is also now centrally tested via the use of national tests taken at ages 7, 11, 14 and 16 (or Key Stages 1, 2 3 and 4). The average test scores of each school are made publicly available in newspapers and on the web, creating so called "league tables" of school performance. Whilst the national curriculum may have reduced the autonomy of schools, it has also generated more information for parents on the quality of each school, and may have thus enhanced the operation of the quasi-market. Even at the primary-school stage, parents are encouraged to act as consumers. They have been given greater choice of where their son or daughter can attend school and more information about the quality of different schools. The government has also attempted to increase school performance and accountability via the regulatory inspection regime and the setting of key targets of educational attainment.

The analysis later in this chapter suggests that, relative to other countries, the performance of the top end of the UK education system has been improving in recent years. Yet there is little hard evidence linking this improvement to any or all of the numerous reforms introduced during the last two decades. Moreover, the quasi-market in education has potentially reinforced inequality within the education system (see Chapter 6, Machin and Vignoles (2004) and Hoxby (2003a) for a discussion of US evidence). Lower socioeconomic groups that already accessed lower-quality schooling appear to do so to a greater extent now despite increased consumer choice. For instance, there is empirical evidence that good schools cause house prices to rise. As school performance and house prices are related, students from lower socioeconomic groups will tend to attend lower-quality schools (Gibbons and Machin 2003, 2004). High socioeconomic groups also appear to have better information on and understanding of school performance, for example via league tables (West and Pennell 1999). If wealthier parents act on this information, choosing for their children to attend the best schools, then there is a clear tension between strategies to raise standards and policies to reduce inequality. Socioeconomic background also relates to school quality and pupil performance in other ways. For example, attending a school with few children from low socioeconomic groups is highly beneficial for pupil performance (Feinstein 2003). If parental choice leads to greater socioeconomic segregation across schools, such peer-group effects will further reinforce socioeconomic disadvantage. These are all issues that are taken up further in the next chapter on schools and teachers. Here they provide a policy context for the discussion about the outputs from the UK education system that follows in Part II. Firstly, however, we discuss other important aspects of the UK education system.

2.2.3 The Private Sector

At the same time that growing demand for education and increased emphasis on improved quality and academic achievement was altering the shape of the state sector, changes were also occurring in the private-education system. Although the proportion of pupils in private education has remained remarkably constant since the 1970s (7% in 2001), private expenditure on education saw a fivefold real-terms increase over the same period (Glennerster 2002). In the last few years, fees have been increasing in real terms by about 3.5% per year (Green 2003). Given that student numbers in the private sector have not grown substantially, this represents a substantial increase in the per-child funding levels in private schools.

The huge growth of resources in the private sector contrasts strongly with the fiscal limitations faced by the state-education system.[6] There is no denying the huge gap in both inputs into, and outputs from, the two sectors. For example, in England in 2000 the pupil–teacher ratio in private schools was 9.9:1, compared with 23:1 in state primary schools and 17:1 in state secondary schools (Green 2003). Equally, whilst 60% of pupils schooled through the private system in the 1980s and 1990s attained postsecondary degrees, only 16% of state schools pupils did so (Green 2003). It seems likely that such large differences in resourcing levels between the two sectors would have contributed to these substantial differences in outcomes. Of course, differences in achievement between the two sectors also relate to the more general issue of socioeconomic inequality in the UK education system discussed

---

[6]See Green (2003) and Glennerster (2002) for a more detailed analysis of the gap in educational expenditure between the state- and private-education sectors, and the real decline in state-school expenditure per child since the 1970s.

above and in more detail in Chapter 6. In any case, it is fair to say that such a vibrant and successful private-education sector also draws vocal and committed parents out of the state-education system, with potential consequences for standards in the state sector.

In the discussion that follows about the outputs from the UK education system, one therefore needs to be aware that aggregate figures are presented, which include outputs from this successful private sector.

2.2.4 *Vocational Education*

Perhaps in stark contrast to the success of the private sector, vocational education in the UK is seen as a particularly problematic area. It has long been argued that the main issue in the UK education system is the neglect of the long tail of academic underachievers. These are generally students who leave school at age 16 with few or no educational qualifications. Part of this neglect is related to the problems inherent in the provision of vocational training in the UK.

The system of vocational training and qualifications in the UK is complex and has changed substantially over time. Certainly there is no unified system of vocational education, as is found in some other countries such as Germany. There are hundreds of different vocational qualifications currently available, many of which appear to have very low economic value. Different training providers offer very different qualifications, with quite different requirements in terms of achievement. This has left students, parents and employers somewhat confused about the content and economic value of different vocational qualifications (see Chapter 9 of this book for a more detailed discussion).

Despite this, full-time vocational education is chosen by around 25% of all 16 and 17 year olds in the UK. This has risen from just under 15% in the mid 1980s (West and Steedman 2003). Vocational education therefore represents a sizeable part of the UK education system. However, the expansion of full-time vocational education has come largely at the expense of part-time, work-based education and training rather than academic qualifications. Academic full-time study remains the most popular choice at age 16/17 in the UK.

Part of the instability of vocational education in the UK stems from an unsuccessful attempt to achieve so-called "parity of esteem" between vocational and academic education. Numerous reforms have been introduced, all in an effort to improve the status of vocational qualifications, as compared with their academic counterparts such as A levels. Of course, the instability that this continual reform generates itself undermines the value of vocational qualifications.

In the UK in the 1960s vocational education typically consisted of one day a week of study at a further-education college, in conjunction with an apprenticeship. This system led to qualifications being provided by different awarding bodies depending on the industry. During the 1970s and 1980s the UK apprenticeship system virtually collapsed in the traditional apprenticeship sectors. Various initiatives attempted to replace the traditional apprenticeships (West and Steedman 2003) with yet more qualifications, increasingly taken full time at further-education colleges and with no work-based element. These initiatives are too numerous to mention but the most recent reforms of note are the development of National Vocational Qualifications, or NVQs, and General National Vocational Qualifications, or GNVQs.

Introduced in 1988, NVQs were originally intended as competence-based qualifications. They were designed to certify existing occupational knowledge and skills and were targeted at those in work. Many criticisms have been aimed at NVQs, in particular that they are too low level and do not require sufficient vocational knowledge and skill. GNVQs, on the other hand, were introduced in 1992 and were designed to be largely classroom-based taught vocational qualifications. GNVQs covered broader occupational fields (OECD 1999) and were much less task-specific than NVQs. The aim was to provide an option that would enable students to either enter the world of work directly afterwards or to continue with further study. GNVQs have had some success in terms of enabling vocational students to progress on to HE (around 6% of those enrolling to do a postsecondary degree have Advanced GNVQ qualifications). However, they are still not popular with employers (OECD 1999).

The key problem associated with NVQs, and indeed GNVQs, is their lack of value in the labour market (see Chapter 9 for a full discussion of the value of vocational qualifications, and also see Dearden *et al.* (2002*a*)). Recognition of this problem has also led to yet more attempts to reform the vocational education system. For example, the introduction (in 1995) of the Modern Apprenticeship Scheme was designed to provide a high-quality vocational option for more-able students. Modern Apprenticeships are modelled on the German dual system of apprenticeship, and are aimed at young people (age 16–19). The apprenticeship prepares the worker for an NVQ level 3 qualification and generally lasts around three years. The UK apprenticeship rate is now greater than that of France, Finland and the US, although still well below the levels in Germany and Denmark, and there is recent evidence that where an apprenticeship leads to an NVQ level 3 qualification it bestows a substantial wage premium (McIntosh 2002). More recently, new vocationally oriented GCSE qualifications have been introduced, with the aim of providing a more work-relevant curriculum for the 14–16 age range. Vocational AS and A levels have also been introduced for the 16–18 age range. This rapid change has certainly not simplified the system of vocational education in the UK and there continues to be much policy concern about the establishment of a high-value vocational-training route.

2.2.5 Work-Related Training

In contrast to the problems associated with vocational education, the evidence on the extent of and benefit from work-related training in the UK is altogether more positive. It is often argued that the continued education and training of adult workers is an important part of sustaining the highly skilled workforce needed by today's economy. Evidence suggests that, compared with other countries, the workforce in the UK receives relatively high levels of training (Green 2003). For example, the training participation rate amongst the adult population in the UK in 1995/1996 was 40%, compared with 35% in the US (in 1999) and 30% in Germany (in 1997). Adults in the UK also receive more hours of training than adults in most other countries,[7] around 45 hours on average (OECD 2001a). In the UK, as in other countries, younger workers are more likely to receive training than older workers, service-sector workers receive more training than those employed in manufacturing, and employees in large firms receive more training than those in smaller firms.

There are also gender differences in training participation. Males in the UK are more likely to receive training than females, although this is also true of a number of other countries such as Germany and Switzerland.[8] Gender differences in training receipt are reduced as the education level of individuals increases, so that for workers in the UK with postsecondary degree level qualifications the participation rate and the hours of training received is higher for females than for males. The latter finding highlights the most alarming aspect of adult learning in the UK: training tends to reinforce skill differences produced by the education system, rather than reduce them. Thus, in the UK, as in other countries, those with the least formal education receive the least training in later life.

In terms of the benefits of training, the UK evidence suggests that work-related training conveys a substantial earnings premium (Machin and Vignoles 2001). A spell of work-related training yields a wage gain of around 5–15%, depending on the duration and nature of the training. More recent evidence from the UK does suggest, however, that the group of workers who are selected by firms to receive training is highly select and that although these workers do gain substantially from training, those not selected to receive training would not have gained from it anyway (Vignoles et al. 2004). What this implies in policy terms is that firms are adept at selecting workers to be trained and at providing effective training. Hence training per se is not a universal policy solution to the problem of low skills since, if it is left to the market, workers with the poorest skills are much less likely to get training.

---

[7]With the exception of Denmark, where the mean number of hours of training is 91, New Zealand (68 hours) and Norway (66 hours).

[8]The participation rate of males and females in a number of countries is more even. For example, Norway and Ireland have relatively equal participation rates. In Denmark, Finland and Australia the female participation rate is actually higher than the male rate.

2.3 How Well Is the System Doing?

Having discussed some of the institutional features of the UK education system, and presented some evidence on the particular challenges it faces, we now undertake a systematic examination of the educational outputs from the system and make some comparisons with other countries. While outputs such as qualifications gained are often thought to be the most important measure of educational achievement, it is very difficult to measure and compare qualifications across countries (Barro and Lee 1993, 2001; Steedman 1996). In particular, data on educational attainment are very problematic, since different countries use different definitions of what constitutes a particular level of education. For example, Steedman (1996) suggests that there is significant underreporting of qualifications in a number of OECD countries, largely due to the exclusion of many vocational qualifications from the statistics. The other major difficulty is that one has to assume that a certain level of educational attainment is similar in quality across countries (e.g. attaining an upper secondary education is assumed to mean that the person has reached the same level of attainment across different countries). Yet clearly the standards reached vary both across and often within countries. Although the UK education system relies on externally validated measures of achievement, such as O levels and A levels, many systems, such as the US, do not. Thus we cannot be sure that a high-school graduate has reached a certain level of attainment, even comparing students across the US, let alone across countries.

Despite these difficulties, it is desirable to place the UK's level of educational achievement in some kind of international perspective. A partial solution to the problem is the use of the International Standard Classification of Education. The ISCED classification is not without its own difficulties (Steedman 1996) but at least it provides some kind of consistent comparison system. Broadly, ISCED levels 0, 1 and 2 refer to lower secondary education or below ("drop-out"), ISCED levels 3 and 4 correspond to upper secondary (high-school graduation), and ISCED levels 5, 6 and 7 signify postsecondary degree or above.

However, the cut-off point between ISCED levels 2 and 3 is particularly problematic for the UK. According to ISCED definitions, level 3 should include qualifications that give access to university-level study or that require completion of a two-year course of education/training following completion of compulsory education. Yet the UK government has included people with five good (grades A–C) GCSEs in the ISCED level 3 category, despite the fact that these qualifications do not (at least at the point of obtaining them) lead to higher education and do not require two years of post-compulsory study. Including good GCSEs in ISCED level 3 makes the UK's attainment at this level look substantially better than many of its competitors.

Table 2.1. Qualifications held in the workforce, 2002/2003 (percentages).

	At least postsecondary degree	At least "A level"	At least "good GCSE"
Germany	19	68	85
France	22	41	77
UK	25	44	64
US	34	57	73

Notes. Source: Steedman *et al.* (2004). UK and US results are for 2002; France and Germany for 2003.

Steedman (1996) has tried to overcome this problem and we therefore start with her assessment of the UK's educational attainment level. Table 2.1 shows the percentage of workers in particular qualification groups in the UK relative to a selected group of countries.[9] It shows that the UK performs well at postsecondary degree level education, but very poorly at lower levels.

Of course, Table 2.1 includes only a few comparator countries. However, a more global analysis by Barro and Lee (2001) paints a similar picture and the good UK performance at postsecondary degree level is confirmed by OECD data on graduation rates from type A[10] tertiary education, as shown in Figure 2.3. Figure 2.3 shows that the UK has one of the highest graduation rates from tertiary education amongst the group of countries being considered, and a much higher rate than for the whole OECD.[11] This is not just a recent development, even though the expansion of HE has been very rapid in the UK over the last two decades. Even if one looks at the proportion of graduates in the population as a whole, as in Table 2.1, as opposed to just new graduates, as in Figure 2.3, the UK still does relatively well compared with other OECD countries. The notable exception is the US, which had a much higher graduation rate somewhat earlier.

From an economic perspective it may not be sufficient for a relatively small proportion of the population to be well educated. A supply of labour with intermediate skill levels is also important. Table 2.1 clearly indicates that the UK performs poorly in this regard. Even abstracting from the problems of classifying upper and lower secondary education (A levels and GCSEs), Table 2.1 indicates that 36% of the UK population have not even acquired good GCSEs, compared with only 15% in Germany. Only the US does worse than the UK on this measure. Even standard

[9]Table 9.5 in Chapter 9 shows this table in more detail, giving a breakdown by age and type of qualification, i.e. whether academic or vocational.

[10]This means academic, non-vocational, higher education requiring a minimum of two years of full-time study.

[11]As discussed, we have some reservations about comparisons using this OECD data. Nonetheless, the story that emerges is consistent with the more detailed comparisons by Steedman (1996).

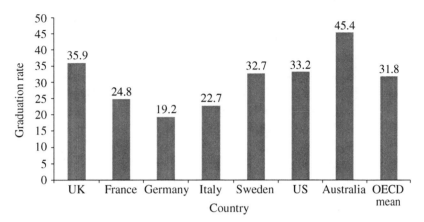

Figure 2.3. Graduation rate from type A tertiary education. Notes: type A tertiary refers to academic, non-vocational, higher education requiring a minimum of two years full-time study. Source: OECD (2004) except US data, from OECD (2001*a*).

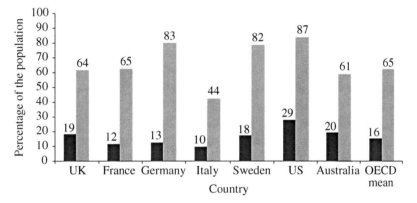

Figure 2.4. Upper secondary (ISCED 3) (grey bars) and tertiary schooling (ISCED 5+) (black bars). Notes: type A tertiary refers to academic, non-vocational, higher education requiring a minimum of two years full-time study. Source: OECD (2004).

ISCED levels, which overstate UK attainment levels, particularly at ISCED level 3, suggest the same story. Figure 2.4 shows the proportion of the population obtaining at least an upper secondary education (A level, or equivalent qualifications), as well as tertiary education (postsecondary degree plus). At the intermediate level the UK performs less well than the other countries examined (with the exception of Australia and Italy) and marginally worse than the OECD as a whole.

The situation gets worse at the lowest levels of skill and education, as we now show. Formal qualifications only capture some dimensions of skill of course and do not inform us about the achievement levels of those people who do not hold formal qualifications. But one can examine the actual skill level of workers in each country, drawing on various sources. The most recent are the Progress in International Reading Literacy Study, the Programme for International Student Assessment (PISA) and the International Adult Literacy Survey (IALS). Collected in 2001, PIRLS data measure the reading achievements of over 140 000 10 year olds in 35 countries. PISA data, gathered in 2000, measure how well 15 year olds across 32 countries perform on tests related to the curriculum that they study at school. IALS data measure *adult* literacy in 12 countries in 1995.

These data sources suggest different things and highlight some of the difficulties in making these types of international comparisons (in particular, the sample of countries in each dataset is very different). Testing adults who have already left the school system (IALS) suggests that the UK does relatively badly, compared with other countries, in both literacy and numeracy. Table 2.2 shows the relatively poor literacy and numeracy performance of adults in the IALS data. This poor performance is present for all age groups.

PIRLS data on the other hand indicate that English schoolchildren are among the most able readers in the world at the age of 10 (Twist *et al*. 2003).[12] This finding is consistent with evidence from PISA which suggests that the UK achieves the highest scores in both reading and mathematics for the countries listed in Table 2.2, and some 13% higher than average for all PISA countries. Given that the IALS and PISA tests were so different perhaps it is not surprising that we get these conflicting results, and certainly this exercise illustrates the inherent difficulties in assessing the skill levels in different countries. IALS measured the skills of a sample of the working-age population in 1995, whilst PISA examined the reading and mathematics achievement of 15 year olds in 2000. Thus this conflicting evidence may be down to differences in the tests, differences between the samples (particularly in terms of age) or perhaps a genuine improvement in skill levels between 1995 and 2000, although the latter seems unlikely in such a short time period. What seems much more likely is that since PISA samples UK children at age 15 during the compulsory phase of schooling and at this stage they are performing reasonably well. The problems within the UK education system are more acute from age 15 onwards. Given the high UK drop-out rate at age 16, it could simply be that insufficient numbers of students are continuing their education beyond 16 and some fraction of those who do continue do not gain good skills during the post-compulsory phase.

We can use the IALS data to determine whether the UK really does have a long tail of very low achievers, compared with other countries. To do this we measure the real skill levels of workers with each level of education. Crudely put, we determine what

---

[12]However, PIRLS data indicate that England also had an extremely wide distribution of reading scores with a long tail of low-achieving pupils.

Table 2.2. Numeracy and literacy performance by age from IALS.

| | % of adults at IALS level 2 or above | | | | | |
| | Numeracy | | | Literacy | | |
	Age 16–25	Age 26–35	Age 36–45	Age 16–25	Age 26–35	Age 36–45
Belgium (Flanders)	93	91	83	92	88	80
Switzerland (German)	93	87	81	93	83	76
Netherlands	92	93	90	92	94	91
Sweden	95	96	93	96	95	93
Germany	96	95	94	91	88	86
Ireland	82	80	77	84	84	79
UK	78	80	81	83	82	83
US	74	80	82	77	80	81

Notes. OECD, *Literacy, economy and society* (1995), pp. 152, 154. Based on IALS measurement of "quantitative literacy" and "prose literacy".

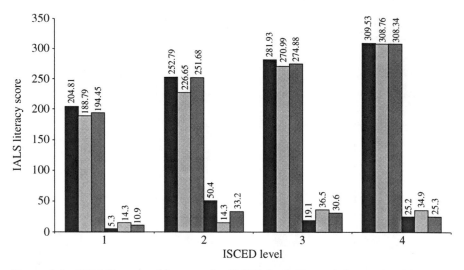

Figure 2.5. IALS literacy achievement by ISCED level. For each International Standard Classification of Education level, the six bars represent, from left to right, UK ISCED level; US ISCED level; mean ISCED level; UK proportion at this level; US proportion at this level; and mean proportion at this level.

each level of education "provides", in terms of skills, in each country. Figures 2.5 and 2.6 show that, compared with other IALS countries, UK workers with the lowest levels of education (below GCSE) are no less skilled in terms of adult literacy and numeracy, and indeed if anything are marginally more skilled. At ISCED level 2 (GCSE) there does seem to be a gap in numerical skills specifically, with UK workers having slightly lower skill levels. However, by and large the skills achieved by UK workers at each level of qualification appear to be similar to those achieved in other countries.

The problem, as the data in Figures 2.5 and 2.6 show, is that the UK education system produces a lot more people with the lowest levels of education (although not as low as the US) and, as we have already established, far fewer at intermediate levels. In particular, around half the UK's workforce is at ISCED level 2 (poor GCSE, high-school drop-out), compared with just one-third for all other IALS countries. Thus, relative to the comparator countries, which include the major economies of Northern Europe and the US, the UK does appear to have a relatively long tail of low achievers (see Green 2003). This issue is taken up again in Chapter 9, where the focus is on the type of qualification acquired.

An additional problem is that there is more variability, in terms of skill, *within* education categories in the UK (and even more so in the US), compared with some other Northern European countries. This too applies particularly at the lower end of the education distribution.

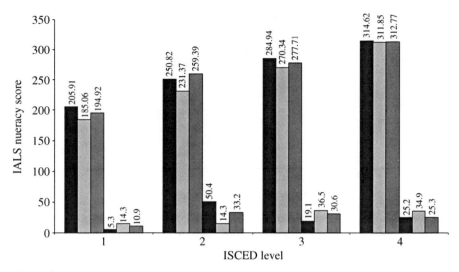

Figure 2.6. IALS numeracy achievement by ISCED level. For each ISCED level, the six bars represent, from left to right, UK ISCED level; US International Standard Classification of Education level; mean ISCED level; UK proportion at this level; US proportion at this level; and mean proportion at this level.

One does not want to overstate the problem of the level of skill of the UK's work-force. The UK system performs as well as the OECD average in terms of outputs, but we have highlighted particular concerns about the output from the education system at the lower end of the distribution. Of course, to judge the effectiveness of the UK education system one would like to compare outputs with costs of production. However, this is extremely difficult, as not only is it hard to find measures which would accurately allow us to do this, but also empirical evidence examining causal relationships between expenditure per pupil and educational attainment across countries has generally not found that higher-spending countries produce more educated workers (Hanushek and Kimko 2001). However, as Figure 2.7 shows, by looking at expenditure per pupil on education against average expected years of schooling we can very crudely establish that the UK is a low-to-moderate-spending nation, with an above-average output from its education system. By contrast, the US and Switzerland are both high-cost systems with average output, while Sweden achieves a high output with above-average spending.

2.4 THE UK EDUCATION SYSTEM AND THE LABOUR MARKET IN AN INTERNATIONAL CONTEXT

Chapter 9 will consider in detail the extent to which the UK education system meets the needs of the labour market, but the final consideration in the current chapter is

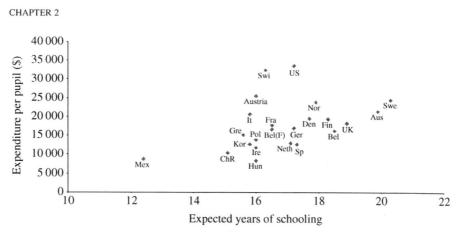

Figure 2.7. Expenditure per pupil (in US$) and educational attainment (expected years of schooling).

to consider this issue in an international context. From a comparative perspective, it is interesting to estimate the economic value of different qualification levels in the UK, as compared with the value of similar qualification levels in other countries. The price of a given qualification level will reflect its relative supply and demand. A very high price for a particular qualification suggests relatively low supply or relatively high demand for that educational output, although determining which is problematic.

There is of course a large literature both providing evidence on, and critiquing, comparisons of rates of return to schooling across different countries (Harmon *et al.* 2001; Psacharopoulos 1994; Psacharopoulos and Patrinos 2002; Bennell 1996). Much of this literature has focused on the returns to an additional year of schooling (primary, secondary or higher), rather than the return to particular qualifications. It provides an overall assessment of the value of a year of schooling in each country, abstracting from the fact that different types and levels of schooling may have different returns in different countries, an issue we return to below.

The results from this literature are somewhat mixed. Early work by Psacharopoulos (1994), which has since been updated (Psacharopoulos and Patrinos 2002), suggested that the social rate of return to schooling in the UK is not dissimilar to the social rate of return to a year of schooling in other OECD countries, although it is somewhat lower for higher education. Psacharopoulos and Patrinos (2002) cite the mean OECD social rate of return to primary education as being 8.5%, 9.4% for secondary education and 8.5% for higher education (derived from various studies using data which span a period from the early 1970s to the late 1990s). The same study finds 8.6%, 7.5% and 6.5%, respectively, for the UK (the data for the UK were from 1986 (see Cohn and Addison 1998)). Evidence on the private returns to a year of schooling in the UK indicates that the returns are higher in the UK, compared with many other European countries. For instance, Harmon *et al.* (2001) suggest the that return to education in the UK (measured in 1994/1996) is high by European standards[13] (around 8%), second only to the return to schooling in Ireland, and certainly higher than the mean return across all the countries considered, which was around 6.5%. This picture is confirmed by evidence from IALS data, which suggest that the return to a year of schooling in the UK is around 10% if no account of ability is made, and around 7.5% if account is taken of the person's cognitive ability (Denny *et al.* 2003). This is relatively high compared with countries such as Sweden, Switzerland, Germany, Finland, Italy, Denmark, Norway, the Netherlands and Belgium, and more similar to the returns in Northern Ireland, Chile, Ireland, the US and French-speaking Canada.

In this chapter we are particularly interested in the labour-market value of different types of outputs from the education system, i.e. different qualifications. We have therefore done some illustrative estimation, which focuses specifically on the return to particular qualifications. We use IALS data[14] to estimate some indicative returns to qualifications across a very select group of countries, namely Germany, Sweden, the UK and the US. Table 2.3 shows earnings differences by skill and qualification level, from a simple statistical regression analysis of IALS data. The table shows the earnings premium associated with A levels or equivalent (high school) and postsecondary degree qualifications across four IALS countries, taking into account basic skill levels (as measured by the IALS survey), gender, age, parental background and hours of work. In all four countries, workers with postsecondary degree level qualifications earn significantly more than those with qualifications below A level. However, UK and US workers with postsecondary degrees earn a larger premium from their postsecondary degree than their counterparts in Sweden and Germany. For example, the premium attached to a postsecondary degree in the UK is around 37% in the IALS sample, compared with 22% in Germany. Lower down the scale, the picture is somewhat different. There is no wage premium to the equivalent of A levels/high-school graduation in Germany, and just a 9% premium in the UK. In the US, by contrast, the premium to this level of qualification is around 42%.

Various explanations are consistent with these findings. Firstly, the relative demand for graduates in the UK may be high. This is in line with arguments that there has been particularly rapid skill-biased technological change in the UK boosting demand for skill (Machin and Van Reenen 1998). If the relative demand for skill is high in the UK, this will boost the price attached to a postsecondary degree in the labour market. It is not clear, however, whether the high wage premium for graduates

---

[13] The other countries considered were Germany (West), Portugal, Switzerland, Finland, Greece, Spain, France, Italy, Austria, Netherlands, Norway, Denmark and Sweden.

[14] See, for example, Denny *et al.* (2000) for a discussion on the problems of using IALS data to estimate the returns to education.

Table 2.3. Earnings differences by skills and qualifications (IALS data).

	Germany	Sweden	UK	US
Qualifications				
A level or equivalent	0.011 (0.068)	0.190[a] (0.042)	0.094[a] (0.035)	0.416[a] (0.103)
Postsecondary degree	0.223[a] (0.098)	0.304[a] (0.046)	0.371[a] (0.038)	0.691[a] (0.105)
Literacy				
IALS 3	−0.072 (0.074)	−0.012 (0.044)	−0.022 (0.041)	0.079 (0.072)
IALS 4/5	−0.068 (0.132)	−0.036 (0.055)	0.037 (0.055)	0.079 (0.081)
Numeracy				
IALS 3	0.077 (0.072)	0.020 (0.044)	0.183[a] (0.042)	0.180[a] (0.070)
IALS 4/5	0.064 (0.119)	0.057 (0.053)	0.256[a] (0.056)	0.260[a] (0.079)

Notes. Earnings regressions were run separately for each country and include both education levels and basic skill-level variables. The dependent variable is log annual earnings. The samples are people in work aged 16–64 in each country. [a] Statistically significant at a 5% level of significance or better. Standard errors are in parentheses. The UK and German earnings data is banded so the regressions for these countries used interval regressions. All regressions control for education, skill level, gender, age, age squared, father's education, part-time status and weeks worked in the year.

in the UK actually indicates relatively high demand and insufficient supply. Indeed, given the evidence that the UK produces a large number of graduates compared with other countries, this seems unlikely as a complete explanation for the relatively high return to a graduate education. Of course, the wage premium for graduates in the UK is partly determined by the wage of unskilled UK workers. The UK is relatively unequal, in terms of its income distribution, and thus the high returns to a postsecondary degree may simply reflect the higher degree of wage inequality in the UK labour market. A similar argument can be made to explain the relatively high return to a postsecondary degree in the US.

Of course, the results relating to A levels would suggest a relatively low demand for these qualifications or a relatively high supply. Given that we know that the UK does not produce as many workers with these intermediate qualifications as other OECD countries, this tentatively suggests that there is a relatively low demand for these qualifications.

There is also a growing literature on the value of skills and abilities across different countries (Denny *et al*. 2000, 2003). Denny *et al*. (2003) use IALS data to assess the return to ability, measured as an individual's average functional literacy (prose, document and quantitative). They suggest that the UK again has high returns to these skills, at least in terms of numeracy, relative to the other IALS countries, second only to the return in the US. This is confirmed in our illustrative analysis in Table 2.3, which also considers the earnings premium that accrues to better literacy and numeracy skills. Thus Table 2.3 shows earnings gaps associated with higher levels of IALS literacy and numeracy. The table shows that log(earnings) are 4% and 26% higher for higher-level literacy and numeracy skills in the UK. This is consistent with evidence in Denny *et al*. (2003) for a wider selection of IALS countries, which confirms that the impact of what they call ability, namely literacy/numeracy, is highest in English-speaking countries (Ireland, the UK and the US). This may reflect the fact that there is an under supply of skilled people in these countries, so those with higher skills are suitably rewarded. The fact that the results for Germany and Sweden in Table 2.3 are not statistically significant may indicate that these countries have a better supply of skilled workers. However, it may also be the case that the high return to skills and qualifications in the UK reflects other underlying features of the labour market that have resulted in a high degree of income inequality, such as the decline in unionization and the reduction in the role of the public sector.

In summary, the data suggest that the reward, in terms of earnings, from having better literacy and numeracy skills is substantially higher in the US, and even in the UK, compared with the other countries considered. The effect of *numeracy* on earnings is particularly strong in the US and the UK. Yet we have already shown that achievement in basic skills is lower in the US and the UK, compared with countries like the Netherlands and Germany. In other words, from our very small sample of countries, it appears that those countries with more unequal earnings distributions, lower basic-skills levels and greater *variability* in basic-skills achievement, the wage premium for skills is higher. Given that the UK is one of the few countries where the majority of people do not learn mathematics beyond the age of 16, the numeracy result in particular may not be surprising. The UK is certainly the exception in allowing students to enter university having done no mathematics beyond the age of 16. In Northern Europe over 80% of 17 year olds in full-time education are studying some formal mathematics, compared with only 25% in England. This does not, however, explain the poor numeracy performance in the US, where 80% of 17 year olds are engaged in formal mathematics study, yet, as we have seen, achievement levels are low. It might therefore be the *standard* of mathematics being studied in the US that is the culprit.

A similar explanation may be found for the relatively poor performance of UK adults in terms of basic *literacy* skills, since most students stop the formal study of English at age 16 in the UK. In other countries, including the US, students tend to continue formal study of their mother tongue up to the age of 18/19, particularly if they intend to go on to university. Nonetheless, the curriculum at 16–19 can only provide a partial explanation for the poor basic skills performance of UK workers. It is still the case that around 40% of students leave full-time education at age 16 in the UK. The explanation for the poor skills of this group obviously lies in the standard of their education up to the age of 16.

2.5 Conclusions

The UK's education system has been subject to much change and reform since World War II, particularly in recent decades. It has expanded dramatically, particularly at university level. Furthermore, in the drive to raise standards, the UK education system has been at the forefront of the movement to introduce market forces into education. With a twin-pronged goal of greater parental choice and better school accountability, the UK has strived to improve the productivity and efficiency of its schools.

What has all this change achieved in terms of performance? We have shown that the UK spends a moderate amount on education, but achieves an above-average performance in terms of the expected average years of education. The UK performs particularly well at the upper end of the distribution, with one of the highest graduation rates amongst OECD countries. However, we have identified significant problems at the lower end of the education distribution, and in particular the high proportion of workers leaving with GCSE qualifications or less (high-school drop-outs) and the variability of basic skills amongst less-educated workers. We also presented evidence that there are relatively high returns to certain qualifications in the UK, such as postsecondary degrees, as well as atypically high returns to basic skills, compared with other European countries. This may reflect upward wage pressures arising from excess demand for these qualifications and skills, or alternatively the high returns may be driven by the greater inequality in the UK earnings distribution, again as compared with other countries. In any case, it is not at all clear, as we will discuss throughout this book, that any of the achievements (or indeed the problems) of the UK education system are causally related to the reforms discussed earlier in this chapter.

PART 2

Who Gets More Education?

School and Teacher Effectiveness

By Arnaud Chevalier, Peter Dolton and Ros Levacic

3.1 INTRODUCTION

A crucial issue for the economics of education concerns the way in which schools affect educational attainment. If schools are differentially effective, then the school attended matters for children's educational attainment and, depending on who benefits most, can serve to reinforce or counter family and social influences. A central feature of research into the general issue of school effectiveness is an aim to discover which factors are associated with more-effective schools and more-effective teachers, and to suggest potential policy levers based upon this.

This chapter builds on the discussion in Chapter 2 by discussing the features of the UK education system that are pertinent to an understanding of school quality and effectiveness. A particular focus is placed on policy changes that have occurred in the last 30 years, which have attempted to increase the accountability of UK schools and to introduce elements of a quasi-market into the education system. The effectiveness of these market reforms is discussed, before moving on to a critical review of the school-effectiveness literature. The chapter ends with a policy discussion.

3.2 FEATURES OF THE UK SCHOOLING SYSTEM

The UK state-schooling system is essentially centralized, with all pupils following a common National Curriculum and sitting nationally set public examinations between the ages of 7 and 16. In this system all teachers are paid using national pay scales. Each school's budget is largely dependent on the number of pupils it has. However, the educational budget is administered by the Local Education Authorities (LEAs), who may set their own educational priorities. Thus variations in school funding between LEAs are possible due to compensatory additional educational funding being given to geographical areas with high levels of economic and social deprivation.

Various types of school coexist in the UK. Within the state sector around 85% of schools are mixed-ability comprehensives, although some LEAs still allow streaming of their pupils[1] and some schools select on ability or other criteria. The private system of independent schools, which provides for about 7% of pupils, is relatively autonomous, but still broadly follows the National Curriculum. Such schools select, stream[2] and teach by ability and are free to charge fees.

In the last three decades there have been a myriad of reforms designed to counteract the perceived failure of the UK educational system (in absolute terms and relative to other OECD nations). As already noted in Chapter 2, the underlying objective behind many of these reforms was to create a quasi-market in the provision of publicly funded education by granting more choice for pupils and parents and more accountability in the education process (see Glennerster 1991).

These reforms were certainly intended to increase post-compulsory staying-on rates, qualification attainment and the effectiveness of schools to deliver improved child outcomes across the ability spectrum. Perhaps the most radical changes in the education system came with the 1988 Education Reform Act, which introduced the National Curriculum. This specifies, in a highly prescriptive manner, the form and content of subjects to be taught in schools. The 1988 Act also required Local Education Authorities (LEAs) to delegate financial management and the appointment of staff to the governing bodies of schools and increased parental representation on these governing bodies. It also allowed some schools to opt out of LEA control altogether. These schools had more control over their budget and also received their funding directly from central government.

At the same time, published league tables (of school examination results) were introduced. These league tables regularly appear in newspapers and are easily accessed by parents. The ethos of greater parental choice underpinned their introduction, on the grounds that the increased supply of information to parents about school performance would increase competition between schools and thus increase accountability. To ensure that such competition would not lead to a reduction of quality, the Education Act of 1992 introduced the Office for Standards in Educa-

---

[1] This is a remnant of the previous stratified system discussed in more detail in Chapter 2, where children used to be tested at age 11 (via the well-known "11 plus" exam). This stratification of education was mostly dismantled in the 1970s and replaced by a system where most children attend the same "comprehensive school" regardless of academic aptitude. The 1976 Act required LEAs to introduce comprehensive schools in place of schools split by the 11 plus examination. This act was repealed in 1979 and so to this day there are some LEAs (33 out of 148) in which selective state grammar schools still exist (see Jesson (2000) for further details). The distribution of pupils in 1971 was 39% secondary modern, 36% comprehensive, 18% grammar and 7% technical. By 1991, these percentages were, respectively, 10, 85, 5 and 0 (MacKinnon and Statham 1999).

[2] The system of using differential teaching by ability – often in separate classes – is usually called streaming in the UK but is known as tracking in the US. We use these terms interchangeably.

tion (OFSTED). This administrative body has responsibility for inspecting every state-funded school in England at least once every four years.[3]

These changes have raised a number of key questions relating to the effectiveness of schools and the utilization of resources in schools. The focus of this chapter is on four key questions.

(a) What is the role of the market as a resource-allocation device in education?

(b) How do we measure school and teacher effectiveness and what is the evidence on what makes some schools and teachers more effective than others?

(c) What does the empirical evidence tell us about the link between educational resources (and the quality of provision) and subsequent pupil outcomes?

(d) Once one accounts for difference in pupil intake, do selective schools achieve better results?

3.3 INCENTIVES AND QUASI-MARKETS

The general aim of the 1988 Education Reform Act was to introduce a more competitive quasi-market approach to the allocation of resources in the education system.[4] The idea was that popular schools would be allowed to expand without limit (given capacity limitations) and unpopular schools would be forced to improve or face possible closure. The principle of parental choice and devolved school funding linked directly to pupil numbers establishes the conditions under which, theoretically, a quasi-market can operate. This approach was designed to provide teachers and schools with appropriate incentives for efficiency and effectiveness.

Empirical evidence from the US (Chubb and Moe 1990) is supportive of the view that decentralized schooling systems can produce better results, measured in terms of educational outcomes. But this can come at a cost: Barlett (1993) reports that US moves to a more decentralized system resulted in large shifts in the distribution of resources between schools. That is to say, inequality in school resources increased significantly. Schools in the poorest inner-city areas received reduced funding, whilst school funding increased in more prosperous areas of the county. It is not only financial resources that were affected. For example, the appointment of proactive parent governors in middle-class areas is straightforward, but finding any parents willing to do the job in deprived areas is difficult. Therefore access to good governance becomes polarized.

Over and above this, comparing schools in a systematic and meaningful way requires some clear metric of school performance. Many researchers (Goldstein

---

[3]OFSTED's role has since been extended to include the inspection of independent schools, nurseries, teacher-training institutions and LEAs.

[4]See Adnett and Davies (2002) for a description of the "market-led" reforms in the UK.

1997*a*; Rivkin *et al.* 2002) have come to the conclusion that a value-added measure or "student level gain score" is the most appropriate measure of school performance. The justification for this is that crude league tables of raw exam scores do not provide an accurate measure of the effectiveness of a school, because one needs to take account of the prior attainment of pupils. Otherwise one is looking at a mixture of attainment and pupil social mix, owing to the fact that the raw material or inputs that the teacher and school have to work with is highly variable across schools (and even within schools over time). Moreover, there may be problems of measurement errors in point-in-time exam scores (see Kane and Staiger 2002). Furthermore, even if one uses value-added measures of improvements in exam scores, these do not reflect the other factors outside the control of schools, such as family background, that also affect gains in academic performance.

Closely related to these issues are those considered in economic models of incentives, which stress that schools are multi-output organizations and have many objectives beyond improving simple exam scores. Like other public services, schools are characterized by there being multiple principals with varying objectives (Dixit 2002; Besley and Ghatak 2003, forthcoming). For example, schools are concerned with the emotional and physical development of their pupils. They are also responsible for teaching them life skills, such as health and financial management (Dixit 2002). These tasks may be sacrificed if undue attention is placed on exam results and other measures of cognitive ability.

There is now widespread evidence that incentives work in education (see Barlett (1993) or Adnett and Davies (2002) for reviews). Given this, the challenge is to try and design contracts with incentive structures that are not subject to distortion or "gaming". The education production process is very reliant on teacher labour as the most important factor of production. In practice it is very difficult to write complete labour contracts in education to generate the appropriate incentives for teachers. To a large extent this is an orthodox principal–agent problem where one needs to try to design incentives to minimize, or eliminate, information asymmetries and conflicts of interest between principal and agent.[5] However, there are several extra dimensions to this problem in education.

However, the central problem of public-sector educational provision is that the education system has multiple objectives. Dixit (2002) lists the multiple goals of public education as

- imparting basic skills of literacy, mathematics and science for communication, reasoning, and calculation;

---

[5] Milgrom and Roberts (1992) provide a clear textbook exposition of principal–agent models.

- fostering the emotional and physical growth of children;
- preparing students for work, by teaching them vocational skills and attitudes suitable for employment;
- preparing them for life, by teaching them skills of health and financial management;
- preparing them for society, by instilling ideals of citizenship and responsibility;
- helping them to overcome disadvantageous circumstances at home, including in many cases poor nutrition and poor study environments; and
- providing an environment free from drugs and violence.

Dixit suggests that, although these goals are not mutually contradictory, they do compete for resources. As such, they are alternative outputs in the educational production process and teachers' effort put into one of these objectives may detract wholly, or in part, from one or more of the other goals. The second essential feature of any education system is that it has multiple principals. As a consequence, actions of any individual teacher (the agent) could be affected by many other people (the principals) who are in a position of influence. Most specifically, the wishes of parents, head teachers, teacher unions, local or federal authorities, taxpayers, employers, religious and ethnic pressure groups, governors and even pupils influence the actions and decisions of individual teachers. However, Dixit (1997) shows (under regularity conditions) that the existence of several principals makes the overall incentives for the agent much weaker. This weakening of incentives occurs because each principal will seek to divert the agent's effort to his most preferred dimension. Obviously, the more principals that are involved with competing interests the more diluted will be the incentive structure for the agent.

The more complex nature of the implications of a principal–agent model applied to schools therefore generates incentive issues that need to be resolved. On a practical level in the UK case, there has been a fierce public debate on how schools can be made more accountable. The system of school accountability works through several channels: the publication of school examination results; the (theoretical) right of parents to send their children to any state school; the presence of parent governors on school governing bodies; and regular school inspection by OFSTED to monitor standards.

Any system of accountability should create incentives. However, such incentives may not always have desirable consequences. For example, it is unclear whether the mere publication of information on standards in schools will provide an adequate incentive for efficient resource allocation. Surely a necessary (but not sufficient) condition for such efficiency is that this accountability be directly linked to the power of consumers to choose alternative providers in a competitive market. Dolton (2002) suggests that *effective accountability in education* necessitates that

  (i) the education system provides consumers with full information to make decisions;

 (ii) consumers have the power to influence the balance of priorities across the multiple goals of educational provision;

(iii) the consumers have the means to choose alternative providers in a competitive or quasi-competitive environment;

(iv) any incentives which operate on education providers do not act to distort their incentives regarding their provision in ways which are counter to the wishes of consumers.

At the heart of effective public-service provision is the possibility of competition amongst providers. Unless there are alternative schools for parents to send their children to, there is no incentive mechanism for each school to compete in the quasi-market. Another problem occurs where private and state schools coexist, as an "exit and voice" issue arises (see Hirschman 1970). This problem is that there will not be an effective mechanism for change if the most influential parents choose to "exit" from the state schools to the private schools rather than "voice" their views in an attempt to change the state schools.

The other relevant point is that whatever measure of school performance is published, it is this measure that schools will be most concerned with. This can be problematic if, for example, publishing data on the proportion of each school achieving five or more good GCSE exam scores causes teachers and schools to focus disproportionate attention on students on the margin of achieving this, and disregarding the very high achievers (who will achieve this anyway) and the very low achievers (who will never make the grade). However, we currently know little about the practical importance of this and this is an area requiring further work.

In the UK it is still early days to assess the overall effect of the quasi-market, but there are a limited number of studies that suggest that efficiency improvements can be directly attributed to the quasi-market. Bradley *et al.* (2001) find that schools with the best examination performance grow most quickly and that increased competition between schools has led to improved exam performance. The US discussion on school choice (e.g. through vouchers) is also relevant here (see the contributions in Hoxby (2003a)). However, in a similar vein to the US experience, increased efficiency has come at the cost of a rise in inequality. Aspects of rising inequality include greater segregation between schools, as measured by the proportion of children eligible for free school meals (Bradley and Taylor 2002), and significantly higher house prices in localities with the best-performing schools (Gibbons and Machin 2003).

3.4 SCHOOL AND TEACHER EFFECTIVENESS

Other than the quasi-market reforms, there are of course more-general and long-standing questions about what makes a school effective. A key starting point is that school effectiveness is a relative concept. One definition of an effective school is one in which students progress further than might be expected from consideration of its intake (Mortimore 1991). Thus, to estimate relative effectiveness, researchers need data on pupil-level attainment at two points in time, together with information on the characteristics of the pupils and schools. This information is sufficient for estimating a "basic" school-effectiveness model. In the education field these are often set up in a multilevel or hierarchical modelling framework, where the levels are defined as pupils and schools (and in some cases LEAs as well). The advantage of this approach is that the variance in the attainment of pupils can be partitioned between levels. A common notion (Goldstein 1997b) is that only schools that have statistically significant differences in the size of their effect on attainment can be designated as "effective" or "ineffective".

The same approach can be used to study classroom effectiveness under the condition that data on at least two parallel classes in each school are available. A comprehensive model of school effectiveness (Teddlie and Reynolds 1999) thus also includes process factors at school and classroom level. School process factors relate to the school as an organization and encompass its leadership, decision-making, staff–pupil and pupil–pupil relations, parental involvement, attitudes, expectations and norms. Process factors are also defined at class level and relate in particular to how the teaching is conducted and the interactions between pupils and teachers, and of pupils with each other. One of the aims of school-effectiveness research is to identify school and classroom processes that are not just related to school composition and pupil background but which have an independent effect on pupil attainment. This is a difficult undertaking because of the problems of measuring processes and taking account of correlations between processes and school and pupil factors.

Studies of this "comprehensive" model of school effectiveness are relatively rare because they require a large-scale longitudinal research design with intensive fieldwork. Such studies that do exist have had to collect data on processes from interviews, surveys and detailed observation, particularly of teaching. Basic studies based only on pupil and school data (i.e. those excluding these process variables) are more numerous.

The two most influential English studies on school effectiveness concluded that schools certainly matter for children's outcomes. Rutter *et al.* (1979) undertook research based on 12 inner-London secondary schools over four years, while Mortimore *et al.* (1988) based their research on 50 inner-London primary schools over three years. The authors established that "schools matter". In particular, at primary level, after controlling for prior attainment and pupil factors, the school attended accounted for 9% of the variance in reading attainment after three years, and 11% of the variance in mathematics attainment. The maximum difference between the least and most effective schools was 25 points out of 100 in reading and 12 out of 50 in mathematics (Inner London Education Authority Research and Statistics Branch 1986). In particular, a child from a manual working-class family in the most effective school did as well as a middle-class child in the least effective school.

In secondary education, the school accounted for 10% of the variance in attainment and pupil factors accounted for 33%. The school variables identified as affecting effectiveness were similar to the list produced in the literature review by Sammons et al. (1995): head teachers' leadership; teachers' shared vision and goals; a learning environment; focus on teaching and learning; purposeful teaching; high expectations; positive reinforcement; monitoring progress; pupils' rights and responsibilities; home–school partnership; and school-based staff development.

Later, "basic" studies using national datasets with large school numbers have confirmed these results and found that schools account for between 5% and 18% of the variance in attainment (Sammons 1999). It is also found that after controlling for prior attainment and school composition measured in terms of eligibility for free school meals, pupils in all-girls schools, denominational schools and specialist schools do slightly better at GCSE (Levacic 2002; Schagen et al. 2002). These effects could either stem from the processes associated with particular pupil compositions, which in turn are the result of selection into schools, or be entirely due to omitted pupil factors associated with the type of families choosing and being chosen by such schools.

Most (but not all) studies confirm that schools are not differentially effective for different types of pupil (Jesson and Gray 1991; Smith and Tomlinson 1989). Generally there is a reasonable amount of stability in secondary-school effects on overall outcomes and for basic skills in primary schools (Sammons 1999) but less so for subjects at secondary schools, between which there tends to be greater variance, indicating that the effectiveness of departments and teachers within schools is more variable than the total school effect (Fitzgibbon 1991; Sammons et al. 1995).

An important issue for investigation is whether the school effect is due to the aggregation of random class-level effects or whether the school as an organizational unit exerts an influence through its leadership and climate on teaching and learning in classrooms. There are few UK studies on the class effect, especially at secondary school since this requires linking pupils to classes, which vary by subject.

There is more UK evidence for primary schools, where the class–teacher link can be made more easily. For example, Blatchford et al. (2002) study 368 Key Stage 1 (age 7) classes in 220 schools in England and find that for literacy, 20% of variance is at school level, 21% at class level and the rest at pupil level after controlling for prior attainment and class size. For mathematics the equivalent estimates were 15% and 22%, respectively, and 62% at pupil level. While "basic" models of school effectiveness can, with class-level data, identify the relative size of class-level effects, they cannot account for it without further evidence, in particular on teacher effectiveness.

Teacher effectiveness is defined in a similar way to school effectiveness and requires first accounting for the effects on pupils' learning over which the teacher has no influence. It is the extent to which pupils' attainment differs from that predicted by factors beyond the control of the teacher, such as pupils' prior attainment, background characteristics, school and class compositional effects, and resourcing (e.g. class size, other adult support in class, teaching materials). The existence of differential teacher effects, which has strong anecdotal support, is confirmed by research (Luyten 2003).

Economists have taken an agnostic view on the determinants of teachers' quality and have mostly focused on pupils' test-score improvement as a measure of an individual teacher's quality. The idea is that if the pupils of a given teacher usually improve more than pupils of similar initial ability, then this teacher must have some characteristics associated with quality of teaching. The evidence on what makes for a good teacher is limited, especially in the UK. There is some US evidence on this issue, however. For example, Rivkin et al. (2002), following three cohorts of Texan pupils, find that variations in the average teacher quality within schools accounts for at least 7.5% of the variation in test-score gains. Although variation in test score between teachers is stable over time (Aaronson et al. 2002), suggesting that it truly captures idiosyncratic aspects of teacher quality, only 10% of it is explained by observable characteristics such as qualifications or experience (after the first two years).

Given that differential teacher effects exist, the next question is how to account for them. There are two foci of inquiry: one is to investigate the practices of teachers in classrooms to identify approaches used by more- and less-effective teachers; the second is to examine the characteristics of the teachers themselves. From a resourcing perspective, the characteristics of interest are cognitive ability, qualifications, experience and age – factors that are rewarded in the labour market.

In the last 30 years, there have been a handful of major UK studies involving observations of teachers in classrooms over two or more years, which record aspects of their practice.[6] These are then analysed with pupil progress measures and other pupil-level data to find teaching approaches that are significantly related to pupil progress. These studies are all of primary pupils, reflecting the fact that a single

---

[6]The studies are the ORACLE project in the 1970s (Galton and Simon 1980), the ILEA Junior Years Study (Mortimore et al. 1988) (the only one to nest a study of teacher effectiveness within a school-effectiveness study), the "One in Five" study (Croll and Moses 1985) and the Primary Assessment, Curriculum and Experience Study (36 teachers over four years in 18 schools) (Pollard et al. 1994).

teacher teaches a primary class for all or most of their lessons. The findings of these studies are relatively consistent and have resulted in the advocacy of a set of "middle-range" strategies for teachers, which are discussed in Croll and Hastings (1996) and Muijs and Reynolds (2001).

From the perspective of the economics of schooling the most interesting of the research findings concerns teacher–pupil interactions. The teacher typically spends 80% of his/her time in class interacting with pupils, however it is the time the pupil spends interacting with the teacher that appears to be key in determining the effectiveness of teaching. When a very high proportion of the teacher's time is taken up with individual pupil interactions the time each pupil has to interact with the teacher can be as little as 2%. To be effective, whole-class teaching (teaching the entire class as one group) needs to engage the pupils by keeping them actively on task. The findings concerning the efficacy of whole-class teaching ran counter to the popular policy in the 1970s and 1980s of pupils working on their own using worksheets, often seated in groups but not interacting with each other to learn.

A more recent study of primary mathematics teaching (Muijs and Reynolds 2000) supports both the existence of significant teacher effects and the positive effects on pupils of "direct teaching". This study included 16 primary schools taking part in the Gatsby Mathematics Enhancement Programme, which promotes the use of direct-teaching methods in mathematics, and 3 "control" primary schools, which were not involved. Teaching the whole class was not in itself effective, but was effective when done by a teacher using the set of effective approaches. Being taught by the most effective compared with the least effective teachers contributed to between 11% and 25% of the predicted mathematics score depending on the year group and test. Of the unexplained variance in attainment only between 0% and 9% was at teacher level, while a very high proportion of the explained variance in attainment (62–100%) was attributed to the fixed teacher characteristics. The research findings, coming from the US in particular, concerning the efficacy of a set of teacher behaviours included in the "direct" teaching approach have been influential in the creation of the National Literacy and Numeracy Strategies, though these were not extensively evaluated using experimental research designs. An exception is Machin and McNally's (2003a) economic evaluation of the National Literacy Project (NLP), where the literacy hour was introduced in about 400 English primary schools in 1997 and 1998.[7] This resulted in children being exposed to the literacy hour in these schools for two years before the national roll-out took place. Their analysis shows substantial improvements in reading and English took place (for example, reading scores rose

---

[7]The literacy hour is an initiative introduced nationwide in September 1998 in primary schools to tackle the problems of functional illiteracy. The programme involves a set of practices to teach reading (and potentially other subjects) more efficiently (see Machin and McNally (2003a) for details).

by around 0.09 of a standard deviation) for a policy that is not very costly (just over £26 per pupil per year, at 2004 prices).

To judge teacher effectiveness, and to underpin the assessment of teachers for the performance-related pay scheme that was recently introduced in the UK (see next chapter for details), teachers deemed to be effective were recently observed first hand, and asked to respond to various questionnaires (DfEE 2000). The effective teaching skills identified in this study are not dissimilar to those found in previous academic research: high expectations, time on task, lesson flow, planning, methods and strategies, pupil management, time and resource management, assessment, homework. School climate encompasses clarity, order, standards, fairness, pupil participation, support and feelings of safety.

From an educational production perspective, it is to be expected that pupil progress is positively affected by the amount of time the pupil is actively engaged in learning. Indeed, time on task is one of the factors found to be significant in teacher-effectiveness studies. An important strategy is therefore to keep as many pupils as possible engaged in active learning concurrently, and whole-class direct teaching aims to achieve this. In this way the loss of teacher time in larger class can be offset by more effective whole-class teaching. This causes some complications in any assessment of the impact of class size on pupil outcomes and provides a plausible explanation for the lack of consistent evidence that reducing class size improves learning outcomes, as discussed in the next section.

3.5 THE IMPACT OF RESOURCES

The previous section showed that schools and teachers matter. This section focuses on how, by considering the impact of resources on pupil outcomes. One of the most researched questions in the school-quality/school-effectiveness literature is the impact of smaller class sizes on pupil outcomes and this forms the bulk of the evidence on this issue. Reductions in class size have the advantage of being visible, easily understood and easy (but costly) to implement, and benefit from the broad support of parents. As an anecdotal example of its popularity with parents, most private schools advertise their lower class size compared with state schools.

Some of the existing literature has considered other components of school resourcing and quality, typically looking at observable measures such as expenditure per pupil, and teachers' experience, qualification or pay. However, pinning down an effect from some of these other resource measures can be problematic. For example, teachers' salaries in the UK are nationally determined on a pay scale with a yearly increment, and thus variation in average teachers' salaries across schools mostly reflects the seniority of staff in that school rather than their quality per se.

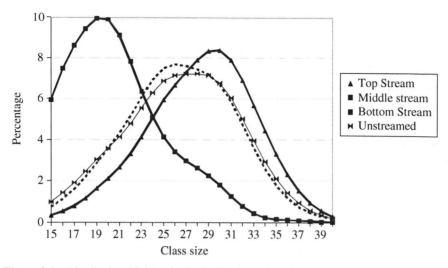

Figure 3.1. Distribution of class size in English by stream. (Source: Iacovou (2002). Reproduced with the agreement of the author and publisher of the original work (Taylor and Francis Ltd, http://www.tandf.co.uk/journals).)

Hence most of the focus here is placed on class size as the key resource measure of interest.

The main conceptual difficulty in estimating the effect of resources on educational achievement (or on economic outcomes when an adult) comes from the observation that parents and schools take decisions regarding the school attended by the young person, so that school quality or the level of resourcing is not randomly allocated to a pupil. Furthermore, schools stream students and allocate students with more learning difficulties to smaller classes in order to prevent them disturbing more-able pupils (as in Lazear 2001) or to provide them with more teacher attention.

Figure 3.1, reproduced from Iacovou (2002), shows that in the UK schools do allocate lower-ability individuals to smaller-sized classes. Hence pupils in smaller classes may have lower achievement. The figure shows the distribution of class size in English at age 16 by ability stream. For schools not practising streaming, the distribution of class size follows a normal distribution and the median size is around 28. For schools streaming by ability, the distributions are skewed and the median class size for pupils in the bottom stream is 20, but reaches 30 for pupils in the top stream.

These issues make the class-size literature controversial and much of the UK evidence reports little or no impact of class size. The usual approach is to use school- or pupil-level data and involves estimating the impact of class sizes, or teacher–pupil ratios, on educational or economic outcomes from statistical regressions. Table 3.1 summarizes the existing studies. All in all, the table shows rather patchy and weak evidence. The most optimistic findings are that for younger children, smaller class sizes are associated with higher test scores, but these effects are not permanent and fade as the pupil ages. But smaller class size/pupil–teacher ratios can be associated with other positive outcomes (e.g. in Dustmann *et al.* (2003), pupils, especially boys, taught in smaller classes are less likely to truant).

There is a much bigger literature on class-size effects in the US. Statistical-regression work reports findings consistent with the UK research and often fails to find much of an effect (Hanushek 2003). However, there are certain studies that do a better job of getting around the conceptual difficulties associated with identifying class-size effects on educational outcomes. Krueger (1999) and Krueger and Whitmore (2001), for example, consider the Tennessee project STAR (Student Teacher Achievement Ratio) class-size experiment where children were randomly allocated into classes of different size. They show substantial beneficial effects on pupil performance for the relatively large class-size reductions that took place in the experimental setting. For example, Krueger (1999) reports a reduction of eight students per class to improve student test scores by 0.20, 0.28, 0.22 and 0.19 of a standard deviation for kindergarten, first-, second- and third-grade children, respectively. One should also note that half of the effect of the class-size reduction disappeared the first year students were put back into larger classes.

Angrist and Lavy (1999), in their study of class size in Israel, also adopt a superior methodological approach, exploiting rules about class sizes to generate a quasi-experimental modelling approach. They take advantage of a long-established rule in Israel (Maimonides' rule) where classes that move above a threshold of 40 students are split into two smaller classes. Like the experimental work, they also report sizeable benefits from class-size reductions, with an improvement of 0.18 of a standard deviation for fifth graders and an effect around half that size for fourth graders. These better-structured studies do suggest that class-size reductions enhance educational performance, suggesting that resourcing, if modelled appropriately, can matter for children's educational attainment. But even this remains controversial. Hoxby (2000), for example, uses a similar approach to Angrist and Lavy using US data, and finds no impact of class size on test scores.

A different way of ascertaining whether school quality matters is through attempting to evaluate how much parents are willing to pay to get their children into better-performing schools. A smaller literature than the class-size work has studied this and finds that parents are often willing to pay substantial amounts in terms of higher house prices to live closer to better-performing schools. These studies are predicated on the notion that quality of schooling is not directly observable to researchers, but that parents have better information. In the UK, school choice is heavily determined by where the pupil lives. Obviously, parents' decisions about house purchases are

Table 3.1. UK studies on class size/teacher–pupil ratios.

Study	Type of Data	Measure	Findings
School-level studies			
Bee and Dolton (1985)	309 secondary private schools	PTR	No impact on A levels, but significant negative impact on the percentage going on to do a postsecondary degree
Bradley and Taylor (1998)	All state secondary schools	PTR	Insignificant impact on school performance
Graddy and Stevens (2003)	256 secondary private schools	PTR	10% reduction in pupil–teacher ratio raises A-grade A levels by 3.6%
Pupil-level studies			
Blatchford *et al.* (2002)	9000 children in the first three years of school (ages 4–7) in 368 classes in 220 schools in England	CS	A decrease in class size of 10 (at sizes below 25) associated with a gain of about 1 year in the achievement of low attainers and of 5 months for other pupils
Chevalier (2003)	Programme for International Student Assessment (PISA)	PTR	For boys, a decrease in the pupil–teacher ratio by 10% (1.5 pupils at the mean) increases test scores by 4–6 points (1% at the mean score); insignificant for girls
Dearden *et al.* (2002*b*)	NCDS	PTR	No significant impact on exam results except for negative effect on men from secondary moderns and lower-ability women
Dustmann *et al.* (2003)	NCDS	PTR	Significant impact on exam results when school type not included; insignificant once school type included
Feinstein and Symons (1999)	NCDS	PTR	Insignificant impact on exam results
Iacovou (2002)	NCDS	PTR	0.29 of a standard deviation reduction in age 7 reading; no impact on age 7 mathematics
McVicar (2001)	Survey of school leavers in Northern Ireland	PTR	Positive (and significant) relationship between pupil–teacher ratio and staying on at age 16

Notes. NCDS is the National Child Development Study, a survey of all children (around 18 500) born in a week of March 1958 that were surveyed at ages 0, 7, 11, 16, 23, 33 and 42. "PTR" stand for pupil–teacher ratio and "CS" stands for class size.

affected by various characteristics of the neighbourhood like low crime, shopping and amenities, but quality of the local school is also likely to be an important factor.[8]

Gibbons and Machin (2003) look at this issue for English primary schools and find substantial effects on house prices. Increasing the average test score in the area by 5 percentage points adds 4.4% to the value of the average house in the South East and the North of England, and 2.7% in the South West of England. These effects are of very similar magnitude to Black's (1999) US work on elementary schools in Boston.

A second UK paper, by Rosenthal (2003), maps data on individual house prices (from a nationally representative building society) to the nearest non-selective public secondary school. This detailed dataset allows him to control for the dwelling characteristics. Rosenthal's estimates of the effect of school quality on house price are one-tenth of those found for primary schools by Gibbons and Machin. Some of the difference may be due to parents valuing a primary school more since an early intervention has higher returns (Reynolds *et al.* 1996) but a major part of the discrepancy between these two studies is likely to stem from differences in the catchment areas associated with primary and secondary schools. Since catchment areas are smaller for primary schools than secondary, we would expect to see a greater effect of primary-school quality on neighbouring house prices compared with secondary schools.

Additionally, Gibbons (2002) finds that pupils located in schools in higher-income areas did significantly better than pupils in schools in less-well-off areas. However, once the specific characteristics of the area are taken into account (especially neighbourhood composition and residential selection on prior school performance), the relationship between average incomes and school performance disappears. In other words, it is the characteristics of the people living in a particular area, not the incomes they earn, that determine school performance.

3.6 SELECTION AND PEER EFFECTS

Thus far the focus has been on factors that influence pupil attainment, with particular emphasis on the effectiveness of schools and teachers. Yet there remains an important input into the schooling process that merits greater attention, namely other pupils. Peer-group and selection effects are important issues in many education systems, and have historically had a particular prominence in the UK, owing to its long history of school selection, with the elite grammar schools catering only for the top 20%

---

[8]Living within the catchment area of a school is not the only criterion used by schools and may not guarantee a place at the school of choice, but it nevertheless increases the odds substantially (see Gibbons and Machin (2003) or Rosenthal (2003) for a detailed description of the school-selection process in England).

of the ability distribution. Even long after the demise of most grammar schools, selection and peer groups have remained a topical issue. Indeed, as parental school choice has become increasingly important (if only in rhetoric), there are growing concerns about schools selecting only the most able students ('cream skimming') and the resulting negative peer effects on other worse-performing schools.

In the research evidence on selective schooling the most pressing question is whether selective schools actually perform better than other types of school. There is a substantial literature that attempts to answer this question by measuring the educational and economic returns to selective schooling. For the UK, Dustmann *et al.* (2003) estimate that even after accounting for age 7 and 11 test performance and parental interest, pupils attending grammar or private schools obtained 0.8 more O levels than pupils in comprehensive schools. Similarly, Dearden *et al.* (2002*b*) estimate large financial returns from attending a selective school for men, but not for women. This selective school premium persists even when controlling for highest qualification obtained. For example, Naylor *et al.* (2002) estimate that university graduates who went to an independent school receive an earnings premium of 3% compared with other similarly qualified university graduates. This premium is driven by attendance at the top 20% of private schools and is positively related to fees paid.

Yet this literature is quite controversial (Jesson 2000). Harmon and Walker (2000), for example, dispute these findings and find that attending a grammar school only had a positive effect on earnings for individuals with low mathematical ability. What is problematic about this result is the notion that individuals with low mathematics ability at age 7 would have passed the entrance exam for grammar school. This suggests that either mathematics scores at age 7 are not good predictors of future mathematics performance or that this estimate is biased due to lack of data on other factors that influence achievement. In any case, isolating the effect of attending a selective school from the impact from having a better peer group is quite problematic in such studies. This is equally true of studies that evaluate the effectiveness of private-sector schools. For example, Naylor *et al.* (2002) found that the distribution of parental social class was a significant determinant of the magnitude of the independent-school earnings premium.

Furthermore, there is also some evidence of positive effects from grouping pupils by ability. For example, Feinstein and Symons (1999) estimate that having a "better" peer group increases a child's test score in English at age 16 by 9%. Equally, pupils in schools that "stream" students also do better in test scores in English at age 16 by 3.5%. (This same study found a grammar-school effect of 7%, consistent with the other evidence cited earlier in this section.) Such large peer-group effects are indeed cause for concern, given the evidence that increased parental choice in schooling has brought about greater inequality in socioeconomic intakes between schools.

3.7 Conclusions

Research findings suggest that the market-led reforms of the English and Welsh education system have – for the most part – created incentives in the system to improve school performance. However, there are clear indications that they have created some problems, particularly by reinforcing and strengthening inequalities in education that were present before their introduction.

The question of why some schools and teachers are successful remains high on the research and public-policy agenda. Whilst educationalists have pinpointed school ethos and classroom organization, as well as teachers' behaviour, economists have found mixed results for characteristics that are more easily quantified. This chapter has highlighted the key findings and pinpointed where the literature currently stands.

On school effectiveness, there is evidence that the school a pupil attends matters in a number of dimensions. Part of this is due to differential teacher effectiveness. In terms of resources, the pupil–teacher ratio has been found, at best, to have only a limited impact. The magnitude of any such effect in existing UK work is dwarfed by the effect of other school characteristics like grammar- and private-school status. However, the effects of selective schools are also controversial and significantly affected by the evaluation method used to account for the decision to attend a selective school.

On teacher effectiveness, the characteristics that make a good teacher are not easily observable by researchers and do not include those that are used to reward teachers: an issue that is discussed at length in the next chapter. Parents may have better information regarding the quality of schools and teachers since there is evidence that they are ready to pay a significant premium to live in the vicinity of a good school. Parents as economic agents seem to perceive that school quality, or what they view as school quality, matters for their child's education. Of course, whether this accurately reflects school quality is another important, yet unresolved issue, but it is evident that parents in their quest to get their children a better education link choice and accountability to what they observe, namely "good results' and "good peers".

The Labour Market for Teachers

By Arnaud Chevalier and Peter Dolton

4.1 INTRODUCTION

No book on the economics of education would be complete without an analysis of the teacher labour market. As discussed in the previous chapter, teachers are important in their impact on pupil attainment. The functioning and organization of the labour market for teachers is also important due to its potential effect on school effectiveness, children's human capital acquisition, and ultimately the growth of the national economy. This chapter analyses this important labour market, looking at policies and data from the UK (mainly England) to illustrate some more generalizable points about the supply and demand for teachers.

To some extent, the market for teachers functions like any other labour market, with schools acting as employers of teachers. However, the teacher market, like the market for some other public-sector occupations such as health professionals, is characterized by the state having both monopoly power in the provision of credentials (the state determines who is qualified to teach) and near monopsony power in the recruitment of teachers (since most teachers are employed in state schools). Furthermore, teaching is highly unionized and wages are generally determined by the government. Over the past 50 years, the UK has experienced recurrent crises in the recruitment and especially the retention of teachers. In 2002, for example, the DfES reported that annual turnover and wastage of teachers had reached 16.5% and 9%, respectively. Teacher shortages have been cyclical and regular in occurrence, and may be attributable to a number of factors, not least of which is the perceived low wage of teachers relative to other occupations in the public sector. Furthermore, shortages may be acute in particular subjects, such as mathematics, science and modern foreign languages, or in specific geographical locations like inner London, where the "outside option" in terms of an alternative career is preferred.

The main questions of interest in this chapter are as follows.

(1) What policies most effectively address the problems of recruitment and retention of teachers?

(2) Since teaching is predominantly a female occupation, what are the implications of the feminization of the occupation for modelling teacher labour supply and for teacher incentives?

(3) What is the best way to reward teachers?

(4) How can one (acknowledging the constraint of a national pay scale) address shortages in specific subjects or geographical areas?

(5) What is the relative impact of non-pecuniary conditions on recruitment and retention?

4.2 Patterns of Change in the Teacher Labour Market

4.2.1 Teacher Demand

The first key element in the demand for teachers is the demographic pattern of pupil numbers. The total number of primary and secondary pupils in UK state schools from 1946 to 2000 has fluctuated considerably, from a low of around 3.5 million pupils in 1947 and 1985 to a high of nearly 5 million in the mid 1970s. These trends were carried over to secondary schools, causing a peak in the number of secondary-school pupils in 1979. Additionally, the beginning of the period shows a large increase in secondary-school attendance as the compulsory school-leaving age was raised from 14 to 15 in 1947 and further to 16 in 1973. Specifically, these reforms had the effect of increasing the number of secondary-school pupils from 1.1 million in 1946 to 3 million by 1972.

The second demographic trend affecting the demand for new teachers relates to the age distribution of the stock of existing teachers. Figure 4.1 reports the age distributions of primary and secondary teachers in 2000. Currently, the retirement age for teachers is 60 with various options to stay on longer and is moving to 65 in the future, but teachers can retire as early a 55. A substantial fall in the number of teachers is observed at the early retirement age of 55 and only a minimal number of teachers remain in the profession after the age of 60.

England is also characterized by having an ageing teaching population, especially in primary education. 40% of all teachers are aged 45–55, and those aged above 55 account for another 6% of the workforce. Within the next 10 years, nearly 50% of the current workforce would be expected to have retired. At the current level of recruitment into teaching, a large shortage of teachers is therefore predicted. To some extent the government can influence the retirement plans of existing teachers, for example by reforming pension rights. For example, a change in the pension scheme in 1997 made it less financially advantageous for teachers to claim early retirement and led to a fourfold reduction in the proportion of teachers retiring before 60 (Eurydice 2002).

Several additional features add further complications to the consideration of the demand for teachers. Firstly, the financial administration of education at a local level is performed by LEAs. This means that, although central government sets overall spending limits and determines teachers' salaries, it does not have day-to-day control over how many teachers a local authority may employ. Secondly, since the 1988 Education Reform Act, schools may be financially autonomous with devolved budgets. Hence it is at the level of the individual school where decisions about teacher recruitment are taken, based on the actual (or predicted) income derived from expected student numbers. Finally, it is the case that the determination of desired pupil–teacher ratios are influenced by educational criteria and salaries negotiated with trade unions. Therefore it is not surprising that the setting of salary scales, and attempts to meet target pupil–teacher ratios, could be incompatible with the constraints of government spending limits. In these circumstances a school's capital budget for buildings and equipment may have to be cut, to "balance the books". This also gives rise to relatively large variation in pupil–teacher ratios and per-pupil funding across different regions of the country and compounds difficulties associated with assessment of the aggregate demand for teachers.

4.2.2   The Market for Teachers 1946–2000

Given the complicating factors determining supply and demand, the calculation of the exact extent of the shortage (or surplus) of teachers can be problematic. For example, the government's own estimates of current shortages are sometimes based on the numbers of existing vacancies. These are often inconsistent with figures relating to the shortfall of demand over supply based on using desired pupil–teacher ratios and their own published pupil numbers.[1] In Figure 4.2 the demand for teachers is calculated by taking desired pupil–teacher targets, as published by the government, and multiplying them by actual pupil numbers. Teacher supply is taken from the government's own data on the number of teachers in service, and the excess demand – or teacher shortage – is the gap between demand and supply. Following this simple procedure suggests that in 2000 there was a national aggregate shortage of some 34 000 teachers.

Figure 4.2 shows that there has been an excess demand for teachers almost continuously throughout the post-war period. The main problem has been for secondary-school teachers, although the difference in excess demand between primary- and secondary-school teachers disappeared towards the end of the 1990s. The 1970s are the only time in the post-war period where a (small) excess supply of teachers was

---

[1] For example, the official vacancy rate for teachers in the maintained sector was 1.3% in 2002, equating to a shortage of approximately 5000 teachers. Figures based on vacancies also hide the use of non-qualified teachers and thus understate the shortage of teachers.

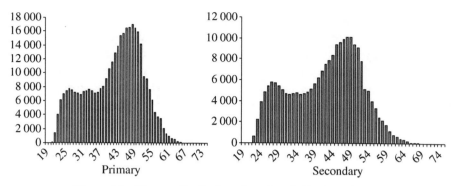

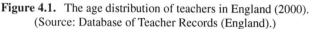

Figure 4.1. The age distribution of teachers in England (2000).
(Source: Database of Teacher Records (England).)

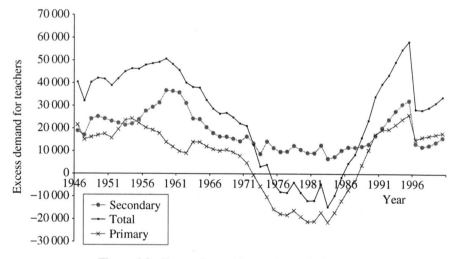

Figure 4.2. Excess demand for teachers: 1946–2001.

apparent. In some cases, the demand for teachers appears to change sharply from one year to the next. This is not due to demographic change, but to modification of the official desired pupil–teacher ratio. Since a shortage of teachers in the UK appears to be a permanent feature, the remaining discussion focuses on the determinants of the supply of teachers.

4.2.3 *Teacher Supply: Quantity*

All teachers in the UK must be qualified. In England, a teaching qualification can be obtained after a four-year university degree in Education or after a one-year post-graduate qualification following a university degree in any subject. Newly qualified teachers must register with the General Teaching Council (GTC) as a pre-requirement to work in the maintained sector and gain Qualified Teacher Status. Ultimately, the government has some control over the stock of teachers (at least in the medium term) since it can determine how many places are provided on courses at universities to train teachers.[2]

There are many factors operating on the choice of whether to become a teacher or not. Teacher-training courses are not always filled, and attendance varies by subject. In the mid 1990s, there were around 20% fewer students than targeted in Initial Teacher Training courses for secondary-school teachers, although this shortage has decreased to approximately 6% more recently. By subject the shortage is highest in mathematics, foreign languages and geography with shortfalls ranging between 20% and 30% in 2000/2001.

Measures to increase the retention of trainees and new teachers have been at the forefront of the political agenda on education. The most prominent measures are repayment of student loans for up to 10 years and a hardship allowance for students in shortage subjects committing to become teachers, bursaries for undertaking and completing the Postgraduate Certificate in Education (PGCE) and "Golden Hellos" of £4000 for new teachers in shortage subjects.

It is evident that the flow of newly qualified teachers does not necessarily indicate the level of overall supply. Focusing on those currently working as a teacher (Zabalza *et al.* 1979) ignores individuals who are available for (and possibly seeking) work in teaching, but who are not currently employed as a teacher. One can calculate supply as consisting of those entering the profession and those remaining in teaching from the previous year. For example, Dolton *et al.* (2003*b*) report that in 2000, 18 000 new entrants and 6000 re-entrants joined the teacher workforce. The difficulty, however, is not only recruiting teachers, but also keeping them in the classroom. Some trainees drop out and others decide not to become teachers. Smithers and Robinson (2003) showed that for 100 registered trainees, 88 passed the final examination, but only 59 were teaching a year later. After three years, only 53 of the original trainees were still in the classroom. This wastage adds to the costs of providing teacher training but also negatively affects child performance as inexperienced teachers are shown to be less effective in assisting pupils to achieve educational outcomes (Dolton and Newson 2003).

4.2.4 *Teacher Supply: Quality*

One of the most important, recurring debates in education is whether teacher quality is high enough. Whilst teacher quality is notoriously difficult to measure, the

---

[2]For example, it is clear that part of the reason for the increase in the supply of teachers after 1963 was the rise in the number of places on training courses.

previous chapter assessed the work on the importance of teachers, concluding that some teachers do consistently perform better than others over time, highlighting that teacher effectiveness is an important determinant of pupil attainment.

However, even if it is unclear whether teachers with better personal academic records or qualifications are necessarily better teachers, there is a concern about the difficulties experienced in recruiting teachers from the top end of the ability distribution. There is some evidence in the UK (Chevalier *et al.* 2001; Nickell and Quintini 2002), as well as in the US (Corcoran *et al.* 2004; Lakdawalla 2001), that current teachers are being drawn from further down the educational achievement or ability distribution than they were in the past. This clearly matters for teacher recruitment and for pupil performance. The issue of how one might recruit better or smarter teachers, and provide them with appropriate incentives, is thus an important one. It is this we turn to next, beginning with a discussion of what has happened to teachers' relative wages through time.

4.3 TEACHER PAY

The main element in the UK strategy to increase teacher recruitment and retention has been through offering financial incentives. Since teaching competes with all other professional occupations open to graduates, it is evident that governments therefore need to take into account changes in the graduate labour market when determining teacher wages. Thus it is not only pay in teaching that matters but teachers' pay relative to potential "foregone" earnings associated with an alternative career.

Figure 4.3 shows the relative earnings of teachers compared with average non-manual earnings from 1955 to 2000. The decline in the relative earnings of teachers is evident from the figure.[3] Since 1992 teachers' pay has fallen by 6% relative to average non-manual earnings (although the decline "bottomed out" in the late 1990s). Examination of the longer-run pattern of change reveals that the pattern of teacher pay exhibits a cyclical repetitive pattern, namely a period of sustained decline, followed by a dramatic increase, usually as a result of a major government report which investigates the crisis in teacher supply.

---

[3]Data on earnings are available from two sources, the October survey of earnings and, since 1968, the New Earnings Survey (NES). With respect to average earnings of all employees, the two surveys give similar estimates over the period in which they are both in existence, and so the reported average earnings is a simple average of the two estimates. For specifically non-manual earnings, the DfES's *Labour Market Trends* (formerly the *Employment Gazette*) reports an index based on the October survey until 1970, and from then onwards on the NES. However, the resulting estimate is considerably above the estimate of non-manual earnings supplied by the NES, thus, we only display teachers' earnings relative to the non-manual average from 1968 onwards using the NES.

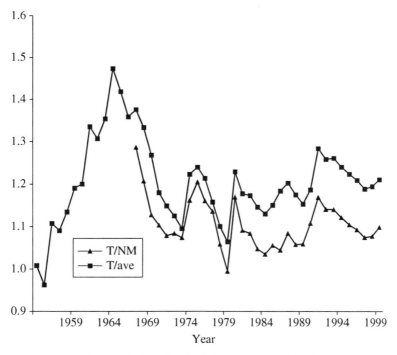

Figure 4.3. Teachers' relative wages 1955–2000.

Figure 4.3 clearly shows the process of "catch-up" following a decline in relative earnings, the most notable example being the average pay rise of 29% following the Houghton report in 1974. This was followed by 4–5 years of decline in real teacher pay before the Clegg Commission award of 1980 restored 1974 relativities. Comparing teachers' earnings to those of other public servants, teachers' pay has also declined by 11% relative to the earnings of policeman since 1981 and by 25% relative to nurses since 1973.

4.4 WHO BECOMES A TEACHER?

A perspective on the decision to enter the teaching profession is provided by the analysis of cross-section, point-in-time data on individuals (recording career decisions, pay, educational achievements and other socio-demographic characteristics). These data permit an examination of the potential supply of teachers by the analysis of the individual decisions that "would-be" teachers make along with those graduates who choose an alternative career. In terms of a model of occupational choice (Zarkin 1985) the expected utility of career alternatives is appraised before a job choice is made. A critical part of the choice concerns the way that expected earnings affect occupational choice.[4]

In this work, relative earnings in teaching compared with the non-teaching alternative have a marked effect on the occupational choice of graduates. In particular, the lower relative wages are (or wage growth is) in teaching, the less likely a graduate is to choose that career. Relative earnings impact both on initial career choices and on choices made later in an individual's career. Dolton (1990) also found that there is considerable inertia to remain in teaching, and suggested that this effect may be partially due to the different individuals' subjective evaluation of the relative pecuniary and non-pecuniary rewards to teaching. Chevalier *et al.* (2001) gave an overview of the market position for teachers in the UK from 1966 to the mid 1990s using graduate cohort data from five separate cohorts of university graduates: 1960, 1970, 1980, 1985 and 1990. The use of these data allowed these authors to simulate the effect of possible teacher pay rises over time. They find that relative wages in teaching compared with alternative professions have a significant impact on the likelihood of graduates choosing to teach, although the impact depends upon the market situation at the time. The wage effect on the supply of teachers is strongest at times of low relative teachers' wages, or following a period of decline in those wages. It is also strongest for those individuals who have more recently graduated. For example, increasing the wages of teachers by 10% would have led to an increase of nearly 10% in the supply of teachers in the mid 1980s but only 2% in the mid 1960s or early 1990s.

Labour-market conditions at the time the occupational choice is made are also important. Work by Court *et al.* (1995) based upon the Labour Force Survey found that aggregate labour-market conditions, particularly unemployment levels, are important determinants of teacher supply. The most recent evidence from Dolton *et al.* (2003*a*) reconfirms these findings with time-series data over the whole post-war period. Notably they find that the supply of graduates to teaching is counter-cyclical with most graduates' perception of teaching (and willingness to enter the profession) improving when graduate prospects are poor in alternative occupations and when graduate unemployment is high.

Whilst relative pay affects the decision to become a teacher, it also affects the decision to remain a teacher. Modelling the decision to leave teaching, Dolton and van der Klaauw (1995) show that the higher the relative earnings of teachers, the less likely they are to leave teaching. The importance of relative wages in teacher turnover decisions is examined by simulating a uniform 10% increase in relative monthly earnings. This leads to a 9% reduction in the total exit probability at five

---

[4]Most commonly, researchers estimate a (reduced-form) earnings equation and then relate occupational choice to a predicted earnings level (i.e. where occupational choice and earnings are simultaneously determined (see, among many others, Dolton 1990; Manski 1987; Hanushek and Pace 1993)).

years of tenure, or a total retention rate of 69%. A 25% increase raises the percentage of teachers still in teaching after five years to 73%.

Work based on US data suggests that raising teacher pay could improve the quality of the stock of teachers. Figlio (1997), accounting for school and district character-istics, concludes that districts offering higher starting salaries recruit teachers from more selective higher-education institutions. In particular, the author finds that a 1% increase in teachers' salaries increases the probability of recruiting a teacher from a selective higher-education institution by approximately 1.58 percentage points. Using information from the National Longitudinal Survey of Youth, Manski (1987) finds that a 10% increase in teacher earnings, coupled with a threshold on SAT scores, would maintain the current supply of graduates choosing to become teachers but they would originate from a higher part of the SAT distribution.

Attracting more-able students to teaching is not the only difficulty faced by policy makers. Since individuals with higher ability generally command higher wages in the labour market, high-ability teachers are at a higher risk of leaving the profession than less talented teachers (Stinebrickner 2001). To negate the lure of improved outside opportunities on "able"-teacher retention, fast-track programmes have been introduced in the UK with the aim of recruiting and retaining the most able graduates by shortening pay scales while providing them with additional training, support and supervision.

4.5 FEMINIZATION OF TEACHER SUPPLY

Another important aspect of teacher supply is that teaching is a career that is relatively popular with female graduates. A crucial aspect of the distinction between male and female occupational choice is that often women are simultaneously making decisions about starting a family and hence deciding whether to participate in the labour market. This is particularly true in teaching since it is argued that a teaching career has complementarities with family formation, particularly in the ease with which one can return to teaching after a career interruption. Dolton and Makepeace (1993) find that the choice of teaching as a career is intimately related to the decision to participate in the labour market for women. This is true in the sense that unobserved factors, which make a woman more likely to select a career outside teaching, make her less likely to participate in the labour market and vice versa. This generates a positive correlation in the teaching occupational choice decision and the decision to work.

Feminization of the teaching profession does add some difficulties to the planning of the supply of teachers as many women will at some point interrupt their career for family reasons; 12% of primary teachers who resign do so for maternity or family-care reasons (Smithers and Robinson 2003). Strinebrickner (2001) also estimates that, relative to men, women are more likely to exit teaching. Policies to facilitate work and child-rearing, such as subsidized childcare or reduced workload, therefore have scope for increasing teacher supply.[5]

Analysis of the role of non-pecuniary factors in the choice of occupation has been conducted by Dolton *et al.* (1989). They show that such factors are generally very important in the choice of teaching as an occupation, and in particular these factors seem to be more important for female than for male graduates.

4.6 INCENTIVES AND TEACHER REWARDS

While the evidence shows that raising pay impacts positively on the supply of teachers, it is not informative on how one can think about designing an optimal pay package to guarantee a supply of high-quality teachers (see a review on these issues by Lazear (2003)). Numerous authors advocate the lack of efficiency of across-the-board pay increases (see, for example, Odden and Kelley 1997). Raising the pay of existing teachers is inefficient since it is unlikely to radically improve their performance. In the UK, a form of performance-related pay (PRP) was introduced in 2000. It is intended to boost teachers' earnings, whilst making the increase in pay dependent upon teachers demonstrating effective performance in their jobs.

The performance management arrangement in the UK PRP system has two main elements. Firstly, each teacher is appraised annually by his or her senior line manager, on the basis of previously agreed objectives. At the second performance review stage, the assessment is used by the head teacher as a basis for teacher pay decisions in the coming year.

However, PRP does not apply to all teachers but only to the most experienced who have reached "the threshold", which is at the top of the pay scales for classroom teachers (approximately six or seven years into their careers). The idea is that individuals who can prove themselves to be effective teachers, assessed against a set of nationally agreed criteria, will "cross the threshold", receiving an immediate £2000 pay rise, and access to a new higher pay scale for classroom teachers. Around 80% of teachers who were eligible for the threshold payment when PRP was introduced in 2000 applied for it, and around 97% actually received it.

It is unclear whether PRP is the appropriate vehicle to solve problems in recruitment and retention of teachers. For example, PRP may not be the best vehicle to improve teacher performance, since the outcome of interest, pupil achievements, is multi-dimensional and depends on the effort of a group of teachers rather than single individuals (Holmstrom and Milgrom 1991).

---

[5]A childcare allowance of up to £150 a week per child is offered to returnee teachers undertaking a training course for up to 12 weeks.

Of course, it is by and large an empirical question as to whether performance-related pay schemes actually improve teacher performance. Evaluation of PRP in the UK is not possible since the scheme was introduced nationally. Evidence from elsewhere in the world tends not to support performance-related pay schemes. With the exception of Lavy's (2002) evaluation of an Israeli school-based tournament, there is little international evidence that financial incentives for teachers improve students' outcomes. In fact, over time, most performance-related pay schemes for teachers have collapsed (Murnane and Cohen 1986) and there is evidence that the ability of PRP to motivate staff was limited (Marsden 2004).

4.7 VARIATIONS ACROSS SPACE AND SUBJECT

The fact that teachers' pay and conditions of service are determined for the whole market presents problems with the supply of teachers for particular subjects or in specific geographical areas. This is due to there being large specific market differences found within each subject and in each region of the country. This can lead to a position where there are shortages in some subjects, or in some areas, and excess supply in others.

As was discussed earlier, training places for teachers specializing in mathematics and languages are continuously surplus to actual take-up, despite there being a wealth of financial incentives to induce people to enrol. On the other hand, other subjects like physical education are always oversubscribed. Because outside options for teachers with high ability in mathematics or languages tend to be higher, they are also more likely to leave the profession (Lazear 2003). Smithers and Robinson (2003) confirm that teachers in mathematics, information and communication technology (ICT), languages and English were disproportionately more likely to resign. Furthermore, amongst all graduates, there is evidence that the average wage return to a mathematics degree is higher (39%) than for many other subjects (Walker and Zhu 2001). This means that the opportunity cost of being a teacher may be a lot higher for a mathematics graduate than for a history graduate in terms of the foregone earnings in alternative jobs.

As with other public-service professions, there have also been shortages of teachers in certain areas of the country, most markedly in inner London and the south east of England. Official vacancy rates are two to three times higher than the national average in London, despite London being the area relying the most on temporarily filled positions. Chevalier et al. (2001) estimate that a graduate with mean characteristics is 15 percentage points less likely to be a teacher if he or she lives in London. Teachers in London are also more likely to leave or transfer to other schools than teachers in other geographical area (Smithers and Robinson 2003). Official turnover and wastage rates in 2002 were, respectively, 20% and 11% in London compared with 15% and 9% for England. The recruiting difficulties in London are thought to stem from the better wage opportunities in other jobs for potential teachers (and the upward pressure on living costs associated with a more competitive labour market in such areas). From April 2003, a specific salary scale has been defined for London replacing the previous London allowance. On the lower pay scale, teachers in London are paid about £3500 more than in the rest of the country; the pay differential for teachers on the PRP scale is up to £6000.

Budget permitting, schools in fact have the capability of adding some flexibility to teacher salaries. A range of recruitment and retention allowances, with a total value ranging from £1000 to £5400, can be offered to assist towards relocation, travel to work or provision of care for dependants. These allowances can be offered in case of recruitment difficulties. Thus, it will be possible for a school to offer this allowance to a new or established mathematics teacher but not to other teachers in the same school. However, it is possible that recruiting difficulties in London have more to do with the job conditions in inner-city schools than outside job opportunities and living costs.

4.8 Non-Pecuniary Conditions

It has long been asserted that many people become teachers due to the non-pecuniary benefits offered by joining the profession (long summer holidays being the classic, but not only, example). However, more recently, with the advent of the quasi-market and increased accountability, it has been argued that these non-pecuniary benefits have become less attractive. For example, it has been suggested that the extra burdens of the national curriculum and the rigours of the OFSTED inspection procedures (which involve increasingly detailed monitoring of pupil progress) have caused an excessive increase in the administrative burden on teachers. Moreover, it is commonly stated that increased workload and unruly pupil behaviour are important issues that are dissuading individuals from entering or remaining in the profession. There was such concern over this issue that the government commissioned an independent report into teacher working conditions (Coopers and Lybrand 1998). This report suggests that teachers are more overburdened with paperwork than they could or should be. Interviews of teachers leaving the profession also confirmed that heavy workload and school characteristics ranked more highly than salary as a reason for quitting (Smithers and Robinson 2003).

Other evidence from Chevalier et al. (2002) suggests that teachers are less satisfied in their jobs with respect to key attributes associated with the conditions of work than comparable graduates working in other fields. Teachers are particularly dissatisfied with pay and hours worked. Compared with other graduates, teachers are 12 percentage points more likely to claim to be dissatisfied with the number of hours worked. Compared with other employees, teachers' hours of work are concentrated during term time with an average working week of 52 hours. For over 40% of the leavers surveyed by Smithers and Robinson (2003) nothing could have made them stay. For the others, change in workload or school characteristics were more likely to be cited than salary as an inducing factor to stay.

4.9 CONCLUSIONS

A perennial problem for any state-education system is how to ensure a steady supply of quality teachers. A key public-policy issue is how to provide enough reward to induce high-quality individuals to become teachers and stay in the profession. Despite an array of financial incentives, there has been an excess of teacher-training places, especially in subjects where the economic returns are high outside teaching.

A striking feature of the recruitment process in the UK is that half of those enrolled as teacher trainees are not in the classroom three years after gaining their teaching qualification and beginning work as a teacher. The wastage of teachers is observable at all career points but is especially high early on in the career. This is usually thought to stem from the relatively low pay of teachers, but non-pecuniary aspects also matter.

Over the years there have been various attempts at providing differential pay for teachers, but since 2000 this has been focused upon performance-related pay. While moves to introduce incentives into the wage structure of teachers seems, in principle, to be a good idea, there are many theoretical and practical reasons why it remains very unclear whether a performance-related system is effective for teaching. Finally, while most governments' policies to retain teachers have concentrated on financial incentives, surveys of teachers reveal that earnings are not the only determinants of their dissatisfaction. Heavy, and increasing, workloads and unruly pupil behaviour are commonly cited as reasons given to justify the decision to exit the occupation. If one wishes to get a high-quality teaching profession in place, all of these difficult issues need to be addressed.

Post-Compulsory Education and Qualification Attainment

By Damon Clark, Gavan Conlon and Fernando Galindo-Rueda

5.1 INTRODUCTION

In differently organized education systems, different numbers of people choose to continue their education after the compulsory school-leaving age. It is often argued that in some countries, like the UK, too small a proportion of students decide to stay on in full-time education, and this has led to a high proportion of the population having low-level or no educational qualifications, with a consequent lack of basic and intermediate skills. It is therefore hardly surprising that policy makers have consistently aimed at improving staying-on rates and subsequent educational attainment, while also trying to provide a set of meaningful learning alternatives to those leaving education early.

After discussing recent trends in enrolment rates in post-compulsory education in the UK, this chapter proceeds to consider academic and vocational paths for further education, offering a discussion of qualification attainment from these routes. It also examines issues of access and funding for higher education (HE), which has traditionally been considered to be one of the better-performing sectors of the UK educational system.

5.2 CHANGING PATTERNS OF PARTICIPATION IN POST-COMPULSORY EDUCATION

Figure 5.1 shows trends in two measures of participation in post-compulsory education. It plots the staying-on rate into full-time further education at age 16 (in England) and the fraction of young people entering HE relative to the entire cohort in Great Britain (sometimes called the Age Participation Index (API)).

The figure shows that the staying-on rate increased steadily until the mid 1970s, and had a step change towards the end of the 1980s, with a flattening off at the end of the 1990s. The sharp increase in staying on at age 16 in the late 1980s follows the reform of the examinations system with the introduction of the General Certifi-

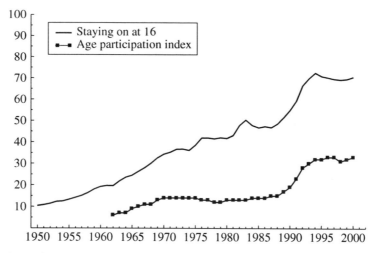

Figure 5.1. Long-term trends in staying on at 16 and Age Participation Index (API). (Notes. Authors' own calculations of staying-on rates in full-time education, based on series provided by the DfES. For related official statistics on education trends, see http://www.dfes.gov.uk/trends/. Staying-on rates refer to England. API also includes Wales and Scotland.)

cate of Secondary Education (GCSE). The GCSE became the public examination taken by pupils at school-leaving age (at age 16), and it represented something of a departure from the previous O (Ordinary) level system (see Gipps and Stobart 1997), in that everyone took the same examination (regardless of ability) and thus (at least in theory) could achieve the top grade. This seemed to facilitate a sharp increase in both the performance of students in their examinations at age 16 and consequently their likelihood of staying on after the compulsory school-leaving age.

The higher-education participation measure in Figure 5.1,[1] the API, is characterized by two periods of rapid growth. The first expansion occurred in the mid 1960s, following a government report into HE that advocated substantial expansion (Robbins Report 1963). The second period of expansion followed the end of the "binary divide" between traditional universities and polytechnics in 1992 (discussed in Chapter 2). During the entire period there is a rapid rise in HE participation, from around one in twenty in 1960 to one in three by 2000.

---

[1] In 1997–1998, the API for Scotland was 46%, considerably higher than for England and Wales, where the API is 32%. Participation in Northern Ireland is also higher than in England and Wales. (Source: parliamentary questions 24 March 2003. The Stationery Office.) In this chapter we try to distinguish specific features for different countries where relevant. Data limitations constrain the analysis in many cases to the UK, and institutional differences often restrict us to England or England and Wales alone.

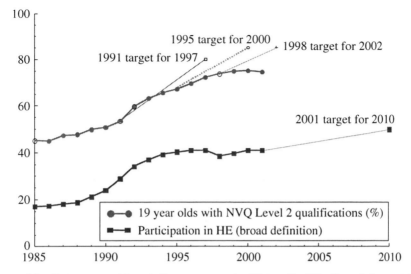

Figure 5.2. Outcomes and targets for young people. (Notes. Qualification-attainment data provided by the DfES. The question on which the series is based changed in 1993 and 1996. HE participation data based on the narrow measure (the API) spliced using the 2001 figure for the broader IER definition (see above), given by David Normington (DfES) to the House of Commons Education and Skills Select Committee, 30 January 2002.)

Figure 5.1 does pinpoint some slowdown in education participation in the late 1990s. If this slowdown in enrolment growth continues, qualification-attainment levels in the UK are unlikely to improve. In recognition of this fact, the Conservative government in 1991 set ambitious targets for the proportion of young people to achieve at least a level 2 qualification (which equates to five or more higher-grade GCSE passes or one A level pass or the vocational equivalent, i.e. a National Vocational Qualification (NVQ), level 2). In 1998, this became one of the new Labour government's five key education targets. Later on, the government also committed itself to move towards 50% participation in HE by 2010.[2] However, consistent with the slowdown in enrolment growth at age 16 since the mid 1990s, both attainment amongst 19 year olds and participation in HE have increased only slightly since that time.

As Figure 5.2 shows, the various targets set by governments have consistently not been met. Indeed, if these targets are ever to be met, decade-long trends must be reversed. Whether this can happen and the factors that might bring about this reversal are the key questions with which this chapter is concerned.

---

[2] As measured by the government's Higher Education Participation Rate (HIEPR).

5.3 Staying On after the Compulsory School Leaving Age of 16

It is of particular importance to be able to explain the broad trends in the staying-on rate graphed in Figure 5.1, with a view to assessing how these might evolve in the future. The recent history of staying on into further education in the UK can be thought of in terms of three phases: the period before 1988, characterized by a gradual increase in participation; the sharp participation increase between 1988 and 1993; and the subsequent slowdown.

Analysis of the staying-on rate can be undertaken by assuming that individuals choose between staying on in full-time education at age 16 against the pool of possible alternatives. We can assume that the staying-on rate is demand-determined as, by law (the Education Act of 1944), all school leavers are legally entitled to stay on if they choose to. In this context, it is helpful to view the staying-on decision as a cost–benefit calculation: school leavers will stay on when the returns reaped in the future (higher wages and/or a reduced risk of unemployment) exceed the costs incurred in the present (the small direct costs of books and materials, the large indirect costs of foregone earnings as well as other non-monetary costs such as net effort, dislike for studying, etc.). This follows Becker's (1964, 1967) analogy between this type of "human capital" investment and the investments in physical capital (such as factories and computers) made by firms.

Expected returns to staying on will depend on the value that school leavers expect their future employers to place on education. As has been said, the costs of staying on may be non-monetary as well as monetary. Young people may enjoy or dislike education irrespective of its potential financial gains. Indeed, many view this as the main channel through which family background (e.g. parental social class) influences the staying-on decision. Academic ability, part of it presumably inherited, plays an important role by determining how difficult it can be for a student to achieve a given qualification if they do decide to stay on.[3] In terms of marginal costs, more academically able people will find education less difficult and thus less costly, but education will, on the other hand, be "more expensive" in terms of the opportunity cost of study (i.e. foregone earnings during the study period).

Of course, family background may also affect the monetary costs of staying on, since wealthy parents may subsidize their children's education. From a quantitative perspective, however, we would expect the most important monetary cost to be foregone earnings, which will depend crucially on the state of the local labour market, as measured by the rate of youth unemployment, as well as the individual's own ability and motivation. When school leavers cannot find jobs, they have little to

---

[3] As hypothesized by Ben-Porath (1967) and others, human capital increases the efficiency with which more human capital is produced.

lose by staying on in education. Hence we would expect the state of the local labour market to impact on the staying-on decision.

This discussion suggests that three factors may influence the staying-on rate: individual ability, family background and the state of the labour market.[4] To disentangle these effects and assess which are the most important, we can conceptually partition the factors mentioned above into individual characteristics (such as exam achievement, family income, parental education), and external factors (principally economic conditions such as youth unemployment). We now discuss some of the more important factors in turn, starting with some key individual characteristics.

5.3.1 Individual Ability

Intuitively one would expect that an individual's ability would determine to some extent whether he or she stays on in education after age 16. However, testing this empirically is not straightforward. There are many relevant dimensions to ability and whatever measure is considered it will reflect both individual inherent attributes and also the outcome of earlier educational experiences. Thus, in practice, data availability determines what particular ability measure we can use.

Exam achievement is by far the most widely available measure of academic ability. The headline measure usually considered in the UK is whether an individual obtains five or more good grades (A*–C) at O level/GCSE. Figure 5.3 plots this measure of exam achievement alongside the staying-on rate. Given the close connection between the two series, it is not surprising that, in research based on micro (typically cross-sectional) data, a strong positive correlation has been found between exam achievement and staying on. Rice (1999) uses Youth Cohort Study (YCS) data to show that for a school leaver with a base set of characteristics, the predicted probability of staying on increases from 0.084 (0.172) for boys (girls) with no GCSE passes to 0.869 (0.884) for boys (girls) with more than five GCSE passes at grades A*–C. However, one can of course question whether exam achievement drives staying-on rates or vice versa, i.e. the decision to stay on at school may determine an individual's exam performance if, for example, individuals who decide to leave full-time education have a reduced incentive to work hard in order to gain GCSE passes. On the other hand, Payne (2001) notes that many school leavers postpone the staying-on decision until after their examination results are known.

---

[4]These factors are not necessarily independent, as they may interact in a number of possible ways. For example, more-educated parents may transmit simultaneously higher ability through genes, a more positive taste for education through transmission of values, and better financial resources. Given space constraints, we do not discuss these aspects in detail. For the same reason, we also abstract from related issues such as neighbourhood effects, school characteristics, etc.

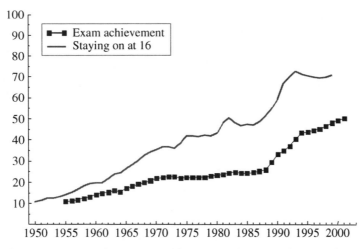

Figure 5.3. Staying on at 16 and exam achievement. (Notes. Staying on as in Figure 5.1. Exam achievement series measures the proportion of school leavers achieving five or more higher-grade GCSE (or O level) passes. Data for 1994–2000 from DfES Statistical Bulletins. Before 1994, data are taken back using a series very kindly provided by Duncan McVicar (see McVicar and Rice (2001) for details).)

An alternative is to use data from tests administered to children earlier on in their lives and see how such test scores relate to the subsequent staying-on decision. The two main UK birth cohort studies (the National Child Development Study, NCDS, which is a cohort of all people born in a week of March 1958, and the 1970 British Cohort Study, BCS, which is a cohort of all people born in a week of April 1970) include data on individuals' general ability as determined by tests taken by cohort members during childhood (age 7, 11 and 16 for NCDS and age 5, 10 and 16 for BCS). Micklewright (1989) uses reading and mathematics test scores at age 16 that are less likely to be correlated with the staying-on decision than exam results. He finds, as we would expect, that ability measured in this way is strongly correlated with the decision to stay on. We illustrate the relationship between staying-on rates, attainment and ability, using the composite measure of cognitive ability applied in Galindo-Rueda and Vignoles (2003, forthcoming).[5]

Figure 5.4 shows, for the 1958 and 1970 cohorts, the expected probability of staying on at 16 (i.e. the probability of being enrolled in full-time education after one's 16th birthday) and the probability of obtaining an academic qualification (A levels or higher), for a given level of ability at the age of 11. The higher the individual's ability at age 11, the higher his or her likelihood of staying on and

---

[5]This variable provides an indication of an individual's position within his/her own cohort in terms of cognitive ability, resulting from a set of ability test scores, and has been normalized to a unit standard deviation and zero mean.

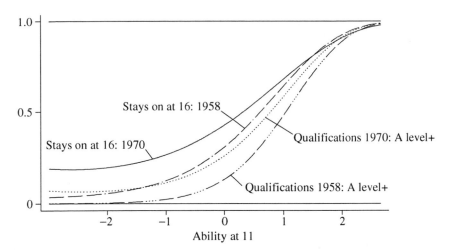

Figure 5.4. The changing effect of ability on staying-on rates and qualifications. (Source: Galindo-Rueda and Vignoles (forthcoming). Notes: predicted probability of staying on in full-time education at 16 (enrolled in October after turning 16) and probability of attaining a qualification level equal to or higher than A level (A level+), for cohorts born in 1958 and 1970. Probabilities calculated from logit estimates of dependent variables on a polynomial in ability for NCDS and BCS cohort members. Men and women combined.)

achieving higher-level academic qualifications. Because the figure shows both the 1970 cohort and the 1958 cohort, we can also examine cross-cohort changes. We find that there was a growth in staying-on rates and in attainment between the two cohorts, but mostly for individuals of lower and intermediate ability levels.

5.3.2 *Family Background*

Another individual characteristic that impacts on educational decisions and attainment is family background. Family background effects on education participation have important implications for intergenerational mobility and are of substantial policy interest. (Chapter 6 will cover these issues in more detail.) However, in contrast with the effects of ability, the nature of the impact of family background on staying on is less clear-cut.

Rice (1999) finds that even controlling for "ability", parental social class exerts a strong effect on staying on. Amongst those with medium levels of exam achievement, the predicted probability of staying on increases from 0.28 for those where the head of household is semi-skilled/unskilled, to 0.55 where the head of household is a professional worker. However, the Youth Cohort Studies contain no data on family incomes, and thus the research relied on parental occupation as an indicator. In an earlier paper using Family Expenditure Survey data, Rice (1987) concludes that family income has no effect on the staying-on rate for boys, but has a fairly large

77

positive effect for girls. Micklewright (1989) uses the NCDS data discussed earlier to address potential biases from omitting detailed background characteristics. He finds that once ability and school type are controlled for, the effects of family income are statistically insignificant. This does not imply that other measures of family background are not important, however, like Rice (1987), he finds that parental social class (combined with parental education) has a very strong impact on participation.

Although this particular evidence would suggest that family income may not in itself be an important determinant of staying on, there are a number of reasons why we should be cautious. First, the studies under consideration refer to cohorts leaving school in the mid 1970s, a period when the staying-on environment was fundamentally different. Secondly, family income data are especially prone to measurement error, and as mentioned above, income effects may be silenced by including too many controls highly correlated with income. Third, evidence from a UK government scheme to encourage young people to stay on (the Educational Maintenance Allowance (EMA)) suggests that paying school leavers from low-income households a modest amount to stay on in school does have an effect on participation (DfES 2001), but at the time of writing we do not know the impact on attainment. The importance of using this kind of robust evaluation evidence in policy-making is discussed at length in Chapter 10.

Parental income and social class are not the only family-background characteristics that influence staying-on behaviour and qualification attainment. Parental education, age and household composition are well known in the literature as being highly correlated with these outcomes. Parental attitudes are also deemed important in explaining attainment, but from a policy point of view, they are not as easily influenced as, say, household income.

To conclude the analysis of the effects of parental background on staying-on behaviour, we again use the information from the two birth cohort studies to make comparisons of the impact of parental income on staying on for a given level of early cognitive ability (age 11). We use parental income quintile as a time-comparable measure of a household's relative position in the income distribution.

Figure 5.5 shows the probability of staying on for individuals of different ability levels, for both the 1958 and the 1970 cohorts. It shows separate curves for children from high-income families (quintile 5) and low-income families (quintile 1). The gap in the probability of staying on between children from the top and the bottom of the income distribution, which is fairly constant over the ability distribution in 1958, widens substantially, particularly for those with high ability, by 1970. Another way to view this is to consider how participation has increased between 1958 and 1970. The staying-on rate for able but poor students does not increase over time, though the staying-on rate for rich but less able children increases substantially. This pattern of increasing complementarity between parental income and ability is

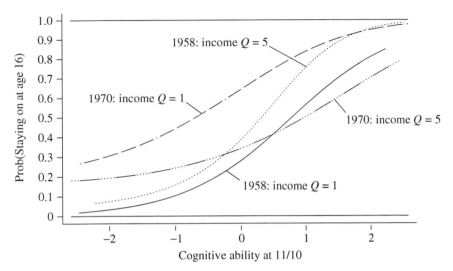

Figure 5.5. The changing effect of ability and parental income on staying on. (Note: predicted probability of staying on in full-time education at 16 by parental income quintile, for cohorts born in 1958 and 1970. Further details as in Figure 5.4.)

almost exactly the same for post-compulsory attainment, as discussed in Galindo-Rueda and Vignoles (2003, forthcoming). During the period considered, being part of a family with higher parental income became a more important determinant of an individual's qualification attainment, whereas the opposite was found to be true for ability.[6]

5.3.3 *The Labour Market*

Although the individual characteristics already discussed go some of the way to explaining trends in participation over time, much remains unexplained. This includes the stagnation of participation during two cyclical episodes (in the mid 1970s and the early 1980s) and the absence of any increase in the staying-on rate since 1993. A promising explanation for these phenomena is the state of the labour market, in particular the level of youth unemployment and changes in the benefit entitlement for the under 18s that made it harder to claim unemployment (via the 1988 Social Security Act). In support of the hypothesis that school leavers are more likely to stay on when youth unemployment is high, Figure 5.6 illustrates the very tight correlation between the sharp participation increases of the mid 1970s and early 1980s and increased unemployment induced by the recessions during these periods.

---

[6]Nevertheless, ability continues to play a key role in determining staying-on behaviour and qualification attainment.

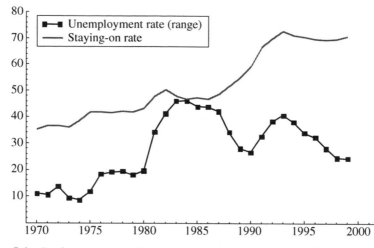

Figure 5.6. Staying on at age 16 and youth unemployment. (Notes. Staying on as in Figure 5.1. Unemployment based on the Labour Force Survey definition from 1984–1999 and imputed backwards using the estimated claimant count rate.)

Generally, the relationship between unemployment and staying on is quite strong. The exception is a brief period (1988–1990) in which, as discussed above, the introduction of GCSE examinations and changes in benefit entitlement rules[7] appear to have dominated the "negative" impact on participation of declining unemployment. In a similar vein, we might speculate that the absence of any post 1993 upward participation trend is due to modest improvements in exam achievement being more than offset by large falls in unemployment. This contrasts with the early 1990s episode, when both improved exam achievement and increased unemployment may have served to dramatically increase participation.

McVicar and Rice (2001) and Whitfield and Wilson (1991) use time-series data to assess the quantitative importance of the state of the labour market on the staying-on rate. Building on the analysis of Pissarides (1981, 1982) and Whitfield and Wilson (1991), they find that participation is increased by higher returns to a postsecondary degree (a measure of the financial returns to staying on) and lower overall unemployment levels. Using data over a longer period, McVicar and Rice (2001) find smaller effects from differently measured versions of the same variables. This paper also controls for a broader range of variables, including exam achievement and family income. Whilst they find that family income has little impact on participation, exam achievement has a large positive effect, and can jointly explain much of the rapid participation growth witnessed over the period 1988–1994.

---

[7] These changes to the welfare system made it harder for young people (age 17) who were out of work and not in full-time education to claim any state benefits, such as unemployment insurance.

Regarding the magnitude of the estimated effects, both papers find unemployment elasticities for boys in the region of 0.1, with smaller effects found for girls. These estimates imply that, from 1985 levels of participation and unemployment (the reference point used by Whitfield and Wilson (1991)), it would require a five percentage point increase in youth unemployment to increase participation by one percentage point. Although the papers use very different measures of the returns to staying on, Whitfield and Wilson (1991) report an elasticity of 0.3 with respect to postsecondary degree level earnings returns. This is a large effect, implying that a 10% increase in the return to a postsecondary degree induces a 3% increase in participation.

Clark (2002) takes a somewhat different approach to analysing this issue. He uses a 20-year panel of regional data to exploit the variation in staying-on rates and unemployment over time and between regions. His key finding is that local unemployment has a much stronger effect on the participation decision than was previously thought. For boys, the elasticity is roughly double that previously found, although for girls the effects are weaker. He also finds a large positive effect of returns to staying on for boys (elasticity of 1.177) but no effect for girls. Finally, Clark (2002) finds a significant negative effect of cohort size on staying on (elasticity −0.05 for boys and slightly larger for girls). This is consistent with a situation where popular courses become oversubscribed, leading to a reduction in staying on.

5.3.4   Summary of Findings on Staying On

To get a feel for the relative magnitude of the various effects that we have discussed, Table 5.1 uses the estimates obtained by Clark (2002) to decompose the change in participation over time. We see that over the period 1981–1988, the actual change in participation for boys was 3.4 percentage points. The predicted change was 3.9 percentage points, which can be decomposed into the effects of changes in several groups of variables. Notable amongst these is the large positive effect (2.3) coming from an increase in the proportion gaining high levels of exam achievement and the even larger negative effect (−2.7) operating via a decrease in youth unemployment. Increased income and reduced cohort size have smaller effects, and there is a large component associated with the estimated yearly fixed effects (4.4), which pick up common aggregate factors not already accounted for. For girls, more of the (negative) overall change is accounted for by cohort size and less by youth unemployment.

Turning to the period of very rapid growth, 1988–1993, column (4) illustrates that for boys, the actual increase in attainment was an enormous 22.8 percentage points. Of the 22.3 percentage points predicted by the model, the bulk of this change operates via improved exam achievement (10.2), increased unemployment (5.8) and cohort size (1.2), with the remainder roughly accounted for by the estimated time

Table 5.1. Decomposition of changes in staying on.

(Percentage point changes in the staying-on rate.)

	1981–1988		1988–1993		1993–2001	
	Boys	Girls	Boys	Girls	Boys	Girls
GCSE achievement	1.723	3.523	10.191	15.371	5.196	9.865
Income	0.356	−0.022	−0.062	0.004	−0.011	0.001
Unemployment	−2.690	−1.129	5.781	1.248	−8.933	−1.290
Returns	−0.290	−0.033	−0.157	0.129	0.112	−0.050
Cohort size	0.447	0.413	1.223	1.130	−0.783	−0.724
Time trends	4.415	−3.630	5.325	6.093	0.381	−3.373
Total explained	3.962	−0.850	22.301	23.975	−4.038	4.430
Actual changes	3.410	−0.861	22.86	24.278	−0.920	0.223

Notes. Figures based on Table 7 of Clark (2002). Time trends refer to aggregate country predictions from year-dummy coefficient estimates.

trends. For girls, changes in exam achievement provide the main driving force, with less of the predicted change accounted for by unemployment, and more by time trends.

The final two columns repeat the exercise for the period in which the staying-on rate remained broadly flat. For boys, the figures suggest this was the result of increases in unemployment cancelling out improvements in exam achievement. In fact the model predicts that staying-on rates should have decreased over this period. In contrast, for girls, none of the explanatory variables can explain why participation did not increase, and so the model over-predicts the growth in staying-on rates under constant elasticity assumptions.

5.4 BROADER CHOICES AT 16

So far this chapter has focused on the staying-on decision, but a richer classification of choices at 16 can be considered. Within the "staying on full-time" group, individuals can pursue academic or vocational courses, and those who leave full-time education may be grouped into those in Government Supported Training (GST), employment and non-employment. Figures 5.7 and 5.8 show this broader range of choices, with the former considering those not staying on and the latter looking at the staying-on group.

Perhaps the most striking feature of Figure 5.7 is the collapse in the employment rate over the period. In the earlier part of the period, a relatively small decrease in the overall proportion of school leavers not staying on masks a huge decline in the employment rate. In the space of three years, between 1980 and 1983, the employment rate of this group falls by more than one-half, with a corresponding increase in

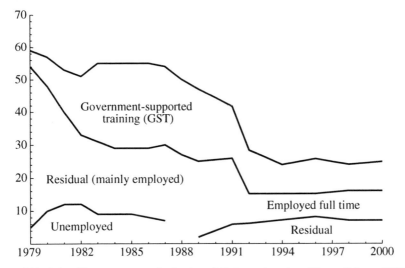

Figure 5.7. School leavers not continuing into full-time education. (Notes. Prior to 1989, the data come from Statistical Bulletin 13/91. Unemployed consists of registered unemployed prior to 1982/1983, and claimant unemployed between 1982/1983 and 1983/1984. From 1989, data are YCS taken from Payne (2001, Chart 4.1). Data from both sources in 1989 are used to take the YCS series forward.)

the proportion of school leavers in unemployment and government training schemes. The latter reflects the rapid growth in the Youth Training Scheme (YTS) introduced in 1983. Later, as the overall proportion not staying on declined sharply (between 1989 and 1993), this was reflected by a decline in the proportion of school leavers in full-time employment, with proportions in the other groups remaining fairly stable. A third feature of the employment rate series is that whilst employment rates fall as the economy moves into recession, they do not increase as the economy recovers. Why temporary shocks to the youth labour market appear to have permanent effects on the school leaver employment rate is a question we will return to.

Turning to the group that stays on in full-time education, Figure 5.8 breaks down education participation into GCE A levels, GCSEs and different types of vocational qualifications (described in Table 5.2). Over the period, most levels of qualification attainment have very stable shares. Only the share of students pursuing GCSE qualifications changed dramatically, in this case falling noticeably, especially during the 1990s.

One paper that models a richer menu of school-leaver choices is Andrews and Bradley (1997). The authors have access to a survey of young people leaving school in the north-west of England in 1991, and these data permit a rich classification of first destinations. They examine six possible first destination states – staying on and studying for academic qualifications (including GCSEs); staying on and studying for

83

Table 5.2. Changes in qualifications available over the period since 1975.

		1975	1988	Arrangements in 1992	2000	2002
NVQ level 3	Academic	A levels [2 years, 5 O levels]	AS levels			
	Vocational	BTEC Nat OND/OND [2 years, 5 O levels]	*NVQ level 3*	GNVQ advanced [2 years, 5 GCSEs]	Vocational A level [2 years, 5 GCSEs]	
NVQ level 2	Academic	O levels	GCSE A–C			
	Vocational	BTEC First Diploma [1 year, none] RSA Diploma [1 year, 5 O levels] *City & Guilds Craft*	*NVQ level 2*	GNVQ Intermediate [1 year, 2 GCSEs]		Vocational GCSE A–C [1 year, 2 GCSEs]
NVQ level 1	Academic	CSEs	GCSE D–F			
	Vocational	BTEC First Certificate [1 year, none] RSA other [1 year, 2 O levels] *City & Guilds other*	*NVQ level 1*	GNVQ foundation [1 year, none]		Vocational GCSE D–F [1 year, none]

Notes. Compiled by the authors from various sources. See the text for more detailed descriptions. The terms in brackets indicate the length of the course and the entry guidelines, respectively. Italicized entries are work-based, as opposed to classroom-based, qualifications.

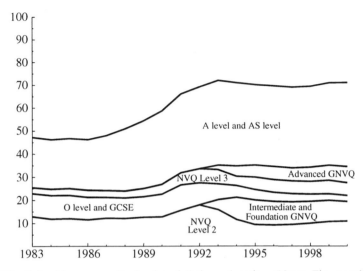

Figure 5.8. School leavers continuing into full-time education. (Notes. Figures taken from various Statistical Bulletins, based on education census data. There is a break in the data in 1994. We use both values for each series in 1994 to adjust the data going forwards.)

vocational qualifications; leaving to employment associated with on-the-job training (of any description); leaving to employment associated with general-skills training; leaving for GST and unemployment – and use a multinomial logistic framework to model these outcomes.

Once more, exam achievement is key and, broadly speaking, the greater it is, the more likely school leavers are to stay on to pursue academic courses, and the less likely they are to pursue all other options, notably youth training.[8] School-level factors are also important, including school size (larger graduating cohorts were less likely to stay on and more likely to engage in youth training) and school-level exam achievement (positively correlated with staying on into both types of course).

Payne (2001) examines data relating to the YCS cohort that left school in 1996. She focuses on those that did not stay on, and specifies a multinomial logit model with three destination states: full-time employment, government training scheme, and not in employment, education or training (NEET). In contrast to Andrews and Bradley (1997) she finds that boys with relatively good GCSE results were more likely to enter GST than full-time employment, although this was not the case for girls. However, for both boys and girls, the probability of being NEET was

---

[8]An increase in the probability of obtaining five or more higher-grade GCSE passes is associated with an increase in the probability of staying on into academic education of 6.1%. For the other options the equivalent numbers are: -8.2% (stay on, vocational), -17.2% (youth training), -28.4% (employment, on-the-job training), -2.5% (employment, general skills training) and -43.6% (unemployed).

strongly negatively correlated with exam achievement. The same effect was found by Andrews and Bradley (1997) with respect to unemployment, a category related to NEET.

What is the connection between the staying-on rates discussed above and subsequent qualification attainment? In other words, do the patterns described above in terms of staying on also hold for students' subsequent education achievement. Figures relating to non-completion of qualifications (drop-out) can be obtained from YCS data (see Payne (2001) for details). Overall, non-completion rates remain large, even when measured on an individual level, although they appear not to vary dramatically by course type.[9] Once again, previous exam achievement seems to be crucial, with family background acting as a mediating factor. Across every type of qualification, prior attainment and completion rates are strongly correlated, as one would expect.

What do these correlations imply about changes in non-completion over time? If we look again at Figure 5.4, we can see that there exists a substantial gap between staying-on rates at 16 and post-16 academic attainment for the cohort born in 1958. With the increase in participation concentrated largely amongst low-ability individuals in the 1970 cohort, the incidence of a gap in non-completion rates, which was more uniformly distributed across the entire ability spectrum, is now more concentrated at low ability levels. Another possibility is that drop out is higher when there are more labour-market opportunities available to school leavers, the assumption being that school leavers "wait" in further education until finding a suitable job.

5.5 Post-16 Qualifications in the UK

The increase in education participation beyond the minimum school-leaving age has already been discussed, but as we have just shown, it is not necessarily the case that this increase in participation has been converted into increased levels of qualification attainment. Furthermore, it remains the case that the rewards in the labour market associated with different types of qualification attainment remain highly variable.

Traditionally in the UK (as in many other countries) there have been two distinct paths of qualification attainment: the academic route and the vocational route. The academic route in the UK has clearly prescribed milestones for progression from one qualification to the next. The content of such qualifications is largely prescribed by government agencies. On the other hand, the vocational route has a more disparate

---

[9]Although YCS data are not broken down by completion and success conditional on completion, data published by the Learning and Skills Council (LSC) and, previously, by the Further Education and Funding Council (FEFC) show that non-completion is between 20% and 25% and has been steady over the period 1995–2000. These data do not include school sixth forms, and are based on qualifications rather than individuals; hence they are not directly comparable with the YCS data (see, for example, Benchmarking Data 1995/1996–1997/1998; Further Education and Funding Council, September 1999).

structure of provision (as emphasized in Chapter 2), with the government traditionally allowing private (and multiple) institutions greater freedom in determining the content and assessment of vocational qualifications. Table 5.2 summarizes (in a coarse, broad-brush way) the qualifications associated with each path.

The result of this historical provision of post-16 qualifications has been that, upon reaching the minimum school-leaving age, individuals who wish to continue their education are faced with an unambiguous choice. The options are either to continue along the academic route and obtain GCE A levels with the possibility of going to a higher-education institution or, by contrast, to undertake a vocational qualification in the hope that the qualification provides the necessary skills that prepare the individual for a job in a particular firm or sector of the economy.

Individuals pursuing the academic route are usually regarded as being at the higher end of the ability spectrum and those aiming for vocational qualifications are considered the less able students. There have been numerous attempts to change the image of vocational qualifications as being for the less able, but most of this "reform" has been undertaken in a piecemeal manner.[10] In practice, the result of the multiple initiatives to change vocational education has led to a plethora of vocational qualifications, whose content and assessment are constantly being questioned by employers, students and the media (as was discussed in Chapter 2). One consequence is that those in possession of vocational qualifications end up on average earning less than those with academic qualifications, even when the level of qualification is controlled for. For example, Conlon (2001) reported an hourly wage gap of 5 percentage points between the academically and vocationally trained at the lowest level of qualification attainment and that the gap between the two groups increased as the level of qualification increased. Similar findings were produced by Dearden et al. (2002a) and McIntosh (2002). In particular, Dearden et al. (2002a) show that the academically trained earn significantly more than the vocationally trained in terms of returns and even when these estimates are adjusted for the time taken to complete the qualification, the gap between the academically and vocationally trained remains positive and statistically significant. There are large differences depending upon the specific type of vocational qualifications undertaken. Table 5.3 shows this, reporting wage gaps for various academic and vocational level 1 and 2 qualifications.

There is a concern that part of the reason for the apparent "failure" of the UK vocational system (i.e. the low wage premium associated with certain vocational qualifications) is due to stigma effects. For example, employers may be of the view that individuals with certain vocational qualifications lack basic skills of vital importance in the labour market. In this situation, employers may prefer to hire an individ-

---

[10] A proper analysis of these changes clearly exceeds the aims and limits of this chapter. For more details see Robinson (1996) and West and Steedman (2003) on vocational qualifications and Gospel et al. (1998) on changes in the apprenticeship system.

Table 5.3. Wage returns to level 1 and 2 qualifications.

Qualification (time taken to complete qualification)	Men	Time-adjusted return	Women	Time-adjusted return
Level 2				
1 A level pass (2.0)	0.296 (0.047)	14.8%	0.317 (0.033)	15.8%
5+ GCSEs A*–C (—)	0.310 (0.026)	—	0.240 (0.020)	—
RSA higher diploma (1.0)	0.064 (0.305)	6.4%	0.187 (0.082)	18.7%
C&G Craft (2.0)	0.147 (0.046)	7.3%	0.116 (0.053)	5.8%
Apprenticeship (3.0)	0.160 (0.024)	5.3%	0.059 (0.036)	2.0%
GNVQ intermediate (1.0)	0.203 (0.068)	20.3%	0.162 (0.065)	16.2%
NVQ level 2 (2.0)	0.077 (0.039)	3.8%	0.101 (0.026)	5.1%
Level 1				
1–4 GCSEs A*–C (—)	0.178 (0.026)	—	0.160 (0.019)	—
CSE (< grade 1) (—)	0.079 (0.032)	—	0.029 (0.025)	—
RSA other (1)	−0.071 (0.131)	0%	0.125 (0.038)	12.5%
C&G Foundation (0.6)	0.061 (0.093)	0%	−0.055 (0.133)	0%
GNVQ Foundation (—)	−0.048 (0.216)	—	−0.134 (0.281)	—
NVQ level 1 (1)	−0.053 (0.078)	0%	0.045 (0.065)	0%
YTS (1)	0.026 (0.193)	0%	0.038 (0.151)	0%
R-squared	0.445		0.446	
Number of observations	7436		8106	

Notes. Sample covers people aged 16–59 from the spring 2002 Quarterly Labour Force Survey. Dependent variable is log of hourly earnings. Independent variables include age, age squared, region of residence, marital status, housing tenure, part-time dummy. The omitted educational group is "no qualifications". Standard errors are presented in parentheses.

Table 5.4. Average ability index by highest qualification.

Academic qualifications	Vocational qualifications					Total nos and % for academic qual.
	0 No qual.	1 NVQ1	2 NVQ2	3 NVQ3	4 NVQ4	
Men						
0	−0.784	−0.623	−0.576	−0.368	−0.127	18.93%
No qualifications	*395*	*113*	*181*	*94*	*38*	*821*
1	−0.545	−0.563	−0.596	−0.353	−0.438	11.16%
CSE/<5 O levels	*165*	*59*	*168*	*74*	*18*	*484*
2	−0.007	0.149	−0.086	0.142	0.336	35.82%
>5 O levels	*422*	*247*	*354*	*360*	*170*	*1553*
3	0.821	0.718	0.661	0.341	0.601	6.73%
A levels	*133*	*55*	*22*	*32*	*50*	*292*
4	1.016	0.945	0.106	0.448	0.639	27.35%
Postsecondary degree/higher	*411*	*180*	*71*	*125*	*399*	*1186*
Total nos and % for vocational qualifications	35.19% *1526*	15.08% *654*	18.36% *796*	15.80% *685*	15.57% *675*	100% *4336*
Women						
0	−0.897	−0.416	−0.653	−0.533	−0.021	13.59%
No qualifications	*365*	*95*	*115*	*33*	*21*	*629*
1	−0.662	−0.350	−0.543	−0.537	−0.307	10.07%
CSE/<5 O levels	*180*	*93*	*140*	*39*	*14*	*466*
2	−0.055	0.024	−0.062	0.059	0.165	39.94%
>5 O levels	*497*	*437*	*461*	*288*	*166*	*1849*
3	0.634	0.553	0.258	0.436	0.601	8.81%
A levels	*103*	*100*	*51*	*48*	*106*	*408*
4	0.913	0.676	0.362	0.356	0.639	27.59%
Postsecondary degree/higher	*298*	*229*	*103*	*129*	*518*	*1277*
Total nos and % for vocational qualifications	31.17% *1443*	20.61% *954*	18.79% *870*	11.60% *537*	17.82% *825*	100% *4629*

Notes. Sample: men and women with ability and qualifications data for 1970 BCS. Ability index derived as first principal component of mathematics, reading and general ability scores at age 10. Cell sizes in italics, below the ability index average for each cell.

ual with a lower-level qualification that is of a more academic nature. The question is whether those in possession of academic and vocational qualifications at the same level of attainment do genuinely possess the same levels of ability or whether the wage gap in fact reflects a real ability gap.

Table 5.4 shows that increasing levels of qualification attainment (either academic or vocational) are associated with higher levels of ability. However, for individuals with a given level of qualification, the academically qualified are more able (as measured by test scores) than their vocational counterparts. This suggests that some of the reason for the low wage premium from vocational qualifications is simply because lower-ability workers take them and these individuals are simply less productive.

5.6 HIGHER EDUCATION

The higher-education sector has experienced extensive changes since the 1960s. Indeed, the university sector has been considered by many to be one of the best-performing sectors of the UK education system. A primary aim of many UK governments since the 1960s has been to increase the proportion of the cohort attending some type of higher-education institution. In the 1960s, this goal resulted in the creation of several new higher-education institutions in green-field sites. The second major expansion of the higher-education sector began at the end of the 1980s. To accommodate the drastic change in anticipated participation, the higher-education sector was substantially reformed in the 1990s. As discussed in Chapter 2, prior to 1992, traditional, research-oriented universities in the UK coexisted with polytechnics, which did not have full postsecondary degree awarding powers and provided courses in more vocationally orientated subjects. In 1992, this distinction disappeared and all higher-education institutions were granted university status and postsecondary degree awarding powers.

A massive rise in participation followed these changes. This is shown in Figure 5.1 at the start of the chapter. Furthermore, as shown in Chapter 2, the UK higher-education participation rate is also higher than for most other OECD countries (and the drop-out rate is lower than that for most other OECD countries). There are a number of possible reasons for this. Firstly, until recently the government paid students' tuition costs, and many students benefited from additional living-cost grants. Secondly, postsecondary degrees in the UK are considerably more specialized and have a shorter duration than in most European countries. This implies that the opportunity cost of participating in HE in the UK has historically been much lower. Finally, and arguably most importantly, the earnings return to postsecondary degree level qualifications is high by international standards (see Chapter 2) and showed a marked increased from the 1970s to the 1990s (see Chapter 9 or Machin (2003)).

5.6.1 *Rationale for Continued Expansion*

The rationale for the continued expansion of higher education has been both economic and social. On the social front, HE has been considered an important channel for improving intergenerational mobility from an initially rigid class system. However, it should be noted that despite the large increase in the numbers entering HE since the 1960s, the increases have occurred disproportionately in the middle classes rather than the working classes (this is the subject matter of the next chapter). On the economic front, it has been argued that the major growth areas in the economy will occur in the high-skill sector and that without more postsecondary degree qualified workers, the economy will be limited in its growth prospects.

There have, however, been two serious concerns about expanding HE. First, who should pay for the expansion? And second, will the benefits associated with HE diminish following consistent increases in the supply of graduates?

Taking the second point first, the increase in HE participation appears to have been met with an increase in the demand for skills on the employer side. Wage returns to a postsecondary degree rose sharply over the 1980s (Machin and Van Reenen 1998; Machin 1999) and, even with the big supply increase of the 1990s, remained relatively constant over the 1990s (Machin 2003; Walker and Zhu 2001). This strongly suggests that the demand for skills has grown at a faster rate than actual supply (see also Chapter 9 for a full discussion of this issue).

However, given the strain on the public purse associated with the increasing numbers attending university and the reduction in funding per capita, these high private returns to a postsecondary degree have also been used as evidence to support the potentially contradictory policy of making individuals pay a larger proportion of the costs, and the general taxpayer less.

Empirical evidence on the returns to a postsecondary degree support the fundamental conclusion of the Dearing report into UK HE (1997) that graduates are substantial beneficiaries of HE, gaining improved employment prospects and pay, and that it should therefore be graduates in work who make a greater contribution to the costs of higher education. Unfortunately, there is no good-quality information available on the extent of the social benefits arising from HE that would allow us to determine what proportion of the total benefits are private returns to individual HE students in the UK. This is of course of central importance in determining the extent to which the costs of HE should be born by the individual, as opposed to the state. From an efficiency perspective, if the social rate of return to HE exceeds the private rate of return, this would suggest that state intervention and funding is required in order to increase the supply of graduates in the economy.

5.6.2 Reforms

The Higher Education Funding Councils for England and Wales (HEFCE/HEFCW) distribute funding from central government to HE institutions in England and Wales, according to the amount and quality of research and teaching these institutions undertake.[11] In the UK there has been a long tradition of HE being free at the point of use for students (i.e. students did not pay for their HE directly). As HE participation increased, this situation became politically untenable. Per student funding fell continually as the number of students increased. In particular, between 1989 and 1997 per student funding fell by 36% (from http://www.universitiesuk.ac.uk/statistics/funding/unitfundingtrendschart89-90to03-04.pdf). In response to these problems, major funding changes were introduced in 1998. Firstly, a means-tested tuition fee was introduced (£1000 per annum), levied irrespective of the institution attended or the subject studied. The level of this fee was increased annually in line with inflation. Students who were not exempt had to pay this cost upfront. Previously, poorer students were also entitled to a grant to subsidize their maintenance costs whilst at university. Such grants were gradually reduced in value in real terms and phased out completely in 1999. Grants were replaced by means-tested loans, repayable on an income-contingent basis after graduation.

In 2003, the Labour government proposed some radical reforms designed to allow universities more freedom to differentiate their fees by institution and by subject. In addition to the variability principle, government proposals in 2003 involved three basic elements.

- Allowing universities to charge potentially higher tuition fees, of up to £3000 per year.
- Removing the requirement to pay tuition fees in advance (i.e. upfront fees).[12] As before, the debt accumulated would be repaid following graduation though the tax system and would be income contingent.
- Introduction of an access regulator to guarantee fairness in the system and to widen access, particularly regarding universities that charge "differential" fees.[13]

---

[11] Scotland has a largely independent HE system from the rest of the UK. Teaching resources are allocated according to the number of full-time students (and part-time equivalent). However, there are several criteria for receiving additional funds depending on the equipment needs of the subjects provided (laboratories, etc.); the type of student ("mature", "part time" and "students on long courses"); and the institution ("London premium", "pensions", "specialist institutions" and "old and historic buildings"). In addition to the funds for teaching, UK universities are eligible for research grants based on the five-yearly Research Assessment Exercise (RAE). There are three components of quality-related research (QR): mainstream QR, research students' supervision funds, and a London weighting premium. The quality of research is rated according to a scale ranging between 1 (worst) and 5* (best), which has funding weights associated with each score. The measure of volume and quality are multiplied to calculate the allocation of resources to each institution.

[12] The student would remain eligible for maintenance loans and those from less-well-off backgrounds would be eligible for non-repayable grants.

[13] Some of these features are likely to be partly modified throughout the process of approval by Parliament, still incomplete at the time of writing this chapter. In spite of this uncertainty, our discussion of the general principles of this reform can help illustrate some of the basic features of HE policies from an economic point of view.

5.6.3 *Concerns*

Whilst removing upfront fees in itself may be conducive to higher levels of participation, particularly amongst credit-constrained students, there are concerns that the 2003 student-finance reforms will reverse the increasing trend of HE participation in the UK by also introducing higher prices for HE. This might imply a disproportionate effect on those from lower socioeconomic groups (in terms of application and attendance rates at both "prestigious" institutions and universities more generally). This is due to students' attitudes towards debt upon graduation, their associated elasticity of demand for HE, and uncertainty relating to future earnings upon graduation.

The next chapter focuses on the problem of the socioeconomic gap in student attainment. Here we note that although it was expected that the massive expansion of the HE sector would result in a narrowing of the gap in the proportion of individuals from the higher and lower socioeconomic groupings attending university, this has not happened. The increasing participation rate in HE has not resulted in a narrowing of the gap in participation between individuals from traditional and non-traditional university backgrounds (see Figure 2.1 in Chapter 2).

5.6.4 *Earnings and University Degrees*

The logic behind increasing the burden of costs on individual students is that the earnings premium achieved by graduates over non-graduates represents a substantial lifetime benefit from HE. Although one can argue about the exact size of the graduate wage premium, it appears to be in excess of any contribution the individual student has thus far been expected to make to the costs of HE. It could also be argued that, from an efficiency perspective, students studying different degree subjects earn different amounts and therefore should be expected to pay according to what they will expect to earn in returns to their HE investment.

Evidence from Walker and Zhu (2001) suggests that there are indeed quite wide variations in the wage differentials that accrue to holders of postsecondary degrees of different subjects, and that they vary by gender. Their evidence suggests that the payoff to a health, law or economics postsecondary degree is sizeable, for example, and there is a very low payoff for education and arts, especially for men. However, there are potential risks in using this information to support the rationale for differential fees. Estimates of the wage premium associated with different postsecondary degree subjects are not as robust as the aggregate estimates of the return to a postsecondary degree. In particular, researchers need to be sure that individuals who choose different subjects at degree level are in other observable and unobservable ways similar if they are to calculate returns to different postsecondary degree subjects. It would be wrong to conclude on the basis of simple mean earnings differences between subjects that it is not financially beneficial to do a postsecondary

Table 5.5. Average point score by university type.

1990 cohort	Russell Group	"Old" universities	"Modern" universities	Other institutions
Women	23.08(4.88)	17.92(6.07)	13.98(5.76)	11.85(6.67)
Men	24.32(4.80)	19.97(5.84)	14.21(6.10)	14.14(7.81)

(Source: Chevalier and Conlon (2003, Table 2). Point scores range up to 30. Average point score displayed, with standard deviations within parentheses.)

arts degree, to cite an example. Constructing an appropriate counterfactual is the key challenge faced by researchers in the education field. Further discussion of this can be found in Chapter 9, where Table 9.7 gives estimates of the return to different postsecondary degree subjects conditional on an individual's prior achievement at A level.

Work by Chevalier and Conlon (2003) has also estimated the differences in earnings according to the type of university attended. HE institutions are divided into whether they are members of the Russell Group[14], "Old" universities[15] or "Modern" universities[16]. A straightforward analysis comparing the earnings of those attending different types of university may simply reflect existing differences of average ability between students in each type of institution, instead of the genuine effect of the type of institution attended. This is illustrated in Table 5.5, which shows the average A level grade point score achieved by graduates of the various types of universities in 1990.

To account for the problem that very different types of student attend different universities, Chevalier and Conlon (2003) note that the admission of students to an institution is not matched perfectly to ability. A proportion of good students are found in less prestigious institutions and, symmetrically, students with mediocre results do attend elite institutions. This imperfect sorting, which may be due to some institutional features or geographic mobility restrictions, allows the authors to pair students at prestigious institutions (Russell Group) with "similar" students in less prestigious universities using statistical methods.[17]

The authors found that after controlling for academic achievement, subject of postsecondary degree and family background, those attending a Russell Group institution (compared with a "Modern" university) experience an additional earnings premium (over and above the average premium from having a postsecondary degree) ranging

---

[14]A self-selected informal alliance of research-oriented universities.

[15]Universities with postsecondary degree awarding powers prior to 1992 not in the Russell Group.

[16]Universities with postsecondary degree awarding powers since 1992.

[17]The authors use propensity score matching to generate these "pairs" of students. See Rosenbaum and Rubin (1983) on how to use propensity score matching as a means of reducing bias where individuals in samples have different characteristics.

from 2.5% to 3.5% for women and between 0% and 6% for men. This financial benefit is also found to be neither dependent on previous academic achievement nor on parental background. It is unclear whether the premium from attending a Russell Group university is due to a larger increase in human capital for those attending such institutions, or whether it is simply a signalling or a networking effect. To disentangle these explanations, the authors also explore variations in earnings growth by the type of institution but these results are ambiguous. For women (but not for men), graduating from an elite institution leads to greater wage growth. The implication of the overall findings is that certain types of HE institution add more to the human capital of their graduates than other types of university. There is therefore an economic argument in favour of the introduction of differential fees.

It is possible to use estimates of wage differentials attributable to the type of institution attended to predict prices in the HE market, if institutions were left with the freedom to set their tuition fees. Under various scenarios, Chevalier and Conlon (2003) estimate a fee differential between Russell Group and "Modern" universities ranging from £2950 to £7250. Interestingly, this range of tuition fees is in line with the current differential observed in the US among private institutions.

Another aspect of the tuition-fee argument that merits attention is the extent to which tuition fees will alleviate any crisis in funding in UK HE. The implications of the introduction of differential fees for students from different family-income backgrounds have been analysed in this context by Dearden *et al.* (2004). They highlight the extent of financial costs to the government from the subsidization of the interest rate (zero in real terms) at which students can borrow money. Depending on the generosity of student bursaries after the reform is implemented, they estimate that the added funding can increase teaching resources only by approximately £1250 per pupil. Many observers suspect this will not suffice to fully alleviate the funding gap in HE and that further regulatory changes may have to follow.

5.7 CONCLUSIONS

The economics of education has historically been most concerned about the economic value of different types of education, i.e. the rate of return to different qualifications or their economic value in the labour market. In recent years, greater attention has been paid to the closely related issue of who gets what type and how much education. To this end, this chapter reviewed the literature on educational decisions and outcomes during the post-compulsory stage of the education process, largely in the context of the UK education system. From this evidence, we can conclude that education participation in the post-compulsory phase of schooling, i.e. staying-on rates at age 16, are driven largely by improving exam achievement, which in turn reflects individual ability and learning during the compulsory schooling phase, with a secular component attributable to family background and a cyclical component due to the local labour market. Thus we can clearly see in this literature the impact of and returns to earlier human capital investments, made during primary and secondary school. Children who have high attainment levels earlier in their schooling are more likely to stay on in post-compulsory education. Furthermore, children from more advantaged backgrounds start school with higher attainment, progress more rapidly during compulsory schooling, and are then also much more likely to stay on at school past the age of 16 and gain higher-level qualifications. The intergenerational nature of this process – children with more educated parents go on to become better educated themselves – is discussed in the next chapter. The evidence presented in this chapter illustrates the point that prior attainment determines future attainment: more able/higher-attaining students get better qualifications and this selection process needs to be fully taken into account when one tries to estimate the value of different qualifications in the labour market (as is discussed in detail in Chapter 7).

Another important issue, which has a high public policy profile, discussed in this chapter is the significant problem that the UK, in common with many other countries, has in the provision of vocational qualifications. It was shown that vocational qualifications are, on average, taken by less academically able students. In the UK the plethora of vocational qualifications available may mean that they also convey limited information to employers about the potential productivity of workers with such qualifications. From a policy perspective, improving the economic value of existing vocational qualifications, whilst also acknowledging the signalling role played by qualifications in the labour market, is a major challenge. Furthermore, pursuing a strategy of gaining equality in status between the academic and vocational routes appears to be particularly problematic, given the evidence presented here that the academic route is preferred by more able students.

This chapter also considered the expansion and reorganization of HE in the UK. Chapter 2 suggested that the HE sector was performing particularly well in the UK, relative to many other countries. However, the expansion of this sector has led to problems in terms of financing. During the 1990s, it became increasingly difficult for the costs of HE to be met by the general taxpayer. Thus, in 1998, England and Wales introduced tuition fees for postsecondary degree courses, which represented a significant policy change, given that HE had always been free up to that time. The economic justification for tuition fees (high private rates of return to a postsecondary degree) were discussed at length in this chapter, as well as the potential problems arising from the introduction of fees, particularly in terms of access to HE by poorer students, an issue that is discussed in the next chapter. Here we note that despite the rapid expansion of the HE sector, there has been no fall in the average return to a postsecondary degree. This suggests that the general policy of expansion may be justified in terms of the labour market's need for more qualified graduate labour. However, the expansion and increased heterogeneity of the student body has led to greater variation in the labour market returns to postsecondary degrees (see Chapter 9), with considerable variation by subject, institution and indeed by gender, in terms of what people get back from their investment in HE. This clearly has important ramifications for the future funding arrangements in HE, particularly in terms of the economic justification for variable tuition fees. To the extent that the rate of return to different postsecondary degrees varies enormously, it would appear economically justified to charge variable tuition fees (by institution and subject). However, we end with a cautionary note. One purpose of this chapter was to show that different qualifications are obtained by different types of individual. One needs to allow for this when estimating the economic value of different qualifications. The estimates of the return to different postsecondary degree subjects generally do not allow for the fact that more/less able students take different subjects. To use this variation as prima facie evidence in favour of variable tuition fees would therefore be a mistake.

Educational Inequality and Intergenerational Mobility

By Jo Blanden, Paul Gregg and Stephen Machin

6.1 INTRODUCTION

The role of education within society is frequently considered in terms of improving the stock of human capital in the economy. As with all valuable resources, however, there is also an issue of how human capital is distributed across society and the potential inequalities associated with any particular distribution. The distribution of educational attainment with respect to parental background is particularly important and contentious.

We know that (on average) the greater the level of parental qualification, the higher the qualifications attained by their children (Haveman and Wolfe 1994; Solon 1999). We also know that those with higher educational qualifications earn more in the labour market (Card 1999). This means that the relationship between educational attainment and family background is a vital factor in how closely related incomes and economic welfare will be across generations. As a consequence, equalization of current educational attainment of those from different socioeconomic backgrounds is frequently seen as an important tool for improving the equality of opportunity in society.

At a given point in time, most societies are characterized by wide gaps in education for people from high- relative to low-income backgrounds. This income gradient is a natural metric of educational inequality. A highly relevant issue in the current policy debate is the extent to which government initiatives can be used to dampen this gradient, thereby reducing educational inequality and fostering more intergenerational mobility.

This is all the more important when one sees what has happened to educational inequality and intergenerational mobility over time. In this chapter we show that, in the last quarter of a century, intergenerational mobility has fallen in the UK, so that family background matters more now than it did in the past, and that a key factor underpinning such change is increased educational inequality, or a steeper income gradient of education.

The chapter reviews this evidence on education inequality and intergenerational mobility in several stages. It begins by discussing recent patterns of change in education attainment, education policy and income inequality, before discussing changes in education policy that have occurred in the last two or three decades. Next it considers how educational inequality and intergenerational mobility are related to one another. The available data are then discussed, and then the key results are reported. The final section offers some conclusions.

6.2 PATTERNS OF CHANGE IN INCOME, EDUCATION AND EDUCATION POLICY

Throughout this chapter we look at how the economic and educational outcomes of children relate to the incomes of their parents, focusing explicitly on how these associations may have changed over time. In this section we thus begin with some background material on recent changes in income and its distribution, before moving on to a discussion on shifts in education policy and educational participation.

6.2.1 *Changes in Income Inequality*

It is now well known that the distribution of income has altered very markedly in the recent past. Figure 6.1 shows income growth at the 10th, 50th and 90th percentiles of the real income distribution for families with children in the UK since 1978. The figure shows faster growth in real income at the 90th percentile relative to the median, which, in turn, grew much faster than income at the 10th percentile. Indeed, real income barely grew at the 10th percentile over the whole period, with declines in real income until the mid 1990s, after which one sees an improvement in the fortunes of those at the bottom end of the income distribution.

Two further points are worth making about this figure. First, it only considers families with children. The reason for this is that we are interested in how family income is linked to children's educational outcomes. It is, however, worth noting that the income distribution for families with children tends to show a greater widening over time than for the income distribution of people without children (although inequality rises for this group as well) and that the average incomes of families with children fell relative to those without children over this time period (see Gregg *et al.* 1999). Secondly, and related to this, the increase in income inequality for families with children was most pronounced in the divergence between the bottom and the middle of the income distribution and hence generated a large increase in child poverty. In 1979, 13% of children lived in households where income was less than half of the national average. By 1996 this had risen to 33% (Gregg *et al.* 1999), a plateau level, which has only started to diminish in the last few years.

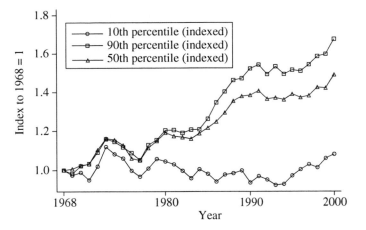

Figure 6.1. Changes over time in the distribution of log(real income) for families with children, UK. (Notes. 1. Own calculation from Family Expenditure Surveys of 1968–2000. 2. Sample is all non-pensioner families with children. 3. Figures are based on net real income.)

6.2.2 *Changes in Education and Education Policy*

As has already been highlighted in Chapter 5, a number of changes were occurring to the education system at the same time as the rise in income inequality was taking place. Several of these are particularly important to the issues of educational mobility that we consider. At the minimum school-leaving age, the most important of these was a reform of the examination system that took place in 1988, with the switch from the GCE O level system to the introduction of the GCSEs. As previously mentioned, this reform moved the education system from one that rationed the number of passes in a given year to one where, at least in principle, everyone could pass (see Gipps and Stobart 1997; Blanden *et al.* forthcoming). Furthermore, the GCE O level system was purely exam based, whereas GCSEs often have a substantial coursework component. It has been argued (see Kingdon and Stobart 1998) that this also facilitated an increase in the pass rate achieved.[1]

This reform of the examination system stimulated a rise in post-compulsory participation. Staying-on rates rose very sharply from the late 1980s onwards. The estimates presented in Chapter 5 reveal that staying on beyond the minimum school-leaving age had begun to rise through the 1980s, from 42% of 16 year olds in full-time education in 1979 to 52% in 1988. However, the pace of change accelerated dramatically after the ending of the rationing system of post-compulsory education

---

[1] This may also have affected the distribution of educational attainment at age 16 (for example, the shift to coursework seems to have been a factor in the strong improvement shown by girls relative to boys (see Gorard *et al.* 2001; or Machin and McNally 2003*b*)).

and the introduction of GCSEs. By 2001, the post-compulsory staying-on rate had increased to 71%.

Higher-education (HE) participation has also risen rapidly in recent years. Figure 5.1 (presented in Chapter 5) shows that, after a slowly rising or steady participation rate in the 1960s and 1970s, there was a strong rise in HE participation from the late 1980s onwards, to the point that HE participation has risen to 33% by the year 2000.

The rise in HE participation was accompanied by fundamental changes in the system of university funding and student finance arrangements. In the 1980s, university fees (in their entirety) were paid by students' Local Education Authorities. In addition, many lower-income students were eligible for maintenance grants to support them while living away from home. This time period effectively represented the high water mark of the extent of state subsidy for HE and the extent of its progressivity.

However, the marked increase in participation meant that these high levels of support could not persist without substantial additional funding. Successive governments were unwilling to provide this and support for student finance dwindled. In 1990 maintenance grants were frozen and began to be phased out in favour of subsidized loans that would be available to all students. As Callender (2003) points out this shifted the public subsidy of student living costs purely from benefiting lower-income students to benefiting all students (the majority of which are from more affluent families).[2]

However, despite the expansion of HE student numbers, universities remained starved of resources. Based on recommendations contained in the Dearing Report of 1998, the government allowed universities to charge students £1000 per year towards the cost of studying, and increased the maximum loan available to students, but still this did not resolve the funding crisis. Greenaway and Haynes (2003) demonstrate that, as participation doubled from 1980 to 2000, funding per student halved.

As detailed in Chapter 5, recent policy reforms will allow universities to raise their fees up to a maximum of £3000 per year. This, and the cost of maintenance, will be met by even larger loans, to be paid back as a proportion of income after the graduate's earnings exceed £15 000. This is likely to be accompanied by increased support for students from lower-income backgrounds, although current proposals of £1000 per year look modest at best.

Proponents of the policy argue that it will have no adverse effects on the participation of those from less-well-off backgrounds as education will not be related to ability to pay at the point of entry. However, one may worry that students from

---

[2]The political economy and redistributive implications of universal subsidies to HE are considered in detail in Fernandez and Rogerson (1995).

lower-income backgrounds will be less likely to participate as the cost of study rises, both because their parents are unable to contribute and because poorer students are more adverse to taking on debt (see Callender (2003) for evidence on the latter).

These are some of the several substantive policy changes that are likely to have affected students and prospective students in the past or will affect them in the future. These are likely to have impacted not only upon the overall increases in education participation and attainment documented in Chapter 5, but also may have differentially affected young people from different family backgrounds. This is one of the main focus points of this chapter and we present empirical work on the extent to which one sees different cross-time patterns in educational outcomes by family income.

Moreover, these policies may well have had different effects, or the magnitude of their impact may have differed, when income inequality is at different levels. If family income influences educational attainment, then as income inequality grows, the gap in educational attainment between those from rich and poor families will widen, simply because the income gap is larger. This income-gap effect is likely to interact with policy. So, for example, under the O level system that rationed educational attainment, this interaction is likely to accentuate the education–income association if inequality increases. But the switch from O levels to GCSEs made the school exam system more inclusive (as now all could achieve the set pass standard) and this displacement effect no longer applies.

By contrast, the increase in university participation was accompanied by a move, from 1990 onwards, toward less state support of students from low-income backgrounds. This is therefore likely to exacerbate relationships between family income and HE participation and attainment as inequality rises.

These two major policy shifts are then likely, in an era of rising inequality, to have driven the relationship between parental income and attainment in opposite directions at different stages of the education sequence. This provides a clear prediction regarding the role of education policy in amplifying or diminishing the relationship between family income and educational outcomes.

6.3 Measurement and Data

Given the discussion so far it is important to establish how one may measure educational inequality and the extent of intergenerational mobility and what data can be used to provide evidence on changes in these phenomena over time. Next we therefore consider some conceptual modelling and measurement questions, and after that consider the available data.

6.3.1 *Concepts and Measurement*

So far this chapter has talked quite loosely about educational inequality and inter-generational mobility. We now place a more formal structure on the questions of interest, and most importantly on how the key concepts can be measured. Crucially, it is important to note that we are concerned with the interface between parental income and individual economic and educational outcomes. In the related, and very sizeable, sociology literature (e.g. Erikson and Goldthorpe 1992), it is very common to consider links between social class and education and the persistence of social class across generations. We believe it to be more important to concentrate on income as this makes the metric much clearer, particularly as over decades the composition of social class groupings is likely to have changed.

First, consider intergenerational mobility. Economists often measure the amount of economic mobility between generations by estimating a statistical regression relating a measure of children's economic status (like labour-market earnings) to their parents' economic status. Suppose that Y denotes the measure of economic status, then a double-log regression formulation for parents and offspring in family i is

$$\ln Y_i^{\text{child}} = \alpha + \beta \ln Y_i^{\text{parents}} + \varepsilon_i,$$

where ε_i is an error term.

The regression slope or intergenerational elasticity, β, can be seen as a measure of the amount of (im)mobility in society (researchers often refer to $\beta = 1$ as complete immobility and $\beta = 0$ as complete mobility). A lower β corresponds to more intergenerational mobility, as children's income is less closely tied to parents' income.

Treating the coefficient β as a measure of intergenerational mobility has a long and distinguished history, beginning with Galton's (1886) measurement of the inheritability of heights across generations.[3] Initial estimates of the intergenerational mobility of earnings showed β to be quite low, at around 0.2, with Becker and Tomes (1986) concluding that "aside from families victimized by discrimination, regression to the mean in earnings in the United States and other rich countries appears to be rapid" (Becker and Tomes 1986, p. S32). Improvements in data and measurement in the early 1990s led to a revision of the consensus estimate in the US up to around 0.4 (Solon 1992; Zimmerman 1992), indicating rather less intergenerational mobility than was first thought.[4]

---

[3] More recently, DiNardo and Tobias (2001) use the Galton data as a classic data source for statistical analysis.

[4] See Solon (1999) for a comprehensive review of the intergenerational mobility literature in economics, including detailed and comprehensive discussion of the research findings in this area.

Solon (2004) has formalized ideas about how education acts as a transmission mechanism underpinning the extent of intergenerational mobility. In a simple version of his model, in generation t, labour-market earnings W are a function of human capital H so that $W_t = \phi_t H_t + u_t$, where u_t is a random error term. If children's human capital accumulation then relates to parental income, we can write $H_t = \psi_t W_{t-1} + v_t$ (v_t being an error term). One can combine these equations to generate an intergenerational mobility function: $W_t = \phi_t \psi_t W_{t-1} + \omega_t$, where $\omega_t = \phi_t v_t + u_t$.

Here the intergenerational mobility parameter is $\phi_t \psi_t$ so that intergenerational mobility will be higher in a given generation t if (a) there are lower returns to human capital for children (ϕ_t is lower); or if (b) children's human capital is less sensitive to parental earnings (ψ_t is lower).

In this context ψ_t is a measure of educational inequality as it is the income gradient we discussed earlier. It is therefore evident from this that more educational inequality corresponds to less intergenerational mobility. If one thinks more generally about the distribution of educational outcomes for people from different income backgrounds, we can also move to different definitions of educational inequality. Suppose we split the income distribution into j quantiles, then we could compare education gaps across quantiles and look at how they evolve through time. In our empirical work below we follow this approach, looking at income quintiles (setting $j = 5$), and defining educational inequality as the gap in educational outcomes of those with parental incomes in the top relative to the bottom income quintile.

6.3.2 Data Sources

The data requirements for studying connections between parental income and the economic and educational outcomes of individuals are stringent. Fortunately there are some rich UK data sources, which enable us to learn something about these relationships by following individuals from birth to adulthood and obtaining a large amount of information along the way. The first of these is the National Child Development Study (NCDS), which consists of the birth population of a week in March 1958 with follow-up samples at cohort member ages 7, 11, 16, 23, 33 and 42. The second, the British Cohort Study (BCS), is very similar in style, covering a full birth population in a week of April 1970 with data collected at ages 5, 10, 16, 26 and 30. Both of these surveys have information about parental income at 16, detailed measures of educational attainment, and measures of earnings at an almost comparable point in time (age 33 in the NCDS, age 30 in the BCS).

These two surveys provide an excellent starting point for looking at educational inequality and intergenerational mobility, and how they have changed over time, but they are not without limitations. For example, the two cohorts made their decision about whether to stay on at school at age 16 in 1974 and 1986. This is rather a long time ago and, although the BCS cohort members were among the young people who were able to take advantage of HE expansion, they were also one of the last groups to be educated under the GCE O level system.

Therefore we feel it is also important to consider more-up-to-date information on young people, certainly for the analysis of educational outcomes. In order to do this, we create a third pseudo-cohort from the British Household Panel Survey. This longitudinal household survey has been running since 1991 and follows all members of the household from age 16 onwards, and includes information on education and family income.

An additional limitation with the use of cohort data is that the results may be specific to individuals born in the relevant weeks. In order to check on some of the patterns in the years between the cohorts and to ensure that the patterns observed are not due to measurement differences in the data, we take a second approach using household-level data from the Family Expenditure Survey (FES). The FES has collected information on education since 1978, as well as detailed income and expenditure data. Of course, the use of household data limits us to studying education at early ages when young people are still in the family home. As such we cannot analyse HE issues in the same way as we can with the longitudinal data sources. We can, however, look at associations between family income and education at school-leaving age and how they have evolved over time. We therefore relate staying-on decisions of 17/18 year olds in each FES year to information on family income.[5]

6.4 Evidence on Changes in Intergenerational Mobility and Educational Inequality

6.4.1 Changes in Intergenerational Mobility

Table 6.1 shows the results from intergenerational mobility regressions for the NCDS and BCS70 birth cohorts. Before considering the results we need to be clear on a couple of issues. First, for data reasons that ensure we are implementing exactly the same regression model across cohorts (see Blanden *et al.* 2004), the actual regression adopted is of cohort members' log(earnings) on log(family income). Second, since income inequality is higher in the second time period, it is important to adjust for changes in inequality when looking at patterns over time: we make this adjustment by multiplying the regression coefficient on log(family income) by the ratio of the standard deviation of family income to the standard deviation of the son's/daughter's income (see Grawe 2003).

---

[5]Family income is defined as the household income less the income of the 17/18 year old, as this will obviously be related to the young person's educational/labour-market status.

Table 6.1. Changes in intergenerational mobility in the UK.

	Intergenerational elasticities (standard errors)			Sample sizes	
	1958 birth cohort	1970 birth cohort	Cross-cohort change	1958 birth cohort	1970 birth cohort
Panel 1: basic model					
Sons	0.17 (0.02)	0.26 (0.02)	0.09 (0.03)	2246	2053
Daughters	0.17 (0.02)	0.23 (0.02)	0.06 (0.03)	1908	2017
Panel 2: augmented model					
Sons	0.10 (0.02)	0.19 (0.03)	0.09 (0.04)	2246	2053
Daughters	0.10 (0.03)	0.15 (0.03)	0.05 (0.04)	1908	2017
Panel 3: income model					
Sons	0.12 (0.02)	0.26 (0.02)	0.14 (0.03)	2110	2015
Daughters	0.14 (0.02)	0.22 (0.02)	0.08 (0.03)	2156	2285

Notes. Taken from Blanden *et al.* (2004).
The basic model in Panel 1 is a regression of log(earnings) of cohort members, $\ln(W)$, on log(family income), $\ln(Y)$, of the form $\ln(W) = \alpha_1 + \beta_1 \ln(Y) + \varepsilon_1$.
The augmented model in Panel 2 adds a set of controls, Z, to this: $\ln(W) = \alpha_2 + \beta_2 \ln(Y) + \gamma_2 Z + \varepsilon_2$. The variables in Z are ethnicity, parental education, family structure, whether father was unemployed during childhood, and mathematics and reading test-score quintiles at age 10/11.
The income model in Panel 3 includes spouse's earnings (W_s) in the dependent variable $\ln(S)$, where $S = W + W_s$ in the regression $\ln(S) = \alpha_3 + \beta_3 \ln(Y) + \varepsilon_3$.
Standard errors are in parentheses.

Three sets of results are shown in the table: Panel 1 relates log(earnings) to log(family income), and the specifications in Panel 2 do the same, but additionally control for a range of cohort member and parental characteristics (namely parental education, family structure, father's unemployment during childhood and cohort members' mathematics and reading test-score quintiles at age 10/11). Panel 3 reports results from a specification relating the log(family earnings) of cohort members to the log(family income) measure of parents.

The results show a very consistent pattern across the panels of the table. For men, they show a substantial fall in intergenerational mobility across cohorts. For example, in Panel 1 the intergenerational persistence coefficient rises by 0.09 (which is a statistically significant rise from 0.17 to 0.26). Analogous (and statistically significant rises) in Panels 2 and 3 are 0.09 and 0.14, respectively. For women the results are more muted, but, nevertheless, for two out of the three specifications

Table 6.2. Changes in intergenerational mobility in the UK: education as a transmission mechanism.

	Intergenerational elasticities (standard errors)		
	1958 birth cohort	1970 birth cohort	Cross-cohort change
Sons (Table 6.1, Panel 1)	0.17 (0.02)	0.26 (0.02)	0.09 (0.03)
Plus son's education	0.11 (0.02)	0.19 (0.02)	0.08 (0.03)
Daughters (Table 6.1, Panel 1)	0.17 (0.02)	0.23 (0.02)	0.06 (0.03)
Plus daughter's education	0.10 (0.02)	0.12 (0.02)	0.02 (0.03)

Notes. As for Table 6.1. Controls for education are whether the individual stayed on beyond the school-leaving age and whether they obtained a postsecondary degree.

presented there is a statistically significant rise in intergenerational persistence, with the range of estimates of the cross-cohort increase being 0.05 to 0.08.[6]

These findings are important in that they show the labour-market earnings of individuals to be more closely tied to family income for the 1970 cohort vis-à-vis the 1958 cohort. As such, intergenerational mobility appears to have fallen across these cohorts.

6.4.2 Changes in Intergenerational Mobility and Education

As already noted in the context of the Solon (2004) model, education may play a role as a transmission mechanism underpinning the extent of intergenerational mobility. This is due to the fact that education raises wages, and because education is correlated with parental income. We have therefore added variables measuring whether cohort members stayed on at school or not and whether they went on to obtain an HE degree to the basic intergenerational mobility regressions (Table 6.1, Panel 1).

The results are reported in Table 6.2. There is, indeed, evidence that highest qualification and staying on matters. For the point-in-time (i.e. within cohort) comparisons, these factors account for around 30% of the intergenerational transmission of income for sons and 40–50% of the transmission for daughters. Moreover, they explain some of the rise in the intergenerational elasticities. For sons, the estimate of the cross-cohort rise falls by around 20%[7] on inclusion of the education variables.

---

[6]For more information on these results and detailed robustness checks see Blanden *et al.* (2004). This work also presents estimates of mobility based on quartile transition matrices that are strongly supportive of the trends reported here.

[7]The numbers in the tables are reported to two decimal places. For this calculation to be made clear (i.e. uncontaminated by rounding) one needs to see the three decimal place numbers: the coefficient falls from 0.095 to 0.078, with the 0.017 fall corresponding to a 20% effect.

Table 6.3. Staying-on rates (proportions) by parental-income group.

| Cohort and year | Parental-income group | | | Educational inequality (unconditional) | Educational inequality (conditional) |
	Lowest 20%	Middle 60%	Highest 20%		
NCDS 1974	0.21	0.27	0.45	0.24 (0.02)	0.24 (0.02)
BCS 1986	0.32	0.43	0.70	0.38 (0.02)	0.39 (0.02)
BHPS 1996	0.61	0.71	0.86	0.25 (0.03)	0.23 (0.03)
Change 1974–86	0.11	0.16	0.25	0.14 (0.03)	0.15 (0.02)
Change 1986–96	0.29	0.28	0.16	−0.13 (0.04)	−0.16 (0.04)
Change 1974–96	0.40	0.44	0.41	0.01 (0.04)	−0.01 (0.04)

Notes. Sample sizes are 5706 for the NCDS, 4706 for the BCS and 1610 for the BHPS.
The conditional model adds controls for family size, sex, parents' age and living in a single-parent family.
Educational inequality in the conditional case is a marginal effect derived from a probit model of staying on beyond 16 including dummy variables for quintiles of family income. This marginal effect is defined as Pr[stay on | top income quintile] − Pr[stay on | bottom income quintile], see footnote 8 of this chapter for more details. Standard errors in parentheses.

For daughters, it accounts for 40% of the cross-cohort rise. Hence, the educational variables seem to explain both point-in-time intergenerational mobility and its evolution over time.

6.4.3 *Changes in Educational Inequality: Post-16 Participation*

We now go on to consider changes in educational inequality. The first educational outcome we consider is staying on beyond the minimum school-leaving age, and the second is postsecondary degree completion by age 23. The focus is on how the association between these two education measures and income has altered over time.

Table 6.3 looks at staying-on rates broken down by parental-income group over the three longitudinal data sources we have. Since the staying-on decision occurs at age 16, the three years we look at are 1974 (for the 1958 cohort), 1986 (for the 1970 cohort) and 1996 on average (for the BHPS individuals). The table shows the proportion staying on beyond age 16 for people from the highest quintile, the middle three quintiles and the bottom quintile of the income distribution for these three years. The measure of educational inequality we then consider is the gap in the proportion staying on between the highest and lowest quintiles. This is reported in the final two columns, first based upon gaps from the descriptive statistics (in the second-last column) and second from statistical models that condition on a number of factors (in the final column).[8]

The table shows there to have been a rise in the staying-on rate for people from all income groups. What is interesting is the way that the distribution of this rise varies over income groups. Between 1974 and 1986 the largest rise occurs for young people from higher-income groups (rising from 0.45 to 0.70), whereas between 1986 and 1996 the largest rise occurs for those from lower-income groups (from 0.32 to 0.61). The consequence of this is that educational inequality rises by 0.14 between the first and second cohorts and falls by 0.13 between the second and third. This result is confirmed by using multivariate analysis to create the conditional analogue, allowing us to control for the effects of sex, family size, parents' age and being in a single-parent family at 16.

Use of the FES to match 17/18 year olds with their family income enables us to consider these changes in more year-on-year detail. The results are given in Table 6.4. Again educational inequality is large at a given point in time with there being sizeable differences in staying-on rates between young people from high- and low-income backgrounds. The change over time is very similar to that found in the cohort data. Unconditional educational inequality was 0.28 for cohorts leaving school between 1977 and 1979. This rose to 0.40 in 1986–1988, before subsequently falling back to 0.26 for those leaving school between 1998 and 2000. The conditional results are very similar.

The time-series pattern of these changes is very interesting in that it ties so closely to the policy changes we discussed earlier. As already mentioned, 1988 was the first year in which 16 year olds took the GCSE qualification. It appears therefore that this policy change had a significant impact on the decisions of 16 year olds in lower-income groups. This is an interesting result, and not altogether unexpected. Pre-GCSE staying on was generally restricted to students with good O level results who would then be expected to continue through to take GCE A levels at age 18. Schools and teachers determined which students took O levels. This was also linked to the type of school attended as the majority of those at grammar schools sat (and passed) more O levels than pupils at secondary modern schools. Hence it seems that the exam reform resulted in a weaker association between income and educational

---

[8]The final column measure is a marginal effect calculated from a probit model of staying on as follows: $STAY = \theta_1 + \theta_2 Q_2 + \theta_3 Q_3 + \theta_4 Q_4 + \theta_5 Q_5 + \lambda C + \xi$, where STAY is a 0–1 indicator of staying on, Q_k is the kth income quintile ($k = 1$ is lowest, $k = 5$ is highest), C is a set of controls and ξ a random error. The conditional measure of educational inequality is thus

$$\Pr[STAY = 1 \mid Q_2 = 0, \ Q_3 = 0, \ Q_4 = 0, \ Q_5 = 1, \ C]$$
$$- \Pr[STAY = 1 \mid Q_2 = 0, \ Q_3 = 0, \ Q_4 = 0, \ Q_5 = 0, \ C] = \Phi(\theta_1 + \theta_5 + \lambda C) - \Phi(\theta_1 + \lambda C),$$

where $\Phi(\cdot)$ is the standard normal cumulative distribution function.

Table 6.4. Staying-on rates (proportions) by parental-income group.

	Parental-income group			Educational inequality (unconditional)	Educational inequality (conditional)
Time period	Lowest 20%	Middle 60%	Highest 20%		
1977–79	0.26	0.37	0.54	0.28 (0.04)	0.26 (0.04)
1980–82	0.33	0.37	0.57	0.24 (0.04)	0.22 (0.04)
1983–85	0.31	0.43	0.62	0.31 (0.04)	0.30 (0.04)
1986–88	0.30	0.44	0.70	0.40 (0.04)	0.39 (0.04)
1989–91	0.45	0.55	0.74	0.29 (0.04)	0.28 (0.05)
1992–94	0.60	0.66	0.83	0.24 (0.04)	0.22 (0.05)
1995–97	0.61	0.72	0.87	0.26 (0.04)	0.23 (0.05)
1998–2000	0.64	0.67	0.90	0.26 (0.04)	0.27 (0.06)
Change 1977–79 to 1986–88	0.04	0.07	0.16	0.13 (0.06)	0.13 (0.06)
Change 1986–88 to 1998–2000	0.34	0.23	0.20	−0.14 (0.06)	−0.12 (0.07)
Change 1977–79 to 1998–2000	0.38	0.30	0.36	−0.02 (0.06)	0.01 (0.07)

Notes. The sample is a cohort of 17/18 year olds drawn from the FES. Total sample size across all time periods is 9994.

The conditional model adds controls for family size, sex, parents' age and living in a single-parent family. Educational inequality in the conditional case is a marginal effect derived from a probit model of staying on beyond 16 including dummy variables for quintiles of family income. This marginal effect is defined as Pr[stay on | top income quintile] − Pr[stay on | bottom income quintile], see footnote 8 of this chapter for more details. Standard errors in parentheses.

attainment under the GCSE system, where in most subjects all individuals are entered to take exams, and if they meet the prescribed standard achieve a grade acceptable to continuing on in the schooling system.

6.4.4 *Changes in Educational Inequality: Higher-Education Participation and Achievement*

Our results for post-16 participation indicate that the UK experienced increased educational inequality up to 1988 and then a narrowing in educational inequality in the period after GCSEs were introduced. A key question is: did this trend extend to HE? It is possible to make arguments either way here. One may believe the school system matters most so that the increased staying-on rates for people from less well-to-do families at secondary level ought to manifest itself in less inequality at HE level. On the other hand, HE is where people have to pay or borrow substantial amounts of money, and student finance became increasingly regressive over the

Table 6.5. Postsecondary degree completion at age 23 by parental-income group.

Cohort	Parental-income group			Educational inequality (unconditional)	Educational inequality (conditional)
	Lowest 20%	Middle 60%	Highest 20%		
NCDS 1981	0.06	0.08	0.20	0.14 (0.01)	0.14 (0.01)
BCS 1993	0.07	0.15	0.37	0.30 (0.02)	0.30 (0.02)
BHPS 1999	0.09	0.23	0.46	0.37 (0.05)	0.37 (0.06)
Change 1981–93	0.01	0.07	0.17	0.16 (0.02)	0.15 (0.02)
Change 1993–99	0.02	0.08	0.09	0.07 (0.06)	0.07 (0.06)
Change 1981–99	0.03	0.15	0.26	0.23 (0.07)	0.22 (0.06)

Notes. Sample sizes are 5706 for the NCDS, 4706 for the BCS, and 580 for the BHPS. The conditional model adds controls for family size, sex, parents' age and living in a single-parent family. Educational inequality in the conditional case is a marginal effect derived from a probit model of postsecondary degree acquisition including dummy variables for quintiles of family income. This marginal effect is defined as Pr[degree | top income quintile] − Pr[degree | bottom income quintile], see footnote 8 of this chapter for more details. Standard errors in parentheses.

period in question. If this matters, one may not see inequality at HE level falling, even if there is falling inequality at earlier stages of educational provision. As it turns out, the results on changes in educational inequality at the HE level are very clear indeed. It is evident that educational inequality at HE level rose very sharply over the period we consider.

Due to data requirements we are only able to explore these changes using our longitudinal data sources: the cohort studies and the BHPS. Table 6.5 presents estimates for obtaining a postsecondary degree by age 23[9] that are analogous to those presented for staying on in Table 6.3. The table shows a large rise in higher-educational inequality (from 0.14 to 0.30) between the 1958 and 1970 cohorts. Of course, this is consistent with the increased income gradient that occurred between these two time periods being important for the fall in intergenerational mobility we saw earlier. However, in contrast to the results for staying on, educational inequality continues to increase through to the BHPS young people in 1999. As such, it appears that higher-educational inequality has persistently risen in the UK since the late 1970s. Put another way, the expansion of higher education has more strongly benefited children from richer families.

So far, the differing effects of parental income at different points in the education system have been considered by examining education inequality at the staying-on and postsecondary degree attainment stages separately. But of course these edu-

---

[9] It is necessary to only consider those who have obtained a postsecondary degree by a fairly young age in order to capture the largest possible sample in the BHPS.

Table 6.6. Sequential models of educational attainment.

Basic controls	log(income) coefficients at different points in the education sequence		
	NCDS	BCS70	BHPS
Staying on	0.24 (0.02)	0.31 (0.02)	0.19 (0.05)
Two or more A levels | staying on	0.13 (0.03)	0.19 (0.02)	0.21 (0.06)
Degree | two or more A levels and staying on	0.14 (0.05)	0.17 (0.04)	0.24 (0.07)

Notes. Estimates are obtained from sequential probit models. Standard errors in parentheses. The basic controls included are sex, parental age dummies, number of siblings, no father figure at age 16. Sample sizes are as follows: NCDS staying on 5706, two or more A levels | staying on 1621, degree | two or more A levels and staying on 751; BCS staying on 4706, two or more A levels | staying on 2179, degree | two or more A levels and staying on 921; BHPS staying on 531, two or more A levels | staying on 400, degree | two or more A levels and staying on 290.

cation transitions are sequential in nature. The relationship between income and postsecondary degree attainment will therefore be a composite of the incremental effects of income on educational attainment that accumulate throughout all the years participating in the education system.

Education decisions made at ages 16 and 18 are not independent of one another and young people will know that not pursuing A levels at 16 will substantially reduce the likelihood of attending university. So it is also interesting to consider conditional education–income relationships. For higher education, of particular interest is whether one gets a postsecondary degree having obtained A levels. Results reported in Blanden and Machin (2004) explore precisely this issue. The authors find evidence of an increase in the association between parental income and HE participation even for those similarly qualified at age 18. Table 6.6 reproduces the key table from their paper, where they report a sequential model of educational attainment. For the group who stayed on at 16 and then went on to obtain two or more GCE A levels or equivalent, the coefficient of log income in a model of degree attainment at age 23 rises from 0.14 in the NCDS to 0.17 for the same group in the BCS to 0.24 in the BHPS in the late 1990s. In other words, parental income has become more important in determining participation in HE over time, even when prior educational attainment is controlled for.

6.5 Conclusions

This chapter has reviewed some of the current evidence on inequalities in educational attainment and intergenerational mobility. Particular focus is placed on how these relationships have changed over time. We illustrate that there have been some strong shifts in educational attainment and intergenerational mobility in the recent past in the UK. In particular, and contrary to some people's initial perceptions, UK society has actually become less mobile in economic status over time.

There are several aspects to this.

- Intergenerational mobility of economic status has declined over time, as the labour-market success or failure of individuals has become more closely connected to parental income than it was in the past.

- Links between HE and parental income have strengthened over time in the UK, demonstrating a significant rise in educational inequality at HE level. This implies that the rapid expansion of the HE system seen in recent years has disproportionately benefited children from richer families.

- Education policy appears to matter in that educational inequality rose at the HE level when student finance became less redistributive, making it relatively harder for children from poorer families in an era of rising income inequality. This is true even for those achieving two or more GCE A levels. This result is despite the fact that the examination reforms that reduced rationing of age 16 educational qualifications seem to have induced an increase in staying on after the minimum school-leaving age, which benefited children from lower-income families disproportionately and countered existing educational inequality at this age.

The results reported in this chapter show the distributional effects of educational expansion to be important and clearly warrant more consideration than they have been given to date. This, of course, has particular relevance at the HE level in contemporary Britain in the light of the current student-finance debate. It demonstrates that it is crucially important to understand how poorer students react to increased loans and fees and what provisions would be needed to prevent them from being further excluded in future. The fact that increased educational inequality is likely to impact on economic inequality in future generations only acts to make understanding these issues all the more important.

PART 3
Economic Outcomes and Education

Measuring the Returns to Education

By Richard Blundell, Lorraine Dearden and Barbara Sianesi

7.1 INTRODUCTION

Over the last few decades, considerable research effort has been devoted to the measurement of the private individual returns to education, namely the individual wage gain from investing in more education. This has resulted in an outpouring of publications, making the returns to education probably the most explored and prolific area in labour economics. At the same time, there has been rising interest from policy makers, leading to much commissioning of studies both by single governments and by international bodies to answer questions such as the following.

- Is it worthwhile to take on more schooling?
- What is the impact of education and training on the labour-market opportunities of individuals, in particular on wages, earnings and employment probability?
- Who goes on to higher education, why, and who should pay for it?
- What skills are valued most by firms?
- What are the wider benefits of education to society as a whole?

In this chapter, we primarily focus on private individual returns, but we also include some discussion of the issues and problems associated with estimation of the social returns to education. Before looking at the issues involved in providing a reliable answer to such questions and presenting and discussing some recent empirical results,[1] this chapter starts by setting out a framework for the way in which the quantification of the individual wage gain from investing in more education can actually feed into education policy. The penultimate section highlights the limitations – in particular those linked to the issues of signalling and general-equilibrium effects – practitioners and policy makers need to be aware of when seeking to use these results for policy purposes.

---

[1] For a summary of the literature from the 1960s and 1970s, see Griliches (1977, 1979) and Rosen (1977). Later surveys are the ones by Willis (1986) and, most recently, by Card (1999, 2001). More evidence on rates of returns to qualifications in the UK is also presented in Chapter 9.

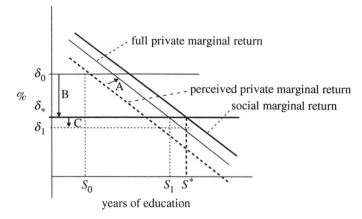

Figure 7.1. Private and social marginal returns on an extra year of schooling, discount rates and optimal educational investment choices. (Notes: S_0 private optimum; S^* social optimum; δ_0 private discount rate; δ^* social discount rate.)

7.2 POLICY RELEVANCE OF THE RETURNS TO EDUCATION

Education can be seen as an investment decision, where individuals give up some proportion of their income during the period of study (in the form of forgone earnings and tuition fees) in return for increased future earning power. More specifically, individuals invest in education until the marginal private return they expect to enjoy from schooling[2] is equal to their marginal private cost (i.e. the individual discount rate or the opportunity cost they face, reflecting, for example, tastes for schooling, risk attitudes, myopia or liquidity constraints[3]). This results in the private optimum S_0 in Figure 7.1.

In terms of education policy, the relevant issue is whether there are any market failures causing the individual to underinvest in education from a social point of view (the social optimum S^* being larger than S_0). In particular, the presence of market failures may result in the individually envisaged private return being lower than the social rate of return, while the private discount rate, δ_0, may be higher than the social discount rate, δ^* (opportunity cost). These discrepancies between the social optimum and private incentives may call for corrective policy action, although different types of measure are likely to be required to best address the various sources of market failure. In the discussion below, we discuss only efficiency considerations

---

[2]Note that this perceived private marginal return includes the individual consumption benefit in terms of pleasure derived from learning.

[3]The subjective discount rate is the interest rate at which future events are discounted in individual preferences; it thus reflects how present-oriented or "impatient" the individual is. The individual's opportunity cost to schooling is the value of the best alternative use of the individual's time (in general represented by forgone earnings) and of the funds used to pay for tuition.

and we leave equity concerns to be addressed separately. Most, if not all, of the problems in terms of efficiency highlighted below are likely to be more acute for individuals from poorer/less-educated backgrounds.

Figure 7.1 is a simplified and stylized representation of how the private and social returns to an additional year of education interact with the corresponding private and social opportunity costs (or discount rates) in determining private and social optimal choices of the quantity of human capital acquired by the individual. The figure and related discussion thus relate to investments in years of homogeneous schooling or, by extension, in the acquisition of a given educational qualification. In Section 7.6 we briefly touch upon further issues involved in comparing the returns to different qualifications. In addition, the figure and discussion pertain to one individual (or to a homogeneous group of individuals in the population). In reality, both the marginal returns and marginal costs are likely to differ between individuals according to their characteristics.

To appreciate the contribution that a sound assessment of the *individual wage gain* from education can give to the issues of underinvestment in education and funding of education, it is useful to discuss Figure 7.1 in the light of three ways of defining the "return to education", and noting that the impact of education on individual earnings is a key component of each:

(1) the net private return, made up of the costs and benefits to the individual, net of any transfers from the state and any taxes paid;

(2) the social return, highlighting any externalities or spillover effects, including transfers (in particular, subsidies to education) and taxes;

(3) the labour productivity return, relating to the gross increase in labour productivity (or growth).

7.2.1 *Perceived and full private returns*

While individuals make their private decisions on educational investments on the basis of what they expect their return to be, market failures may cause this perceived or expected private return to be lower than the full private returns, thus leading individuals to underinvest even from a private perspective.

Market failures of this sort arise due to individuals' lack of information, leading to misperceptions of expected returns. Informational failures may not only relate to lack of information about the nature and extent of the skills conferred by different educational investments and about their labour-market relevance and hence reward, but they may also consist of individuals neglecting other individual benefits of education. In particular, individuals may underestimate the expected returns from their schooling investment by ignoring the large employment benefits arising from education (which has been found to lead to substantially more stable employment histories), as well as the additional benefits from on-the-job training later in life (previous education has been found to be a major determinant of the receipt of on-the-job training).

It is not difficult to conceive that young people, and especially those coming from a low-education and/or disadvantaged background, may not have enough information and/or foresight to assess the full individual benefits of education properly when deciding about their educational investments. The role of the government here is to provide and diffuse accessible information, as well as to change the "culture" around education, so that individuals would base their private decisions on the true private marginal return schedule (measures leading to shift A – see Figure 7.1 and Table 7.1). Comprehensive, precise, reliable and updated analyses quantifying the full returns to education that accrue to individuals in terms of earnings may thus represent very valuable information for the policy maker.

A second set of market failures may lead the private discount rate to be higher than the social one. Individuals, especially if they are young and/or from disadvantaged backgrounds, may not have had a chance to develop a taste for education and, because of their current circumstances, may place too much emphasis on present versus future income streams. This myopic behaviour will lead them to discount too heavily the benefits of a higher income at later dates, so that they may instead end up choosing a job that requires low qualifications but that allows them to be independent and to satisfy more-pressing current needs. Policy measures to tackle this source of market failure (see B in Figure 7.1 and Table 7.1) would consist of changing the attitudes of young people and their families towards learning. Microeconometric analyses along the lines of those discussed later in the chapter can also support a process of change in the way education is perceived (i.e. in tastes for education and recognition of its importance) by attempting to measure other individual wider benefits in terms of less standard outcomes such as health, parenting, informed decisions, access to facilities, political participation, even happiness.

Another way of lowering the opportunity costs/discount rates of disadvantaged individuals is to offer new types and modes of study that are less costly for them, e.g. more flexible and with the possibility of being combined with work (e.g. part-time, distance or e-learning). Again, microeconometric analyses can be fruitfully employed to verify that the acquired skills are comparable with (i.e. rewarded similarly to) those acquired through more traditional routes, as well as to quantify the returns to new types of qualification.

Two other potentially important issues are liquidity constraints and risk. With respect to the former, imperfect capital markets that limit the ability of young people – mostly without collateral or sufficient credit histories – to borrow to finance human capital investment mean that individual decisions are based on a private discount rate that is much higher than the social one. The policy solution to this market failure is loans offered by the government (as discussed in the context of HE in Chapter 5).

As to risk, individuals may lack information about the nature and extent of the skills acquired and about their labour-market relevance, especially in the medium term, which may lead them to discount too heavily the expected returns. Here again, up-to-date and reliable studies on the returns to different qualifications and on how they have been changing over time can provide useful information for policy purposes. However, while estimates generally pertain to average returns, there is a whole distribution of returns, and individuals may feel uncertain as to where in the returns distribution they would be. Only a few recent US studies have tried to learn what kind of information students possess, how they use this information to form expectations, and how they perceive the returns to further schooling. Dominitz and Manski (1996) find that, despite a common belief that the returns to a college education are positive and non-negligible, a sample of students were found to vary considerably in the magnitude of perceived returns. Betts (1996) reports results from a survey of undergraduates, finding that students have a quite clear understanding of the overall returns to education, but individually students have a quite poor picture of the returns. On the basis of a microeconometric model fitted on US data for white males, Carneiro *et al.* (2003) similarly reveal substantial individual heterogeneity in the returns to college (versus high school), much of which is unpredictable at the time schooling choices are made. The study finds that 8% of college graduates *ex post* receive no positive returns to college.

Furthermore, even though potential *ex-ante* returns may be considerable, the consequences of failure for low-income households may be too severe for them to be willing to take the risk. By contrast, society can be expected to have many more possibilities of spreading risk and a much lower risk aversion than the individual. In particular, society knows that, *on average*, more-educated individuals will have gained higher productivity, which in turn will generate higher income and thus tax revenue. An efficient solution to imperfect insurance markets would be income-contingent loans offered by the government, which provide a valuable insurance element, since payments are deferred to when (and if) individuals can afford them.

A final comment relates to the stance at times taken to judge the adequacy and profitability of private investments in education by comparing their returns with the returns on debt and equity. As discussed in more detail in the appendix, this is far from a perfect benchmark. More generally, the wider framework outlined above highlights how individuals' schooling choices are affected by factors quite unrelated to standard financial returns but all of which have important public policy implications.

7.2.2 *Private Versus Social Returns*

Up to this point, we have discussed the scope for the government to remove obstacles – credit/liquidity constraints, risk aversion (especially for poorer households), myopia, lack of information – so as to ensure that individuals are first fully aware of the benefits and are then able to follow their optimizing incentives. We have also mentioned in parallel the role that reliable and up-to-date analyses of individual wage returns can play in supporting this agenda.

Turning now to the optimal sharing of educational *funding*, the relevant question is whether, once individual decisions are based on the full private return (as opposed to the one perceived by the individual) and on the social (as opposed to the individual) discount rate, they still lead to an individually optimal investment in schooling that is smaller than the socially optimal level. If this is the case, subsidies to education are called for (see "C" in Figure 7.1 and Table 7.1), in order to decrease the cost for the individual even further until the private optimal investment decision (S_1) gives rise to the social optimum (S^*).

From a purely economic-efficiency point of view, the relevant issue here is whether there are market failures that result in the full private return being smaller than the social return, leading individuals to acquire not enough education from a social point of view. An important source of market failure (in addition to the fact that the individual will consider returns net of taxes while society will benefit from the revenue return as well) is the presence of externalities, i.e. benefits of individually acquired education that "spill over" to other individuals in the same firm, industry, city, region or economy.[4]

Although the existence of high rates of private returns to education provides an incentive for individuals to invest in human capital, if the *individual* educational investment gives rise to benefits to society over and above the benefits that accrue to the individual, public support for education may be justified on the basis that individuals will not take these wider benefits into account in their educational choices. Subsidies can take various forms, from direct (means-tested) grants to the more subtle difference between the full cost of a course and its fee, or the subsidized interest received on loans to students.

It has to be stressed that it is the deviation of the social return from the private one that should guide state-funding decisions from an efficiency point of view. In other words, even if we knew the social returns precisely, without knowledge of private returns we would have no guidance as to the economically efficient amount of public funding of education.

---

[4] Indirect economic effects from education are, for example, spillover effects from technical progress or knowledge accumulation, better public health, better parenting, lower crime, a better environment, wider political and community participation, greater social cohesion – all of which are in turn likely to feed back into economic growth.

Table 7.1. Sources of market failure in education investments and corresponding policy measures (based on Figure 7.1 and the discussion in Sections 7.2.1 and 7.2.2).

Effect of the market failure	Type of market failure	Policy measures
A full private return underestimated	informational failure	inform on full return: • analyses of returns • **provision of information**
		remove obstacles to attain full private optimum:
	credit constraints	• loans • **new types and modes of studies**
B discount rate/opportunity cost overestimated	risk	• income-contingent loans • **analyses of returns**
	myopia	• **analyses of returns** • **provision of information** • **change the "culture" of education**
C full private return lower than social return	tax externalities	induce individual to attain social optimum: • **subsidy**

Action under A and B moves individual from S_0 to S_1.
Action under C moves individual from S_1 to social optimum S^*.

Note. Policy measures shown in bold are those where a robust, reliable and up-to-date quantification of the individual wage returns from education can prove especially valuable.

123

7.2.3 *Individual Productivity*

We now move on to deal with the third definition of the "return to education" listed earlier, which relates to direct measures of individual labour productivity gains. Despite some of the subtleties involved in estimation that are discussed in the next section, the main finding in the empirical literature is of an unambiguously positive effect on individual earnings from investing in education. Since these higher wages have to be paid out of productivity gains, these real wage increases should provide a lower bound on the likely size of productivity increases. In particular, in a competitive labour market where wages are set to reflect the marginal product of workers, the return to education would act as a proxy measure of the increase in work productivity due to education.

Reliable measures of the individual wage returns to different educational qualifications are thus of further policy relevance in that they highlight the (possibly differential and possibly evolving) rewards that the various qualifications fetch on the labour market. In particular, as far as measures of the individual labour-market return to education are informative of the extent to which formal teaching at school confers skills that are relevant to the labour market (i.e. those for which firms are actually willing to pay), these estimates can convey some information about how in touch a national education system is with firms' needs (the subject of Chapter 9).

Before concluding this section, it is important to anticipate that additional issues will have to be borne in mind when considering these topics, in particular the comparison between private and social returns, and the productivity interpretation of the individual wage gain. A discussion of these caveats – among which general-equilibrium effects and the signalling hypothesis rank highly – is deferred until Section 7.5.

7.3 Methodological Issues

Before turning to the estimates of the returns to education, this section aims to help the reader understand and clarify the methodological issues involved in recovering the causal impact of education on individual outcomes.

It is most natural to begin with the "naive" question: do people with more education earn more, on average, than people with less education? The corresponding "naive" answer is rather obvious: from casual empiricism we can see this to be the case. The aim of early research was to *quantify* such observed educational gain. The early literature on both private and social internal rates of return[5] was simply based on comparing the earnings flows of people with different levels of education.

---

[5]The internal rate-of-return method evaluates the profitability – private or social – of any given investment by looking at the properly discounted flow of benefits and costs arising from that investment. The internal rate of return is given by that discount rate for which the discounted present value of the

Compared with private rates of returns, these estimates of "social" rates of return include the full direct costs of schooling (and not just those borne by the individual) and use *pre*-tax (instead of post-tax) earnings. It should come as no surprise, then, that these "social" rates were consistently found to be *lower* than private ones. These "social" rate estimates should in fact be regarded as a lower bound of the full returns to education, as even though all the costs of education are included, social spillovers (externalities in the form of macroeconomic and social gains) are ignored.

The main methodological limitation of these studies at the private or "social" level, as well as of related approaches,[6] is that they represent purely accounting exercises, quantifying the answer to what we called the "naive" question. However, the relevant question is subtly, but crucially, different: do people with more education earn more, on average, than if *they* had acquired less education?

Ideally, we would measure the return to a certain schooling level or educational qualification (say A) vis-à-vis another schooling level or qualification (say B) by comparing the earnings of an individual when having qualification A and the earnings of the *same* individual when having qualification B. The obvious problem is that, in practice, only one level of education is observed for a particular individual. At the heart of this so-called "evaluation problem" is the need to recover counterfactuals that we do not observe, namely the earnings an individual with qualification A would have commanded had he or she acquired qualification B instead.

It is crucial to understand the difference between the *causal* effect of education – what we are after – and simple correlations observed in the data. Our methodological approach must distinguish between the higher earnings that are observed for better-educated workers being *caused* by their higher education and individuals with greater earning capacity *choosing* to acquire more education. What was potentially wrong with the early internal rates of return studies is that they were comparing the different streams of benefits for individuals who had chosen different educational levels. They were thus implicitly using the (observed) earnings of individuals with education level B to estimate the (counterfactual) earnings of individuals with education level A had they chosen education level B instead.

---

benefits arising from the investment net of its costs equals zero. It can then be compared with the reference discount rate of the decision maker. Detailed research has been conducted on internal rates of return to education in countries around the world (see, in particular, Psacharopoulos 1973, 1981, 1994).

[6] In the age–earnings profile approach, rates of return to education are calculated by equating the present values of the earnings profiles for statistically "standardized" workers who differ in education levels. The effects of schooling and subsequent on-the-job training are, however, confounded and one cannot identify each effect separately (cf. Blaug 1972). In the earnings function approach (Mincer 1974) – one of the most widely estimated models in labour economics – the log of earnings is regressed on years of schooling and on years of work experience (and its square). The procedure imposes some simplifying assumptions but allows separate estimates of rates of return to schooling and rates of return to job training to be obtained. (For a recent appraisal of the earnings function, see Heckman *et al.* (2003).)

To appreciate the reliability of the various estimates proposed in the literature, it is important to understand the potential problems in just comparing mean earnings for groups with different educational levels. First, there is the issue of *selection*. An individual's educational choices are likely to be based on personal characteristics that may well affect the outcome as well. For example, suppose that it is the most able, determined and motivated individuals who choose to obtain more education. Then those individuals who are observed to have more education will be inherently more productive than the low-education individuals, and would thus have earned more than the latter anyway, i.e. even in the absence of their extra education. In this case, the simple difference in observed mean earnings between individuals with high education and individuals with low education will be larger than the return to education, as it will be unable to separate the contribution of this inherently higher productivity – the *composition* of students getting more education – from the contribution of education itself. This procedure will in fact ascribe the whole of the earnings difference to education (the so-called "ability bias").

A second issue, which is receiving increasingly more attention, concerns the extent to which there is *heterogeneity in the returns* to education, i.e. whether the return to education is allowed to differ across individuals. Typically, we do not expect all individuals to respond to education in exactly the same way. Returns may differ across individuals because people differ in the efficiency with which they can exploit a given amount of education to raise their individual productivity.

If there are heterogeneous returns, and if individuals select into education based on their individual returns, then those observed to invest in more education will be the ones with the highest returns. In particular, once we allow for the possibility of heterogeneous returns, defining the "parameter of interest" is central. We distinguish three main parameters, each one answering a conceptually distinct question.

(1) **The average treatment effect (ATE),** representing the impact of a given educational qualification on an individual randomly taken from the population of interest; relevant if the question is whether to make it mandatory for that population to acquire that qualification.

(2) **The average effect of treatment on the treated (ATT),** representing the impact of a given educational qualification on the individuals who have chosen to acquire it; relevant when the "treatment" is voluntary.

(3) **The average effect of treatment on the non-treated (ATNT),** representing the impact of a given educational qualification on the individuals who have not acquired it; relevant if the question is whether to encourage all individuals who are currently not acquiring that qualification to acquire it.

As we will see later, an estimation method will, at times, recover the average treatment effect for a more narrowly defined subgroup of the population (i.e. a local average treatment effect (LATE)).

The methodological problems become even more difficult when attempting to measure the *social returns*. As we will discuss in Section 7.4.2, there is a wide body of literature that tries to estimate the social returns to education using macro growth regressions. These regressions attempt to "allocate" cross-country differences in economic growth to various "inputs", including education. This allows one to recover estimates of the impact that educational investments have had on macroeconomic growth. These macro estimates have the advantage that they should be able to capture externalities that are either ruled out or not properly captured in the standard micro approach. The drawback, however, is that there are many more methodological problems in interpreting the coefficient on education in the macro approach than in the micro approach, and this creates a great deal of uncertainty about the reliability of the results.

A "hybrid" methodology that has recently emerged aims to identify educational externalities by isolating the causal impact on *individual* wages of the *average* level of education in the city or state of residence of the individual (defined as the "social" return), as well as the causal impact on individual wages of individual education (the private return). These micro-based estimation methods have the advantage of being able to obtain estimates of both the private and social returns to education within a particular country. The definition of educational externalities, and thus of "social" returns, in these studies is, however, quite narrow. There are also other methodological difficulties that again place uncertainty on the reliability of the low estimates of social returns that have generally been found in these studies. We will touch upon these issues in Section 7.4.2.

7.4 ESTIMATION METHODS AND RESULTS

The estimation of the individual return to education is probably amongst the most explored and prolific areas in labour economics, and certainly represents the area in which the greatest progress in the economics of education as a specific research field has been made. We discuss it in detail in Section 7.4.1, focusing on recent results for the UK. We then move on, in Section 7.4.2, to review briefly some of the empirical studies attempting to estimate the social returns to education.

7.4.1 *Individual Private Returns*

In the UK, most studies use the repeated cross-section data available in the Family Expenditure Survey, the General Household Survey and the Labour Force Survey.

For example, Gosling *et al.* (2000), Schmitt (1995) and McIntosh (2002) focus on the changing returns over time, but are unable to condition on ability measures such as test scores, nor on family background information. Harmon and Walker (1995) exploit the natural experiment of a change in the minimum school-leaving age to circumvent the need to observe ability and family background variables. Dearden (1999*a*, *b*) and Blundell *et al.* (2000) both use a dataset, the British National Child Development Study (NCDS), which contains detailed ability and family-background measures, but they do not focus on a systematic analysis of the type discussed below.[7] Overall, for the UK, most authors prefer the use of qualification-based measures of educational attainment rather than years of education, as would seem appropriate given the discussion in Chapter 5 about the fact that there are different returns to education for the same years of academic and vocational qualifications, for example.

If one were to browse through the literature on the impact of education on earnings, one would find a wide range of estimates. Even when based on the same sample for Great Britain at a given time – as we shall see with the example of the NCDS birth cohort data – estimates using different methods differ. The main reason for this is that, as outlined in Section 7.3, there are several difficulties that arise when trying to estimate the true causal effect of education on individual earnings: different methods deal with different sources of bias, rely on different assumptions and answer different questions (i.e. recover different average parameters).

In this section, we give a brief intuitive explanation of the main methods used in current research and report results from previous work (Blundell *et al.* forthcoming), where we applied these various methods to a common and rich dataset (the NCDS) to obtain the latest estimates of returns to educational qualifications. (Note that all the results quoted in this section are for men only and are taken from Blundell *et al.* (forthcoming).) The interested reader is referred to that study for further details of the empirical application reviewed in this section.

To frame the discussion, it is helpful to highlight the issue of *selection* again. As we noted in the previous section, an individual's decision about education is likely to be based on characteristics that may affect earnings as well. Some of these characteristics, such as ethnicity or gender, may be observed by the analyst, while some of them, such as motivation or "ability", may be unobserved. The different estimation methods can then be divided into two groups, depending on what they assume about this selection process. A first set of methods (ordinary least squares (OLS) and matching) claim that selection into education takes place only according to characteristics that can be observed – the *selection on observables* assumption.

---

[7]From the 1970s, a body of research, mostly restricted to the US, tried to control for ability bias using army test scores, IQ-type test scores and data on siblings (see Griliches (1977, 1979) and Rosen (1977) for reviews of these early results). The methodological and empirical review by Card (1999) is the main reference for more recent studies.

Table 7.2. Average returns to qualifications (men, NCDS): OLS.

	Basic specification	Full specification
Returns to O levels (versus no qualification)	21.1	14.8
	(17.4; 24.7)	(11.2; 18.4)
Returns to A levels (versus O levels)	9.0	6.4
	(5.6; 12.4)	(3.1; 9.7)
Returns to HE (versus A levels)	28.9	23.5
	(25.6; 32.3)	(20.0; 27.1)
Returns to HE (versus less than HE)	39.8	28.7
	(37.1; 42.5)	(25.7; 31.8)

Notes. Basic specification: ethnicity and region (implicitly, gender and age). Full specification: basic specification plus standard parental background information, tests at 7 and 11, school variables. Numbers in parentheses are 95% confidence intervals. Source: Blundell *et al.* (forthcoming).

The second set of estimators (control function and instrumental variables), by contrast, allow for *selection on unobservables*, i.e. they allow individuals to choose their education also on the basis of characteristics that are unobserved by the analyst.

The intuition behind the simple *ordinary least squares* (OLS) approach is that there are variables X in our data that affect both schooling choices and earnings. This allows us to use regression methods to compare (average) earnings for individuals with low and high education conditional on the same characteristics. In addition to the selection on observables assumption, this method generally imposes the assumption that the returns to education do not vary according to individual characteristics X. Under these assumptions, OLS recovers the average treatment effect for the treated; if there is no unobserved individual heterogeneity in returns, this effect would, by definition, be equal to the average returns for the non-treated and for the population at large.

It is clear that the nature, extent and accuracy of the available observables are crucial for the credibility of the estimates. The NCDS provides a uniquely rich source of information on test scores and family background.

Table 7.2 presents estimates of both the return from undertaking some form of higher education (compared with not doing so) and of the incremental returns to three educational qualifications: leaving after completing O levels or their vocational equivalent; leaving after completing A levels or their vocational equivalent; and undertaking some form of higher education (HE).

The results in the table show significant returns to basic, intermediate and higher qualifications, even after controlling for detailed family background and ability test measures. They also highlight how sensitive the returns to education are to the inclusion of conditioning variables X. In particular, controlling for ability test scores and family influences at an early age significantly reduces the returns, by a factor of almost one-third across most comparisons.

The essence of *matching* is to deal with the process of selection into education by constructing a comparison group of non-treated individuals with characteristics X similar to those of the treated group. This is accomplished by explicitly selecting and pairing to each treated individual exactly one non-treated individual with the same characteristics X.[8] Depending on which group is taken as reference, matching estimators can recover the average effect on the treated, on the non-treated or on the population.

Of course, matching can take place (i) only on characteristics that we can observe and (ii) only if we observe individuals with education and individuals without education who have the same characteristics. The first prerequisite is the selection on observables assumption: we need to observe all those factors that affect both schooling choices and earnings. This is a strong requirement and one that needs careful argument and a rich data source. The second prerequisite is the "common support condition". It requires all high-education people to have a counterpart in the low-education group for each set of observable characteristics X.

Thus, matching, like OLS, requires very rich data for its estimates to be credible; however, unlike OLS, matching does not restrict at all the way in which the return varies according to individual characteristics X. Allowing for completely flexible (observably) heterogeneous gains from HE, matching not only avoids biases that might arise from an incorrectly specified model, but it can also provide additional interesting information as to the average gains for the subgroups of treated and non-treated.

Going back to our NCDS application, the OLS specification, which constrains the returns to be homogeneous, shows a 28.7% average wage gain from taking some form of HE (Table 7.2). The matching estimates in Table 7.3 are more informative. They show that HE graduates enjoy a 26.8% average gain from their HE investment (treatment on the treated). If those who did not continue into HE had instead undertaken it, they would have enjoyed an even higher return of 33.1% (treatment on the non-treated).

This ATNT result cannot, however, be taken at face value. It can be easily checked that, in sharp contrast to the case of the ATT, matching did not perform well in balancing the distribution of observed characteristics X between the non-treated (i.e. those without HE) and the matched subgroup of HE individuals. Note, in particular, that the non-treated group also contains all those individuals who dropped out at 16 without any qualifications. To calculate the ATNT, these drop-outs need to be all matched

---

[8]Alternatively, and more generally, this is done by attaching appropriate weights to the individuals in the non-treated group so as to realign their characteristics X to those of the treated group.

Table 7.3. Average returns to HE versus less-than HE (men, NCDS): matching.

	ATT	ATE	ATNT
Returns to HE (versus less than HE)	26.8	31.3	33.1
	(23.5; 31.1)	(28.7; 34.9)	(30.0; 36.7)

Notes. Controlling for ethnicity, region, standard parental background information, tests at 7 and 11, school variables. Numbers in parentheses are 95% confidence intervals. Source: Blundell *et al.* (forthcoming).

to their most "similar" HE individuals.[9] Considerable initial differences between these two subgroups make it hard to obtain reasonably good matches, and in fact matching did not succeed in choosing an HE subgroup that looked as "low performing" as the full non-HE group. The average wage for the matched HE individuals thus represents an overly optimistic representation of what the non-HE individuals would have earned had they gone on to HE. Thus, even if we believe that the NCDS data are rich enough to satisfy the selection on observables assumption, we know that this estimate of the ATNT is upward biased.[10]

The lesson to be derived from this discussion is that, in contrast to OLS, matching is subject to the common support restriction, which effectively forces the researcher to compare only comparable individuals. The resulting similarity of the two matched samples can easily be assessed; if the two matched groups are still too different in terms of their observable characteristics, the researcher needs to accept the fact that there simply is not enough information in the available data to achieve sufficiently close – and thus reliable – matches. In contrast to OLS, matching can thus help to discriminate between more reliable results and those that should be viewed with particular caution.

We now turn to the estimation of the incremental return to each of the three qualifications by actual qualification. For those with no qualifications, we estimate the returns they would have had if they had undertaken each of the three qualifications (treatment on the non-treated). For those with O level qualifications, we estimate the return they obtained from taking that qualification (treatment on the treated) and the returns they would have obtained if they had progressed to A levels or HE (treatment on the non-treated). For those with A levels, we estimate the returns they

---

[9]By contrast, when estimating the ATT for those with HE, matching was free to ignore those no-qualifications individuals who were not the best matches for the HE individuals; indeed, in the one-to-one version of the matching estimator, individuals with A levels made up 53.6% of the matched controls, individuals with O levels 37% and individuals with no qualifications only 9.4%.

[10]Another issue is that the identification of the ATNT requires a more restrictive assumption than is the case for the ATT. In particular, one also needs to rule out that individuals decide to undertake HE based on their individual unobserved returns from it. If this assumption is violated, and assuming that it is those with the highest unobserved returns who select into HE, the matching estimate of the ATNT would be upward biased.

obtained from undertaking O and A level qualifications (treatment on the treated) and the returns they would have obtained if they had progressed to HE (treatment on the non-treated). For those with HE, all estimates are treatment on the treated. Results are presented in Table 7.4, where we have highlighted the most (and the least) reliable ones on the basis of the achieved similarity in observables between the matched samples. Again, matching allows the researcher to assess the degree of reliability of the estimates. This is in contrast to OLS, which would have hidden and ignored the fundamental non-comparability of some of these groups.

Results from matching show an average wage return of 18% from obtaining O levels compared with leaving school with no qualifications, a further 6.3% return from completing A levels, and a further 24.2% wage premium from then achieving an HE qualification. Compared with leaving school at 16 without qualifications, then, the average return to O levels is 18%, to A levels it is 24.2% and to HE it is 48.4%. An interesting result concerns the returns to O levels by educational group (first column): this disaggregated analysis shows that at that stage, even though those who do acquire some qualification at 16 have the greatest returns from this initial investment, those who drop out at 16 without any qualifications would still have had a hefty average payoff of over 13% from obtaining O levels or their equivalent before leaving education.

As we have mentioned, OLS and matching place strong requirements on the selection mechanism, in particular that selection into education is not based on characteristics that we cannot observe and hence control for. If, however, individuals make a decision about their education based on factors that we do not observe, controlling for observed characteristics X will not be enough to avoid bias in the estimated returns to schooling. Control function and instrumental variables are two methods that can correct for such selection bias and thus yield consistent estimates of the returns to education even in the presence of selection on unobservables.

The *control function* approach is a very powerful method that controls for both selection on unobserved characteristics and selection on unobserved individual returns (see Garen (1984) and Heckman and Robb (1985b) for early examples of this approach). Without going into too much technical detail, the idea is to impose enough structure to allow one to model away the effect of selection. For instance, if individuals who select into education have higher average unobserved ability and/or higher average unobserved returns from education, the unobservable residual in the earnings equation for them will have a positive mean. A "control function" is an estimate of the expected value of this residual conditional on education. The idea is to use this estimate as an additional regressor in the earnings equation, thus effectively including the omitted variable that caused the bias. The control function is obtained by first estimating the schooling participation decision.

Table 7.4. Incremental average returns by highest qualification achieved (men, NCDS): matching.

Highest qualification achieved	O level versus none	A level		HE		
		versus O level	versus none	versus A level	versus O level	versus none
None	**13.2**	**5.5**	**18.7**	*24.8*	*30.3*	*43.5*
	(9.1; 17.3)	**(0.1; 10.1)**	**(13.6; 23.2)**	*(17.7; 31.6)*	*(23.2; 36.3)*	*(36.8; 49.7)*
O level	**17.8**	**5.9**	**23.7**	**24.6**	**30.5**	**48.2**
	(12.9; 22.1)	**(2.3; 9.9)**	**(19.1; 29.4)**	**(20.5; 29.3)**	**(26.6; 34.4)**	**(43.4; 53.3)**
A level	*18.1*	**5.7**	*23.8*	**25.6**	**31.3**	*49.4*
	(13.2; 22.6)	**(2.0; 9.8)**	*(18.5; 28.7)*	**(21.7; 30.2)**	**(27.5; 35.5)**	*(43.5; 54.0)*
HE	*21.6*	**8.0**	*29.6*	**21.7**	**29.7**	*51.3*
	(14.1; 29.6)	**(3.9; 12.6)**	*(22.0; 37.5)*	**(17.4; 25.6)**	**(25.8; 33.7)**	*(43.8; 58.7)*
Any: ATE	*18.0*	*6.3*	*24.2*	*24.2*	*30.5*	*48.4*
	(13.3; 22.4)	*(2.9; 10.1)*	*(19.7; 28.7)*	*(20.6; 28.2)*	*(27.1; 34.2)*	*(43.2; 52.7)*

Notes. Controlling for ethnicity, region, standard parental background information, tests at 7 and 11, school variables (and implicitly gender and age). Numbers in parentheses are 95% confidence intervals. Based on the achieved balancing of the Xs between the matched groups, effects in **bold** are the most reliable and effects in *italics* are the least reliable. Source: Blundell *et al.* (forthcoming).

The power of this method is that under the structure it imposes, one can effectively test for the presence of selection on unobserved characteristics and on unobserved returns. The drawback is that there needs to be some independent variation in the control function, which is most effectively induced by a so-called exclusion restriction, namely the introduction of at least one variable that determines participation in schooling without directly affecting wages. Tuition costs, sibling composition and distance from school are examples that have been used.

If the control function approach is used to "test" the matching estimator in the NCDS data, it suggests that, in these rich data, there is little remaining selection into HE based on unobserved characteristics and on unobserved returns. This latter result interestingly applies only once we control for heterogeneous returns in terms of our (rich) observables X. This evidence suggests that there are enough variables in the NCDS to be able to control *directly* for selection, or, in other words, that OLS and matching with the available set of observed characteristics X are not subject to selection bias.

An alternative and popular method for controlling for selection on unobservables is the *instrumental variable* (IV) approach (see Angrist and Krueger (1999) for an overview of the control function and IV approaches, and Blundell and Powell (2003) for an explicit comparison of them). The idea is to exploit an "instrument", that is an event or a variable which affects schooling attainment but at the same time is unrelated to individual unobserved productivity. In particular one can look for real-world events (so-called natural experiments) that assign individuals to different levels of schooling in a random way, or at least independently of any characteristics (in particular, unobserved ability) affecting earnings. An example is when some educational rule or qualification level (e.g. minimum school-leaving age) is exogenously changed for one group but not for another. Similarly, variables such as birth order, tuition costs or distance to college have often been used as instruments, given that they influence schooling but are not expected to affect wages directly (the exclusion restriction mentioned above).

Care must be taken with IV estimates when the returns to education are heterogeneous, since, in this case, IV identifies a so-called local average treatment effect (LATE): the average return for the very specific subgroup of the population who are induced to take more schooling *because* of the change in the instrument (often referred to as the "compliers" to that instrument). For example, consider using as instrument an increase in the minimum school-leaving age from 15 to 16. In the presence of heterogeneous returns, the corresponding IV estimate represents the average return for those individuals who stay at school until 16 in the presence of the reform, but who would drop out at 15 in its absence. This discussion highlights how different instruments answer different questions, in that they recover the average return for different sub-populations. IV estimates could thus vary widely, as their respective compliers could be a group with very high or very low returns. The nature of the incidence of the instrument within the distribution of individual returns is thus critical in understanding the estimated coefficient, and care should be taken before viewing the IV estimated return as an indicator of the average return for all individuals.

A potentially promising approach in such a context is to look for different instruments that are likely to affect different subgroups in the population, while having a theoretical framework to predict in what part of the returns distribution these complier groups belong. This would allow one to obtain some bounds on the distribution of returns in the population. To illustrate this point, Blundell *et al.* (forthcoming) focus on three different instruments in the NCDS that are likely to affect distinct subgroups of the population. At the same time, they use the theoretical framework of Card (1999) to gauge where in the returns distribution these groups are likely to belong. This exercise suggests a significant degree of dispersion in individual returns (for a more detailed discussion of this model applied to the three instruments as well as the results, see Blundell *et al.* (forthcoming)).

To summarize our analysis of educational returns for men in the NCDS: we found the overall returns to educational qualifications at each stage of the educational process to remain sizeable and significant, even after controlling for selection and allowing for heterogeneity in returns. In particular, we estimate an average return of about 27% for those completing some form of HE. Our IV estimates, however, suggest that there could be significant dispersion in individual returns to higher education. Compared with leaving school at 16 without qualifications, we find an average return to O levels of around 18%, to A levels of 24% and to HE of 48%.

7.4.2 Social Returns

As we have seen above, the social return to education may differ from the private return, and this has important policy implications. If the social return is higher than the private return, then government intervention may be needed to achieve the socially efficient outcome. But how can one estimate the social return to education, and how does it compare with the private one? A number of approaches have been adopted in the literature, which we now briefly discuss (see Sianesi and Van Reenen (2003) for an extensive review and current assessment of this literature).

Macro Studies. There is a literature that has tried to estimate the impact of human capital on national economic growth, or, in other words, the returns to education that accrue at the macroeconomic level. The potential economic externalities to education should, in principle, be captured at this level of aggregation. Although this macro growth regression literature is not as well developed as the research on private returns, it should still provide a benchmark to allow one to gauge some information as to the extent of additional returns accruing at the economy level.

Because the outcome is growth at the country level, the focus is generally on cross-country differences in economic growth, and the aim is to attribute these differences to a number of "inputs", including various measures of education.

These studies almost always find that the contribution (or "social return") of education is positive, but there is a wide variation in estimates. Sianesi and Van Reenen (2003) conclude that, taken as a whole, the literature suggests that a one-year increase in average education raises the level of output per capita by between 3 and 6% and is also thought to yield additional indirect benefits to growth (in particular, by stimulating investments in physical capital and technological development). Tertiary education appears to be the most important level of education for growth in OECD countries. These results suggest that the social returns may indeed be larger than the private ones.

However, there are many more methodological problems in interpreting the coefficient on education in the macro approach than there are in the micro approach. The larger coefficients in the macro literature could be due to endogeneity bias (the reverse impact of economic growth on human capital accumulation), to "aggregation biases" of various sorts, or to the undue imposition of restrictions in the estimation of growth equations – notably of linearity and of homogeneous impact of education. As to the latter, these models generally assume that the social returns are homogeneous across all countries. We already know that the private return to schooling varies considerably across countries, and it is very likely that the social return will vary as well. This makes the use of these estimates for policy purposes quite problematic.

Micro Studies. To get around some of these problems, a literature has recently emerged in the US which, instead of relying on country-level data, uses both individual- and either state- or city-level data to estimate both the private and "social" returns to education. The idea is that education must have some external social (or spillover) effect on individual productivity if otherwise-identical individuals have higher wage outcomes simply because they live in a city or state with higher average levels of education.

A key methodological issue in this approach is that, in addition to individual schooling, the average level of schooling is likely to be endogenous. Workers may, for instance, self-select among cities/states (e.g. higher-ability workers may sort into cities/states with a highly educated workforce). Alternatively, cities/states with unobserved characteristics that generate higher wages for the skilled may attract better-educated workers. In either of these cases, ignoring the endogeneity of average schooling would result in biased estimates of the "social" return.

Moretti (2004) allows for both possibilities, thus treating the average level of education in a city as endogenous; however, he assumes individual education to be exogenous. He focuses on the social returns to higher education, which he finds to be larger for the less-educated groups of workers. Specifically, a one percentage point increase in the share of college graduates in a city's labour force is found to increase the wages of high-school drop-outs by 1.9%, of high-school graduates by 1.6%, and of college graduates by 0.4%.

Acemoglu and Angrist (2000), by contrast, treat both individual and state average education levels as endogenous. Their focus is on the social returns to secondary education. If they ignore the endogeneity of both average and individual education, they estimate a private return to schooling of 7.3% and find that a one-year increase in state average education is similarly associated with a 7.3% increase in the wages of all workers in the state. However, once both average and individual education levels are treated as endogenous, the private return remains unchanged at around 7.5% whilst the social return vanishes.

The final paper, by Ciccone and Peri (2000), uses a different empirical approach, which is more closely associated with the macro growth literature and which does not involve estimating individual private returns. Their unit of observation is the city (rather than the country as in the macro growth regressions). Under the assumption that workers with different human capital are perfect substitutes in production, they find a significant average schooling externality of between 7 and 11%. However, once workers with different levels of education are allowed to be imperfect substitutes, the estimated effect falls to 1% and is not significant at conventional levels.

Whilst these within-country microeconometric studies offer a potentially interesting way forward, they suffer from a number of potential weaknesses. First, there are the well-documented problems of adequately accounting for the potential endogeneity of both individual and average schooling. In addition, the definition of educational externality adopted is very narrow. In particular, positive effects may accrue at a higher (national) or lower (firm) level of aggregation. Furthermore, average education may provide externalities not captured by workers through their wages. In particular, individuals may benefit in a non-pecuniary form (e.g. type of tasks, supervisory effort, quality of working and living environment), while spillover effects may in part accrue to employers instead.

Other Approaches. In a recent report commissioned by the European Directorate, de la Fuente (2003) reports a set of estimates of the private and social returns to education in all member countries. The private returns are derived from standard internal rate-of-return calculations, but adjusted for employment benefits from education and for various transfers (income taxes, employees' social security contributions, unemployment benefits, educational subsidies) as well as allowing for part-time work and differential student unemployment and participation probabilities. As to the social internal rate-of-return estimates, this is the first study seriously trying to incorporate externalities. The estimated social effects are based on results from the most recent macro growth regressions.

The calculations – especially the ones for the social rate – represent a very assumption-intensive exercise. A considerable extent of arbitrariness thus exists, since functional forms need to be assumed and key parameters imposed, often calibrated based on selected or, at times, combined and/or (loosely) "corrected" previous evidence. But the study certainly represents an impressive effort to calculate comparable rates across member countries while taking account of a number of generally neglected factors. (For further methodological discussion of this study, see, for example, Sianesi (2003a).)

The estimated returns are those at the margin for an average production worker with the observed average years of school attainment for the adult population (i.e. aged over 25) in a country in 1990, which for the UK is 10.52 years. For the UK, the interesting result is of a social rate estimate of 10.48% that is actually lower than the corresponding private one of 13.87%.

7.5 LIMITATIONS

The economic framework set out in Section 7.2 has clarified what elements are, in principle, needed to take economically efficient policy decisions. Before concluding this chapter it is important to highlight the limitations one has to be aware of when intending to use the estimates of the returns to education for policy purposes.

7.5.1 Private Returns

The estimates we have discussed provide an indication of the returns individuals reap in the labour market from different educational investments. In Section 7.2.1, we highlighted how the private return perceived by the individual (and even more so the full private return) is likely to include benefits that do not necessarily accrue on the labour market and/or that cannot be easily monetized. In fact, *even at the individual level*, econometric estimates of the returns mostly concentrate on the quantifiable economic benefits of these investments, and thus ignore the unquantifiable benefits an individual obtains from undertaking education. Examples of the latter include the pleasure derived from learning, the non-financial and social advantages of working in a skilled profession, and other non-employment benefits such as better individual health, parenting skills, enjoyment of cultural activities, and wider and more informed choices. If individuals are aware of these non-pecuniary additional benefits and if they value them, they will be prepared to accept a lower monetary return than if only employment-related monetary benefits are considered.

Two findings of particular interest in this regard are those from a recent US analysis that explicitly incorporates non-pecuniary benefits and uncertainty in the standard economic model of college choice (Carneiro *et al.* 2003). First, the authors find a substantial non-pecuniary return to college (i.e. psychic gains from learning and from working in the skilled occupation net of psychic costs). Furthermore, they find that it is variability of these non-monetary factors rather than of financial returns that plays a dominant role in schooling choices. More generally, they show how important it is to account for non-pecuniary benefits when evaluating educational choices: of the high-school graduates, 96% are happy with their choice of not having gone to college (measured in utils[11]), but 85% regret this decision financially.

7.5.2 Signalling Hypothesis

A long-standing debate in the economics of education literature concerns the extent to which education provides individuals with marketable skills that directly enhance their productivity (human-capital hypothesis) as opposed to being a signal of pre-existing productivity (signalling or screening hypothesis).

In its purest form (Arrow 1973; Spence 1973, 1974) the signalling approach rules out any direct contribution of education to individual productivity. By contrast, it argues that in the presence of asymmetric information about workers' productivity, educational qualifications provide signals and offer employers a screening device for identifying high-ability workers. Workers will in turn seek educational qualifications to inform firms of their value. More general screening models focus on the ways in which education serves as a device for signalling pre-existing differences that firms cannot directly observe, while allowing for learning.

The key issue is that in screening models, even after correcting for all characteristics observed by the firm, the coefficient on education in a wage equation may be a very biased estimate of the effects of education on individual productivity, since, in such models, attributes that are not observed by the firm are crucially correlated with the signal, education.[12] This hypothesis thus openly challenges the conventional productivity interpretation of the measured individual wage returns to education (the one we discussed in Section 7.2.3).

For individuals evaluating potential private returns to investments in education, the issue of which theory is the true one is irrelevant: they earn higher wages after education, irrespective of whether this was caused by the content of the course (productivity gain) or by the fact that they obtained the qualification (information

---

[11]A "util" is the equivalent of one unit of satisfaction.

[12]Layard and Psacharopoulos (1974) show that under the screening hypothesis, even a regression that controlled for the *true* ability of individuals could yield a positive return to education even in the absence of any impact of education on productivity.

gain). However, from the point of view of society as a whole, if the screening hypothesis is true, the social returns to educational investments are overstated. In a pure signalling framework, education has a social value only if and to the extent to which the allocation of high- and low-ability workers matters, so that particular combinations of workers are more productive than others.[13] The implication of this is that the marginal social return schedule in Figure 7.1 would shift to the left; if these "credential" effects are strong enough, it could even be the case that the individual is overinvesting in education (i.e. in the signal) from a social point of view.

In spite of their radically different implications at the social level, the human capital and screening approaches are particularly difficult to distinguish. In fact, they are observationally equivalent, in that both suggest that there is a positive correlation between earnings and education and between education and ability, but they produce these results for very different reasons.

As a consequence, the balance of evidence emerging from this debate leads to an inconclusive perspective on which theory is more appropriate (for a review, see, for example, Weiss (1995); for a recent attempt at discriminating between the two theories, see Chevalier *et al.* (2004)). Rather than testing the signalling hypothesis in its extreme version, the relevant issue is most likely to consist of trying to separate out how much of the estimated returns to educational qualifications are due to skill gains as opposed to certificate gains. The extent to which education may have conferred new productive skills as opposed to just a credential advantage is also most likely to differ between types and levels of educational qualifications. This is an issue taken up by the next chapter.

7.5.3 *General Equilibrium Effects*

All the estimates of private returns discussed in this chapter have been obtained from so-called partial-equilibrium estimators. This type of estimator makes three important assumptions.

First, partial-equilibrium estimators assume that individual decisions to invest in education do not affect the earnings of the "skilled" and "unskilled". However, in the case of an educational policy extensively affecting educational achievement in the economy (or in the local labour market if it is "separate" enough), the induced adjustments in the supply of skilled and unskilled workers will depress the post-education earnings of the skilled workers and raise those of the unskilled workers, reducing

---

[13] In this case, education is a signalling device that helps improve the allocation of individuals between jobs by providing information, a valuable commodity for which the market often fails (Stiglitz 1975).

the return to being skilled.[14] The second assumption of partial-equilibrium estimators is that, in their educational investment decisions, individuals do not anticipate these movements in the post-education earnings of the two skill groups. However, if individuals are rational and forward looking, they will both anticipate and take into account these movements in their schooling decision. Finally, these estimators do not take into account that raising taxation to (co-)finance education might have distortionary effects on the behaviour of everyone in the economy.

If these assumptions are violated, estimates from partial-equilibrium approaches will miss these additional effects; they will additionally produce misleading results if the increase in education affects the earnings of the low-education workers as well. How serious this latter problem is depends largely on the scale (relative to the relevant local labour market) of the educational policy, the issue being of course most relevant for universal policies.

But what are the implications of these issues in terms of the private versus social returns question as depicted in Figure 7.1? As regards social returns, they need to be evaluated from a general-equilibrium perspective, taking account of the full cross-effects and interactions that take place in the labour market, as well as of the wider (distortionary) effects of raising taxes to subsidize education. These two factors are likely to *reduce* the social returns to additional levels of education, shifting the social marginal returns schedule to the left.

As to private returns, one can debate whether it is the partial- or the general-equilibrium estimate which best represents private incentives. This question really boils down to what kind of forward-looking behaviour one is willing to assume for the individual, since this will dictate the position of the private marginal schedule he/she will refer to in taking his/her private decisions. Specifically, the general-equilibrium approach would be the appropriate one if it is believed that individuals are rational and perfectly forward looking. Individuals will thus both anticipate the movements in earnings for the various education groups following an educational reform and take such movements into account in their educational investment decision. In this case, the private schedule would also shift to the left, and, for given marginal cost, the individual will choose a lower level of education.

7.5.4 *Time Specificity*

A related feature worth highlighting is that the estimated returns to different educational qualifications will be specific to a particular time period (and location),

---

[14]Provided the demand functions are not perfectly elastic and are stationary. As to the latter, it may well be, by contrast, that the wider availability of skilled workers encourages firms to produce more skill-intensive goods. In fact, the hypothesis of skill-biased technical change is among the main explanations of the recent puzzle of widening educational wage differentials in the face of continuous upward trends in educational attainment.

or, in more general terms, to the earnings set in the labour market. These earnings possibilities will in turn reflect the demand and supply of individuals with these differing human capital attributes, and will do so in a way that depends on the relative substitutability of these different types of human capital (see, for example, Card and Lemieux 2001). For example, the estimates of the impact of different education levels on the earnings of UK men aged 33 in 1991 that we have discussed will be unlikely to be stable across time periods, but will change over time following the evolving interaction between the demand for and the supply of workers at each qualification level. This point, although quite obvious, is often misunderstood in the context of predicting returns to education.

7.6 CONCLUSIONS AND POLICY DISCUSSION

Overall, education seems to be a profitable investment for individuals, although large variation has been found in the observed wage returns by type of qualification. (For a recent survey for the UK, see Sianesi (2003b).) This might suggest that individuals are not choosing their educational investments optimally (in fact, not even from the individual point of view) and that policy reforms are thus needed.

However, in a proper comparison of the private returns to different courses or qualifications, account would need to be taken of the differential net psychic costs, as well as of the differential amount of time needed to achieve the various qualifications. Different qualifications may also imply different degrees of risk. Furthermore, different qualifications may provide a different combination of wage and non-financial returns. Recent work has confirmed that looking solely at average financial returns to education may only tell part of the story. All these considerations point to the possibility that once the *full* individual costs and benefits from the different qualifications are taken into account, the differentials might be much reduced.

As to the desirability of government intervention from a social-efficiency point of view, information on private returns is not enough. In particular, the ranking of the various educational investments may change when taken in terms of their social returns. Different qualifications might differentially benefit society as a whole via their spillover and external impacts. Also, different qualifications may confer skills of a differential degree of generality, which may lead the corresponding increase in individual productivity to be differentially captured by individual wages as opposed to direct measures of productivity and firm profitability.[15] As to the implications

---

[15] Standard economic theory typically distinguishes human capital between general and specific, or more directly in terms of its portability between jobs, firms or sectors. When the acquired skill has a large job-, firm- or sector-specific component (i.e. it has little or no use outside the job, firm or sector) or, more generally, when labour mobility is effectively restricted, firms gain monopsony power, which allows them to avoid passing the full productivity gain on to the employee in terms of wages.

of the signalling hypothesis, it could be that the different premia to different types of qualifications arise since different qualifications confer on individuals a different mix of actual productive skills and of signals of pre-existing skills. Different qualifications may even send out different types of signal.[16]

Whilst we are reasonably confident of the reliability of our estimates of the private financial returns to education, finding reliable estimates of the social returns to educational investments remains an area where a lot more work is needed.

7.7 Appendix: Comparing Private Rates of Return and Real Return on Debt and Equity

An alternative way in which the adequacy and profitability of private investments in education have been assessed (e.g. Harmon *et al*. 2002; de la Fuente 2003) is based on comparing the returns to human capital investments with returns to financial investments. In particular, the favourable comparison between private internal rates of return[17] and the real return on debt and equity has consequently been taken as indicative of the presence of some market failure. Although looking like an attractive comparison, there are a few issues to be aware of.

First of all, this comparison implicitly assumes that the relevant discount rate for the individual is the return on standard financial assets. However, only under a set of very strong assumptions (perfect capital markets, perfect rationality, perfect information, "rational" risk aversion, etc.) will the individual's private reference discount rate equal the interest rate at which every individual can borrow funds and which also represents the return the individual would have received if she/he had invested the same amount of resources into the best alternative available.

To earn the yearly return on financial assets, the young person would have had to invest upfront his/her *entire* yearly wages as well as the direct cost he/she would have sustained for a year in schooling. This is hardly possible: even if he/she does not go to school, the working individual would need to pay for his/her maintenance during the year. Note that there is an asymmetry here, since private returns are,

---

[16] For example, individuals acquiring a vocational qualification may be *perceived* by employers as less able or motivated than their counterparts investing in its academic equivalent. A related concern raised by Conlon (2001) is that while the national administration and common assessment method of academic qualifications gives prospective employers a clear signal about individuals' skills, the local administration and differing assessment methods of vocational qualifications may make them an imprecise and hence risky signal for employers to base their hiring decisions on, which could cause the vocationally trained to pay a risk premium in the form of a lower wage.

[17] The internal rate of return is given by that discount rate for which the discounted present value of the benefits arising from the investment net of its costs equals zero. It can then be compared with the reference discount rate of the decision maker or with the internal rates of return on alternative investments. This methodology thus offers both a rule for deciding on the profitability of an investment and a metric that can be used to order the profitability of two or more alternative investments.

by contrast, calculated taking into account public subsidies for living expenses and other non-tuition costs. In addition, often these are not enough, so that students from disadvantaged families would take on additional loans (at preferential rates (for example, in the UK)). The working individual would have no access to preferential loans to invest the "direct cost of schooling" in the stock market. All this points out that in fact the individual deciding to work would need to borrow the equivalent funds to be able to invest them, something he/she would never succeed in doing at a borrowing rate low enough for the financial return to be the net one from his/her alternative investment. Using the market rate of interest assumes that individuals can borrow against this rate, i.e. that there are no credit constraints. The returns on debt and equity are thus not the relevant benchmark, in the sense that they do not represent the rate at which the individual can borrow for his/her educational investment nor the return to an alternative investment for which there are no upfront funds.

In addition, the question arises as to whether these two investments are really comparable. For the educational investment to be minimally successful, the investor needs to put active effort into the investing process itself (i.e. to study, satisfy course-work, manage exam stress, etc.). Furthermore – and ignoring, for the moment, uncertainty with respect to both the future individual return to education and employment probability – the educational investor will enjoy a return from his/her investment only if he/she works (by contrast, the financial investor need just sit back and see the interest rolling in). The educational return thus rewards not only the taking of risk and the postponement of consumption, but also the (psychic) costs of going through the academic year *and* the necessity to work in order to reap the return. These factors make the investment in human capital intrinsically different from investments on the stock market. The comparison begs the question of whether these two types of investment have similar degrees of risk. In addition, the risk concerning the financial investment is "objective" and, given the relevant information set, applies equally to any given investor; this is not so for an investment in human capital, which is much more idiosyncratic.[18]

There is, finally, the issue of individual myopia or low expectations, which in a sense undermines the perfect rationality assumption. Vulnerable young people might opt for the immediate financial benefits accruing from semi-unskilled and often low-paid jobs rather than thinking of investments; they discount too heavily the benefits from higher income at later dates, so that investments in either education

---

[18]The educational return is not only conditional on successful completion of the course, as well as on being employed, but is also likely to vary according to individual characteristics (e.g. complementary innate or acquired skills). The two US studies mentioned above (Dominitz and Manski 1996; Carneiro *et al.* 2003) do find substantial, and *ex-ante* largely unpredictable, individual heterogeneity in the returns to college.

or the financial market are ignored in favour of immediate consumption, leisure and a sense of independence.

In the wider framework we considered in Section 7.2, individuals invest in education until the marginal return to schooling is equal to their marginal cost, with this opportunity cost being related to the individual's (or to the individual's family's) tastes for schooling, psychic costs from studying, subjective discount rates, access to funds and liquidity constraints. None of these is necessarily related to standard financial returns and all of them have obvious implications in terms of public policy.

Employers' Selection Decisions: the Role of Qualifications and Tests

By Andrew Jenkins and Alison Wolf

8.1 Introduction

Qualifications play a very large part in the childhood and adolescence of citizens in modern industrialized economies. However, the role of qualifications in the contemporary labour market is complex and can sometimes appear quite puzzling.

Consider the following four characteristics of the UK labour market, most (though not all) of which we know to be shared by other European and North American economies.

- There is evidence that employers have substituted graduates for non-graduates in a considerable number of jobs where there does not appear to have been any substantive change in the job's actual requirements (Ashworth 1988; Murphy 1993; Robinson 1997; Chapter 9 of this book, by McIntosh). On the other hand, some jobs have clearly seen significant up-skilling in recent years (Dickerson and Green 2004; Green *et al.* 2002; Felstead *et al.* 2002; Hoyles *et al.* 2002).

- Possession of qualifications is associated with substantial increases in earnings and decreased risk of unemployment compared with the unqualified or less qualified (as illustrated in Chapters 5 and 7). However, acquisition of qualifications in one's thirties (10–20 years after most people enter the labour market) does not appear to be associated with any clear additional gains in income (Jenkins *et al.* 2003; Vignoles *et al.* 2004).

- Many job advertisements do not specify any formal qualifications as either necessary or desirable for applicants, while a high proportion of those job advertisements that do express a desire for graduates do not specify which subject/type of degree applicants should hold (Atkins *et al.* 1993; Jackson *et al.* forthcoming).

- Employers very frequently emphasize "soft" skills (e.g. teamwork, initiative) as very important in themselves and perhaps more important than any academic skills or qualifications (Atkinson *et al.* 1996). In addition, employers frequently express ignorance about the relative standing of different educational institutions/universities, and about the meaning and content of most formal qualifications (Wolf and Jenkins 2002). However, graduate earnings *are* affected by the type of university attended (Chevalier and Conlon 2003) and there are clear differences in the earnings associated with quite detailed levels and types of qualification attained (Dearden *et al.* 2002*a*).

The purpose of this chapter is to attempt to reconcile some of these apparently inconsistent findings.

In evaluating the relationship between formal education and the labour market, qualifications clearly do play a vital role. They are how the education system self-reports and plans its output, especially in countries with formal public examination systems, such as the UK or France. Qualifications are also the way in which employers generally obtain information about what someone has achieved or learned during formal education and training. So, for example, rate-of-return analysis in the UK (see Chapter 7) and, indeed, in most of Europe has evolved and now examines returns to specific qualifications rather than simply to years in education; similarly, government targets for education and training, especially but not only in the UK, are expressed in terms of qualifications achieved.

The process of assessing and awarding qualifications is a major industry in itself, which is increasingly regulated by government. This increased regulation is ostensibly to ensure that high-quality and relevant information is provided to users of qualifications, notably employers. To better understand the labour-market dynamics underlying wage differentials and skills shortages we therefore need to understand how employers actually interpret and use qualifications. Since information relating to qualification attainment is likely to carry the greatest weight at the point of selection into some form of employment, we focus on selection decisions here.

We begin, in Section 8.2, by discussing some theoretical arguments regarding the role of qualifications in employers' selection decisions. Section 8.3 provides an overview of data from employer surveys on the information used in the selection process. Section 8.4 examines the evidence as to how employers interpret qualification data specifically; and Section 8.5 elaborates on this by examining evidence for changes in qualification use, largely based on some recent research on employers' use of selection tests rather than qualifications. The evidence that we present on current UK labour-market practices supports the argument that job selection and allocation take place within broad regulatory environments that may be as important to employers' decisions as are judgements about the productivity of individual workers. Section 8.6 takes up the theme of the heterogeneity of the contemporary labour market, considering how skill demands and the role of qualifications and selection tests vary across economic sectors. Finally, in Section 8.7, we examine the policy implications of current research findings.

8.2 Why Might Employers Use Qualifications for Selection Purposes?

In Chapter 7 the authors posed the "naive" question: do people with more education earn more, on average, than people with less education? The answer, clearly, is yes. Moreover, earnings are higher, on average, for those with formal qualifications than for those without; and also for holders of particular types of qualification rather than others (even when the qualifications in question take much the same length of time to acquire).

Similar patterns hold for employment, so it is obvious that *individuals* have a good reason to acquire both more education, and more qualifications. We pose a slightly different, though closely related, question: why and when might *employers* use qualifications as a basis for employment decisions, over and above those occasions when they are constrained to do so by the law?

Employers will use qualifications to inform employment decisions as long as the qualification provides useful information about a potential employee's productivity levels (Belman and Heywood 1991). Qualifications are thus signalling devices to some extent. The use of such signalling devices depends on the confidence placed by the employer in the value of the signal, i.e. how accurately qualifications actually do reflect a person's productivity level.

In the economics of education, the concept of "signalling" has come to be associated with the idea that education and qualifications are used to indicate worker attributes that are independent of, though associated with, the content of the education acquired (see Section 7.5.2). At their most extreme, signalling models posit a situation in which the value of the qualification signal has nothing to do with the actual skills acquired but is entirely to do either with its association with innate ability, or its association with psychological and personality traits. The anti-schooling literature of the 1960s, for example, argued that employers were quite right to see educated workers as more productive, not because of their skills but because modern schools were designed to produce docile, hard-working employees who were used to boredom and subservience (Bowles and Gintis 1976; Illich 1971). In mainstream economics, the more common concern is with associations between education and differing innate ability (see Spence 1973, 1974). Here, at the extreme, education and qualifications may serve only to signal and identify innate ability. Contrast this with human-capital models, which assume that educational investments make workers more skilled and productive and it is this enhanced productivity that is reflected in their higher wages (see Chapter 7 by Blundell *et al.*).

In the psychological and assessment literature, however, "signalling" is used in a rather different way (see Cronbach 1990; Wernimont and Campbell 1968). The assumption here is that employers are genuinely concerned with the underlying educational content on which qualifications are based. However, employers are still concerned about the accuracy with which particular qualifications reflect a worker's understanding of that content. Is the "signal-to-noise' ratio such that the qualification or score can be used as a reliable and valid indicator that content and skills have indeed been mastered? Government regulation of formal qualifications rests on the assumption that signal reliability in this sense is relevant to employers and will not be assured without government intervention (Blacklock 2003).

Qualifications will obviously be more important in selection decisions the more faith employers have in them as signals. Employers' perception of signal accuracy can, of course, change over time, perhaps as a result of direct experience with new hires or because of perceived changes in the qualification and education system. In principle, qualifications should produce more accurate signals than do length of schooling or training, since they measure outcomes. However, because, in many countries (and notably in the UK) they are used as official targets and accountability measures for public institutions, they may also be highly susceptible to the effects of Goodhart's Law: namely that any measure used for control thereby becomes unreliable.

In practice, the strong relationship between qualification levels and earnings suggests that employers currently treat qualifications as quite clear and powerful signals of productivity. However, it is also important to find out what employers and workplaces actually say they are doing with respect to qualifications; and the following section therefore summarizes data on selection criteria used in UK workplaces.

8.3 QUALIFICATIONS IN THE LABOUR MARKET

A number of large-scale national surveys contain information about qualifications. The Workplace Employee Relations Survey (WERS98) used a nationally representative sample of over 2000 UK workplaces with 10 or more employees. While this will have excluded small professional partnerships, along with other small employers, the sample included sizeable numbers of employers in, for example, health, education, business services and construction – all of them sectors in which formal qualifications are a prerequisite for some appointments (see Table 8.6 for a breakdown of respondent numbers by sector).

For WERS98, employers were asked about the factors that were considered important in recruiting new employees. Respondents were given a list of eight factors, one of which was "qualifications", and were asked to choose all factors that they considered important. About two-thirds of respondents stated that qualifications were important. The most widely cited factors were experience, skills and motivation, all mentioned by more than 85% of employers (see Table 8.1). Qualifications are ranked fifth in terms of how often they were cited (ahead of availability, age and recommendation by another employee).

Table 8.1. Factors considered important when recruiting new employees to UK workplaces.

Factor	Weighted percentage selecting this factor
Experience	89
Skills	87
Motivation	86
References	73
Qualifications	66
Availability	52
Recommended by another employee	36
Age	20
Specific answer not codeable to above	5

Notes. Base: all establishments indicated by question filter. Source: WERS98 (main management interview).

In the Learning and Training at Work 2001 survey (LTW2001), a nationally representative sample of 2235 employers with five or more employees were questioned about the factors that they took into account when recruiting 16–24 year olds. For the recruitment of these young workers, with limited labour-market experience, one might expect qualifications to figure particularly prominently.[1] In fact, only one in five employers referred to qualifications as being important, with the personal attributes of the candidates being most widely mentioned (Spilsbury 2002). However, amongst the largest employers (those with 500 or more employees) qualifications were the most commonly cited factor (see Table 8.2 for details).

Unfortunately, the information obtained from surveys is highly sensitive to the wording employed. This is very obvious with written surveys; but the tightly scripted telephone interviews which are increasingly used for large-scale surveys are even more limited in the type of questions they can ask and the information they can request from what will normally be a single informant. For example, if employers are not asked explicitly about whether they prioritize qualifications, they may note that they use CVs and application forms for selection without explaining whether and how far qualifications feature in these. This is the case in a number of recruitment

---

[1] One would predict that, when direct evidence on worker productivity is available, it will be preferred to a proxy, or signal, however good. In theory, therefore, we would expect employers to give much more weight to qualifications when making hiring decisions about young people who have had little chance to obtain labour-market experience than in decisions involving adults who have (or are old enough to have had) workforce experience. This is certainly consistent with a substantial body of evidence which indicates that low-level qualifications do not do very much to augment the earnings of adults with a history of unemployment and poor academic achievement, whereas holding down a job for a while – even a rather low-skill, part-time one – has a marked positive effect on their future employment and earnings prospects (Jenkins *et al.* 2003).

Table 8.2. Factors taken into account when recruiting 16–24 year olds by size of employer.

	Total (%)	5–24 (%)	25–99 (%)	100–199 (%)	200–499 (%)	500+ (%)
Personality, attitude, flexibility, reliability	45	46	45	37	37	33
Interest, enthusiasm, willingness to learn	24	24	25	27	26	22
Specific skills, ability to do the job	24	23	27	32	30	30
Qualifications	20	18	24	32	34	46
Experience	18	16	23	20	22	20
Interpersonal, communication skills	15	15	17	15	20	18
Appearance	13	14	13	7	8	5
Common sense	11	11	11	8	7	5
Initiative, confidence	9	9	9	9	6	7
Intelligence	8	8	8	7	7	6
References	3	4	3	2	2	4
Other	9	9	8	7	13	9

Notes. Base/coverage: all employers with five or more employees who have recruited 16–24 year olds in the previous 12 months; $N = 2235$. Source: Learning and Training at Work (2001).

studies and surveys (CIPD 1999). Some of the differences between WERS98 and LTW2001 in the proportion of employers mentioning qualifications as being important in recruitment can probably be accounted for by the fact that, in WERS98, respondents were given a list of prompts from which to choose as many as they wished, whereas in LTW2001 (carried out by telephone) they were asked a question without prompts and the responses were subsequently coded up. Unfortunately, neither of these two major surveys asked employers to rank the importance of the various factors, or to distinguish between different types of job within their workplace.

A number of other surveys also provide information on the use of qualifications, though without using a fully representative national sample. In general, they suggest that, just as was the case 20 years ago, employers are often looking for a cluster of affective and behavioural characteristics – more so than for specific skills of the type amenable to formal certification (Oliver and Turton 1982). Atkinson *et al.* (1996) conducted a national telephone survey on recruitment and selection practices as part of a study into the attitudes of employers to unemployed applicants. The results are shown in Table 8.3. Of this sample of approximately 700 employers, 28% set minimum standards for academic qualifications when recruiting and 16%

Table 8.3. Relative importance of criteria in most recent selection decisions (per cent).

	Irrelevant	Minor	Fairly	Very	Don't know
Basic skills (literacy, numeracy)	4	5	25	65	1
Educational qualifications	26	30	21	23	1
Vocational qualifications	35	28	15	20	2
Specific technical competence	23	20	21	35	1
Previous experience in similar job	13	14	31	41	1
Previous employment in similar organization	21	22	30	26	1
Stable relatively continuous job record	18	12	38	30	1
History of employment	48	26	13	9	3
Age	42	30	19	8	1
Health/fitness	8	8	43	40	1
Motivation/attitude/keenness	1	1	13	85	1
Reliability/honesty/integrity	1	1	8	90	1
Reference from previous employer	12	12	35	40	1
Character reference	24	16	25	33	1
Immediate/ quick start	18	16	36	28	2

Notes. $N = 706$. Source: Atkinson *et al.* (1996).

set minimum standards for vocational qualifications. Public-sector employers were much more likely to specify minimum requirements than those in the private sector. Minimum requirements for academic qualifications were more likely in large organizations than in small ones, but there was little difference by size of organization for vocational qualifications.

Conversely, both academic qualifications and vocational qualifications were rated as "irrelevant" or of "minor importance" by over half of all employers. Judging by the proportions rating them of "minor importance", or "irrelevant", academic and vocational qualifications were 12th and 13th, respectively, of the 15 criteria, ahead of only age and history of employment. The most consistently important factors were motivation/attitude, reliability/integrity and basic skills.[2]

---

[2] A surprising finding here is the apparently low weight given to previous history of employment. We surmise that this is because questions were asked in the context of a survey of employers' attitudes to the unemployed: illustrating, once again, the limitations of relying on large-scale survey research in this field.

8.4 WHAT DO EMPLOYERS THINK QUALIFICATIONS SIGNAL?

We argued in Section 8.2 that, when employers use qualifications for selection purposes, this is because of the signals they provide about future productivity; but that such a signal may take a number of forms. This is consistent with the fact that an individual's productivity is itself a function of a considerable number of attributes, some cognitive, others affective.[3] The survey evidence reported above reflects this: employers mention interpersonal as well as technical skills, and emphasize motivation, initiative and reliability as important to selection decisions.

This section reviews research evidence on *which* attributes employers currently interpret qualifications as signalling. This evidence is generally consistent with the proposition that they use qualifications as signals of both cognitive and affective attributes; and, moreover, that within the cognitive domain, some employers use qualifications as signals of specific skills, but others use them as signals of very general attainment, and of ability, rather than of specific learning.

Most of this evidence is, of necessity, indirect. For example, if qualifications are used as signals of general cognitive ability, this means that someone with a higher level of academic qualification is seen as having, in all probability, higher levels of general intelligence or ability than someone with a lower level of qualification. In employers' perceptions, these traits are in turn associated with the likelihood that an individual will need less time to complete and master firm- and job-specific training (Robertson and Downs 1989).

For given qualification levels, job applicants with academic qualifications may be seen as more able than those with vocational qualifications (see Chapter 5). This perception is based in some reality, given the evidence that more academically able students are more likely to choose the academic track leading to a postsecondary degree and less able students are more likely to go down the vocational track (see Chapter 5 herein; Wolf *et al.* 2000; Hodgson and Spours 2003). Young people definitely perceive the selection process to operate in this way. They also perceive that a postsecondary degree as a prerequisite to a good job in the modern labour market. This is a major reason for the international pattern of rising demand for academic qualifications and for qualifications allowing access to higher education, and for rejection by children and parents of early selection into highly specific vocational pathways (Dore 1997; Little 1997; Wolf 2002*a*).

---

[3] In the psychological literature the distinction between these two categories is a conventional one: with cognitive skills and attributes encompassing anything to do with "knowing" in its widest sense, and including perception, conception and analysis; and the term "affective" being used to encompass anything to do with dispositions and emotions, again in the widest sense of these words.

8.4.1 Sheepskin Effects

Hard evidence on how qualifications are interpreted at the time of hiring is very difficult to obtain. A number of studies have looked for "sheepskin" effects, using earnings data to examine whether a diploma or certificate has value in the labour market over and above the value associated with total number of years of schooling completed (Layard and Psacharopoulos 1974).[4]

The procedure here is to estimate an equation of the form

$$\ln Y = \alpha_1 X + \beta_1 S + \varepsilon,$$

where Y is earnings, S is years of completed schooling, X is some vector of control variables (tenure, experience, etc.) and ε is an error term; and also to estimate

$$\ln Y = \alpha_2 X + \beta_2 S + \gamma D + \varepsilon.$$

The estimated coefficient β_1 is interpreted as the total return to schooling, while β_2 is the return net of diploma effects (D). The difference between β_1 and β_2 can be considered as the part of the total return that is due to sheepskin effects.

For the US, Jaeger and Page (1996) showed that sheepskin effects could explain approximately a quarter of the total return to completing 16 years of education and more than half of the return to completing 16 years relative to 12 years. More recently, Bauer *et al.* (2002) applied this framework to Japanese data. The estimated return to additional schooling drops from 6.7% to about 3% when diplomas are included in the model specification, suggesting that more than half of the returns to education in Japan were due to the sheepskin effects of diplomas. In the UK, as discussed in detail in Chapters 5 and 7, academic qualifications consistently show higher returns than vocational ones that take much the same amount of time to obtain; but most vocational qualifications show some positive returns compared with the possession of no formal qualifications at all.

However, the fact that a diploma has an effect on earnings over and above those associated with years of schooling does not, in itself, say anything about how employers use diplomas for selection. The effects might be because collecting a diploma

---

[4]This work has been hampered by the lack of datasets that include information on both years of education and diplomas/certificates achieved, so that some of these studies have simply inferred diploma completion from the number of years of education completed: a process which is likely to lead to biased estimates of sheepskin effects, as in reality the length of time taken to obtain a diploma may vary (Jaeger and Page 1996). More recently, datasets containing information on both years of education and diplomas attained have been utilized to obtain better estimates.

suggests that the holder possesses certain general attributes, but may also reflect the fact that doing so involves acquiring more substantive skills than are gained by simply serving time in educational institutions.[5]

Some additional evidence is available from studies of the American General Educational Development certificate (GED). The US high-school diploma is one of the most important qualifications in the US labour market, with major differences in earnings, employment and life-chances associated with holding, or not holding, the diploma. While most of those who obtain it do so at the end of full-time secondary schooling, the GED offers drop-outs an alternative route. Large numbers obtain this certificate every year. However, in labour-market terms, GED holders are not equivalent to high-school-diploma holders, though they fare rather better than drop-outs without the GED (see, especially, Murnane *et al.* 2000). Within the GED group, those who had fairly high cognitive scores in 10th grade do not seem to do any better as a result of having a GED than comparably scoring drop-outs without one (and both fare worse than diploma holders). However, those who had low scores in 10th grade and obtain a GED do significantly better than their non-certificated low-scoring equivalents. Moreover, foreign-born holders of the GED earn more than those who completed a traditional high-school education outside the US (Clark and Jaeger 2002).

One possible interpretation of these findings is that the high-school diploma has labour-market value as a "general" signal, which the GED does not have, but that, for low-attaining individuals, the additional skills acquired in the course of passing the GED bring substantive rewards compared with non-GED holders with comparable and very poor high-school attainment. However, the results for the foreign-born suggest a clear sheepskin effect, with the GED providing a signal that US employers understand and value when associated with foreign workers whose own qualifications are unfamiliar.

The use of qualifications to infer general attributes is also fully consistent with the observed existence of credentialism and overeducation in the labour market (meaning that employers raise their qualifications requirements even though the nature of the jobs remains unchanged). The extent of overeducation is discussed thoroughly in Chapter 9 by McIntosh, and can be illustrated here by the findings of Felstead *et al.* (2002). They document rising skill requirements in UK workplaces, but also, comparing parallel data in 1986 and 2001, note that, for level 3 qualification holders, the proportions reporting these to be "essential" or "fairly necessary" to do

---

[5]The extent to which this is true may also vary significantly between countries. For example, in Japan, getting into many universities is very hard, but graduating, once there, is fairly easy: so in many cases a university diploma tells people a good deal about pre-university performance but rather little about skills gained while there.

their jobs fell from 77% in 1986 to 70% in 2001, and the proportions who regarded them as "unnecessary" rose from 4% to 10% (Felstead *et al.* 2002).[6]

Evidence that employers (may) treat qualifications as signals of general traits does not, however, preclude their also treating them as signals of highly specific skills. There is a considerable body of evidence showing that individuals who acquire specific vocational training and qualifications, and who then work in the relevant occupational areas, enjoy an earnings advantage over other employees with equivalent numbers of years and level of schooling. Outside the specific vocational area, the value of such qualifications plummets (Neuman and Ziderman 1999, 2001; Tsang 1997).

The evidence discussed so far is all derived from survey evidence, and is correspondingly limited in its ability to document complex decision-making. We are not aware of any research studies of qualification use based on observation of actual selection decisions, but we do have some evidence from in-depth employer interviews. This evidence was obtained as part of a study into the use of psychometric tests for selection (see Section 8.5 below), in the course of which we interviewed managers and external consultants responsible for managing the selection process for 53 private- and public-sector UK organizations (Wolf and Jenkins 2002).

In every case where qualifications were used, it was largely at the shortlisting stage, suggesting that employers believed them to be useful but not perfect signals of productivity. In some cases, highly specific "minimum requirement" measures applied (e.g. for certain types of engineer); more often, qualifications were seen as more general indicators. It was striking that, except in those cases where a few specific (and often sector-specific) qualifications were important, employers consistently made only a few broad distinctions between qualification levels and types. They did not attempt to keep up with the details of qualification reform, and these broad categories were expressed in terms of very well-recognized academic qualifications, such as "5 GCSEs including Maths and English", or "a university degree" (Wolf and Jenkins 2002). Hoyles *et al.* (2002) report a similar preference for a few broad categories and a lack of knowledge of (or interest in) the details of current qualification structures.

This approach is consistent with interpreting qualifications as signals of innate ability, *and* of broad general skills, although most of the respondents who expanded on why they used qualifications referred to general skill levels. US evidence shows a comparable lack of employer interest in highly detailed information on school- and college-acquired skills, with employers unwilling to read either high-school or college transcripts (Wills 1998).

---

[6]They note similar patterns for level 1 qualifications but not for level 2. The strength of this study, as compared with most analyses of possible "overeducation", is that it uses four nationally representative sample surveys to compare trends over time.

The interesting findings of Dolton and Vignoles (2000*b*) on returns to mathematics GCE A level[7] also suggest a lack of interest in qualification content on the part of employers. Although holders of a mathematics A level earn significantly more than comparable employees whose A levels are in other subjects, this difference is not evident at the start of their careers. This suggests that the additional earnings compared with other A level holders are entirely the result of mathematics skills leading to greater productivity within employment, and that employers do not differentiate within the A level signal by subject and content.

Most discussions of qualifications as signals concentrate on cognitive ability and skills. However, qualifications may also be perceived as signals of affective traits or other behaviour, notably perseverance, hard work or conformity (Bowles and Gintis 1976). Direct evidence of the relative productivity of the qualified and the unqualified is very rare indeed, but one such study suggests that employers may be rational if they treat qualifications as a signal of non-cognitive abilities and attitudes. Weiss (1984) compared the productivity, in a manufacturing company, of high-school graduates and non-graduates and found that, for any given day of work, there was no difference. The graduates, however, had better attendance records and were less likely to quit.

Employers commonly use qualifications as one of many potential productivity signals. As noted in Section 8.2, the weight attached to qualifications may depend not just on what they are taken to signal but also on how accurately they do so, and may change over time. UK policy makers in particular have been concerned about whether or not publicly regulated qualifications are perceived as reliable, and whether confidence in them is increasing or decreasing.[8] Compared with France or Germany, the UK has relatively few occupations for which qualifications are a formal prerequisite for employment, or in which gaining qualifications automatically entitles holders to a pay rise. However, government policy on skill supply depends heavily on qualification targets and the development of new awards, and regulatory policy is also increasing the number of occupations for which formal qualifications are required by UK law.[9] The following section discusses what is known about changes in how employers use and interpret qualifications, including whether this

---

[7]Because the academic subjects taken by upper secondary-school students in the UK are separately assessed and certificated (as, for example, "GCE Advanced" level awards, or "A levels"), it is possible to compare returns to different subjects.

[8]For example, England's Qualifications and Curriculum Authority, which oversees all non-university awards offered in publicly supported institutions, has a programme of research examining the general public's confidence in examinations.

[9]For example, by 2005 all UK care homes will have to have a certain proportion of non-nursing employees qualified and in possession of specified vocational qualifications; and qualifications are also being used as part of a new regulatory framework for cab drivers.

reflects changes in demand for skills, or changes in the perceived reliability of qualifications as signals.

8.5 CHANGES OVER TIME

Employer organizations are often very willing to pass judgement on the quality and content of schooling and school examinations, at least in the UK (see Institute of Directors 1994, 2003; Confederation of British Industry 1989, 1994), but there is virtually no good research evidence indicating what individual employers think on this subject or whether it impacts on their actual selection (or promotion) procedures. Nor do any of the surveys discussed in Section 8.3 provide comparable data across substantial periods of time from which one might track changes in the relative importance attached to formal qualifications in selection.

However, during the last 20 years or so, there has been a significant increase in the use of psychometric testing for selection, indicated both in test manufacturers' turnover and in survey evidence (Jenkins 2001). Research into why companies have increased their test use provides a way of investigating, indirectly, changes in the weight placed on qualification signals, and has the advantage that one is not relying simply on stated opinions and attitudes. Employers do not, on the whole, pay directly for the learning process that results in the person having a qualification that can then be used as a signal by the employer. They do pay directly, however, for the costs of selection testing. If we can explain any increase in the weight given to selection-test results, and document any effects on the weighting of qualifications, this should substantially increase our understanding not just of selection decisions per se but also of the underlying demand for skills.

Wide ranges of selection tests are available on the market, but they can be divided into four main groups. General cognitive ability tests measure verbal, quantitative and critical reasoning skills. Tests of specific skills cover areas such as the ability to read diagrams, clerical skills and fault finding. There is also a wide range of both literacy and numeracy tests and of personality tests. The costs of such tests are substantial.

The survey evidence is almost entirely cross-sectional, with a variety of methodologies. It provides strong confirmation that test use has increased steadily and markedly since the 1980s, but little clear indication of why, or of how, this feeds into overall selection decisions (Jenkins 2001). In order to understand the motives behind increased test use, we therefore interviewed staff responsible for organizing selection in 53 UK organizations that used tests during selection. The establishments concerned were all sizeable enough to have some sort of formal human-resources department and they covered a range of industrial and public and private sectors. Most, though not all, had increased their level of test use in recent years; the reverse was true for qualifications. Indeed, one of the most striking findings in these interviews was that well over half the organizations surveyed had either excluded qualifications from the formal criteria on which final selection decisions could be based, or were actively downgrading their use[10] (Wolf and Jenkins 2002).

We had hypothesized that the increased use of tests reflected a declining faith in the qualification signal (perhaps in response to publicity over school standards), or a change in skill demands. We found very little evidence for the first of these propositions: only four respondents commented on the current standard of qualifications (albeit all negatively), though others pointed out that, for most applicants, qualifications tend to have been acquired a long time ago. The evidence for or against changes in skill demand is more complex. The skills tested in general ability tests are very similar to those tested in academic qualifications, and were certainly seen as highly relevant by the organizations studied. Nonetheless, we could not find any clear indication that increased test use was related to increased demand for these skills. Equally, the use of personality tests was linked by many respondents to an increasing confidence among managers that the results were robust, and by some to an increased awareness of which traits were important (probably as a result of the company conducting a formal analysis of core competency requirements). Again, however, we found nothing to indicate that actual requirements for interpersonal skills or other affective attributes had actually changed much in the period under review.

Instead, the majority of employers claimed that they used tests (as opposed to other means of selection) because of their value given the regulatory environment within which selection occurs. The same applied to the move away from qualifications. This was not because of a fall in their perceived accuracy as a signal, but because of concerns that their use as a formal selection criterion might create barriers to access and be viewed as contravening equal-opportunity policies. In other words, test scores are seen as a more objective, fair and legally defensible means of assessing a person's potential to do a job than their qualifications.

Evidence from psychometric tests was regarded as something that courts and tribunals would, in general, accept as valid. If a company could demonstrate that, for example, reading capacity or quantitative skills were relevant to the job in question, then it was generally agreed that evidence from reputable tests of such skills[11] would also be accepted as relevant data upon which to base selection decisions. The same was true of tests of "soft" skills, notably personality measures. This view

---

[10]Leaving aside recruitment to particular jobs for which qualifications were a legal necessity, in over a third of the workplaces qualifications were not viewed as a legitimate criterion at all for use in making recruitment decisions.

[11]Tests from major commercial companies such as SHL carry data about test reliability and validity, including avoidance of adverse impact on minorities; and courts accept this.

derives from a succession of tribunal cases as well as from the underlying legislation and regulations. Analysis of company data in WERS98 supports the argument that companies' selection processes do more than just attempt to infer an individual's future productivity. This research shows that an organization's commitment to practices designed to increase workforce diversity is strongly related to their use of both personality and competency testing. The use of competency testing is also significantly related to whether the organization had recently been involved in grievance procedures and tribunal complaints (Jenkins and Wolf 2002).

Labour-market regulation affects employers' use of qualifications in two major ways. The first way, and the more obvious one, is by requiring possession of a particular qualification for a particular job. There is no modern industrialized society – and probably no contemporary country with a functioning state apparatus – which does not limit the practice of certain occupations to people with the requisite qualification. These societies also regulate the process of providing qualifications, although the extent to which this is a fully nationalized process varies (Wolf 2002b). Those few countries which impose only minimal conditions (e.g. registration as a company) on bodies which offer "certificates", or even "qualifications", nonetheless impose clear restrictions on which qualifications entitle their holders to particular benefits or opportunities.

In addition, in recent decades there has been a major growth in legislation and regulation designed to protect employees against unfair dismissal, biased promotion and pay policies, and to protect all applicants against unfair appointment decisions. The trend is common to both Europe and North America, although the mechanisms have been somewhat different. In the UK, they have generally been developed in response to European directives, while in the US, lawsuits brought with reference to constitutional as well as federal law have been very important (Gifford 1989). Organizations are thus increasingly occupied with the need to be able to demonstrate, in the event of a challenge, that their appointment procedures have been fair both in the criteria used for selection and in the way the appointment procedure was carried out. While only a small minority of UK organizations are actually involved in an employment tribunal in any one year, their personnel and human-resources policies are structured by the desire to withstand such challenges.

The trend towards increased regulation means that employers may be using qualifications less in their selection decisions. On the other hand, many adults will find it necessary to acquire qualifications because of regulatory requirements including health and safety. These developments may help explain why, as discussed in the introduction, obtaining qualifications as an adult at anything below postsecondary degree level appears to have little or no impact on earnings (Jenkins et al. 2003; Vignoles et al. 2004). Many of the qualifications thus obtained may, in fact, relate to jobs that the holder was already doing, but for which they had not previously been certified; while in other cases, a qualification may be obtained because someone moves from an unregulated occupation to a regulated one at an equivalent skill and earnings level.[12] If the trend towards qualification-related regulation increases in the UK, we can expect that qualifications will actually become more important to employers in some sectors, at the same time as playing a smaller role in other sectors. This will further increase the heterogeneity of selection criteria used in the labour market. If, however, employers only use qualifications as selection criteria where required by regulation, this too may impact adversely on the ability of adults who obtain formal qualifications to translate this increased educational attainment into earnings growth.

Rejection of qualifications by many firms as a formal selection criterion does not, of course, mean that the skills acquired while obtaining such qualifications are irrelevant, even at the point of selection. They may feed directly into performance on employer-administered tests. Moreover, qualifications appear to be used informally in shortlisting even in organizations that reject their formal use; and they may also affect the general impression formed of candidates during interview and decision-making. The trend does, however, have implications for government policy on qualifications, and for the likely evolution of qualifications' role in the labour market. We return to this issue in the concluding section.

8.6 A Heterogeneous Labour Market

The research evidence is therefore consistent with the hypothesis that (consciously or unconsciously) employers use qualifications as a signal of productivity; and that many seem to also use them as a signal of general abilities and, in some cases, specific skills. In the UK there is also growing interest in using selection tests rather than qualification evidence, in large part because of regulatory concerns. In contrast, the use of testing in the US may be in decline due to fears about potential racial bias (see, for example, the pressure group website www.fairtest.org).

There are, however, major differences among employers in the characteristics they cite as important during selection. Moreover, while there is evidence of a general trend towards increased test use, many enterprises are not users of any tests while others use a wide variety. These findings reflect the fact that the current labour market is quite diverse in terms of its skill requirements. Some skills appear well suited to formal testing, and certification, and others less so. The usefulness of

---

[12]One might expect that, over time, a new recruit's possession of the requisite qualification would increase their earnings by saving the employer the costs of training. This may indeed become evident in future years, but the training is in fact generally highly or fully subsidized by the state. Moreover, the jobs to which the new regulatory requirements apply are at present largely public-sector positions subject to centralized pay bargaining, so that this will occur only if there is a formal agreement with employers that certification should carry a pay premium.

qualifications and selection tests will therefore depend very greatly on the job for which the employer is hiring. This section reviews evidence for such segmentation in the labour market.

Much discussion of the UK's future skill needs tends to focus on whether or not "unskilled" jobs are disappearing and on how far there is a general increase in the demand for high levels of literacy and numeracy. It is widely believed that generic skills, such as communication skills and numeracy, have become increasingly important in modern workplaces. Dickerson and Green (2004) provide some support for this, drawing on evidence from the 1997 and 2001 British Skill Surveys. Comparing the findings of the 1997 and 2001 surveys revealed that the average level of computer usage and use of most generic skills (such as literacy skills, numeracy, planning skills, problem-solving and communication skills) had significantly increased over this period. This suggests that the demand for such skills has risen over time. Decomposition of the change between 1997 and 2001 suggested that it was largely due to within-cohort rather than between-cohort effects, i.e. it was mainly due to workers gaining skills and not to the retirement of older workers and their replacement by younger ones with more skills.

However, there are clear indications that, while the labour force as a whole may show increasing levels of demand for "cognitive" and generic skills, the type of occupations which have been growing in recent years are not at all uniform in their demands (Turner 2001). Hoyles *et al.* (2002) studied seven sectors with particular reference to their use of intermediate-level mathematics skills and found that in every sector there was increasing use of mathematics and that this was inextricably intertwined with the growing application of IT to products and procedures. However, not all employees were equally affected, and in some jobs there had been a clear decline, in recent years, in the amount of mathematics required.

As Jackson *et al.* (forthcoming, p. 14) point out,

> [while] it is indeed true that professional and various ancillary occupations do in general continue to expand, it is also the case that a similar, or yet more rapid, growth is now occurring in work of a quite different kind; that is, in what have been described as "people" occupations, or as "high touch" rather than "high tech" occupations.

For occupations such as these (e.g. public relations, sales, customer services, entertainment and hospitality), one can hypothesize that qualifications may serve as guarantors of a certain minimum level of competence in generic "academic" skills (literacy, numeracy), and signals of other personality and behavioural traits (as discussed above), but that specific forms of knowledge, of the type that qualifications can certify reliably, will not be necessary.

As Jackson *et al.* (forthcoming, p. 15) suggest,

> the attention that employers give to education in this certifying . . . role
> would seem likely, in modern societies, *to become increasingly vari-*
> *able*.

They analysed a large sample of job advertisements, over 5000 in total, taken from UK local and national newspapers in early 2000. They found that only professional and ancillary occupations are consistently associated with requirements for formal qualifications, although advertisements for technical/operative and administrative/clerical jobs do specify technical-skill and/or cognitive-ability requirements. Jobs that fall into the general managerial and managerial and supervisory categories, along with other sales and personal-services jobs, are associated with requirements relating to effort: experience, social skills and personal characteristics. Qualifications are, overall, a requirement in only 28% of the jobs advertised (including those where the requirement is implicit rather than explicit), but underlying this are sizable differences with qualifications being a requirement for 64% of professional and ancillary jobs and only for 10% of managerial and supervisory jobs in sales and personal services. These results are consistent with an earlier study of graduate vacancies, which found that only 50% of employers specified postsecondary degree subject in any way (Atkins *et al.* 1993) and with the evidence from the survey described by Harvey (1994).

Additional evidence about labour-market heterogeneity comes from surveys of employers' use of skill and psychometric testing rather than qualifications alone. In 2001, detailed data on the use of selection tests from a sample of UK workplaces was collected, including information on the extent to which different types of test were used for different types of employee (CIPD 2001; Jenkins and Wolf 2002). As Table 8.4 indicates, patterns of test use differ quite markedly by employee type, and in directions consistent with job content, although there are surprises in some of the levels of use reported.

Personality tests are very rarely used for skilled manual workers; whereas there is significant use of specific skill and literacy/numeracy tests here – plus a surprisingly high level of use for general-ability tests (higher than for managers given the cost). Specific skill tests are used most often for professionals, as are general-ability and literacy/numeracy tests. The latter are generally quantitative reasoning and communication tests, which test publishers provide at a variety of difficulty levels, including batteries aimed specifically at managers. (Companies are not actually trying to check that potential professional employees can read.) For managers, the highest use is of personality tests, which report on exactly the type of "soft" skill discussed above. The survey, it should be noted, covers recruits of all ages, and not just young people

Table 8.4. Proportion of companies using selection tests by
type of employee (CIPD 2001).

	Professionals	Managers	Skilled manual	Any employee
Specific skills	45.8	29.6	33.6	60.1
General ability	37.9	30.4	33.6	54.5
Literacy/numeracy	30.0	25.3	23.3	44.6
Personality	26.1	38.7	9.1	40.7

Notes. Source: CIPD Recruitment Survey (a representative sample of UK workplaces in terms of workplace size excluding firms with less than 50 employees; $N = 253$).

for whom one might expect qualifications to provide recent evidence of skill levels in some of these categories.

Data for a much larger sample of employers are to be found in the WERS98 data, referred to earlier in this chapter. The WERS98 data provide sector-specific information on recruitment methods, although they do not, unfortunately, specify which sorts of job a given technique is used for – only whether the organization considers the measure important at least some of the time. Even so, as Table 8.5 demonstrates, there are clear inter-sector differences in use of qualifications for recruitment, ranging from 96% in education to 52% in wholesale and retail.[13]

The results for test use again show major differences between companies by industrial sector (see Table 8.6 below). It seems plausible, at the very least, to hypothesize that these differences reflect underlying differences in the skill mix required in different sectors, and companies, including the relative importance of "soft" and other skills, although they may also be affected by other factors which both affect the likelihood of test use and are non-randomly distributed across sectors.

Of course, these sector-related differences may also reflect other factors that vary by sector and that also affect test use. We therefore examined how far an enterprise's use of tests can be explained by a combination of different organizational characteristics (Jenkins and Wolf 2002). These include industrial sector, and a number of other variables (e.g. proportion of professionals and operatives in the workforce) that reflect intra-sectoral differences, which produce different skill demands.

The research indicated that workforce composition did indeed have a significant effect on the likelihood of test use. Even so, and after controlling for a large number of other skill and recruitment-related variables, industrial sector remained significant. Personality testing was significantly more likely in wholesale and retail, financial

---

[13]WERS98 also examines use of tests for selection. Unfortunately, the survey conflates different sorts of skill tests, and asks only about use of "competency" or "personality" measures; nor does the survey contain any questions asking about which groups of employees tests are used for, but only whether the company "ever" conducts tests when filling vacancies.

Table 8.5. Percentage of workplaces citing qualifications as an important factor in recruiting new employees.

Sector	Percentage citing qualifications as important (weighted)	Weighted number of establishments
Manufacturing	61.9	286
Electricity, gas, water	93.2	5
Construction	53.6	92
Wholesale/retail	51.5	421
Hotels/restaurants	55.9	169
Transport/communication	62.7	99
Financial services	69.0	60
Other business services	64.5	247
Public administration	66.6	102
Education	96.0	283
Health	83.6	305
Other community services	43.5	111

Table 8.6. Company testing practices by industrial sector (WERS98).

Sector (number of workplaces)	Proportion using personality tests	Proportion using competency tests
Manufacturing (287)	15.4	52.6
Electricity, gas, water (5)	81.8	72.2
Construction (92)	9.7	33.4
Wholesale/retail (421)	24.7	37.8
Hotels/restaurants (169)	19.0	28.6
Transport/communication (99)	23.5	62.8
Financial services (66)	52.2	71.1
Other business services (247)	18.4	55.0
Public administration (104)	20.3	76.3
Education (283)	9.3	49.7
Health (305)	19.3	44.9
Other community services (111)	18.6	48.4

services, other business services, and (less obviously) electricity, gas and water, while competency testing was significantly less likely to be used in enterprises in the wholesale and retail and hotel and restaurant sectors.

8.7 CONCLUSIONS

One important message to emerge from the literature is that we know surprisingly little about the way in which selection decisions are made. We have to rely heavily on survey evidence that is generated from the responses of one individual per establishment, typically a personnel officer with little direct responsibility for selection decisions. Indirect evidence (largely from analysis of earnings) does suggest that the higher earnings associated with some qualifications partly reflect the skills acquired in the process of gaining that qualification, but that qualifications are also signalling other attributes, such as general ability. As noted above, this is certainly how young people perceive the labour market to operate (see Section 7.4 above and, in particular, Little (1997)). On the basis of the research reviewed here we can expect a continuation of recent trends towards ever-higher formal qualification levels among the young, fuelled by certification's general signalling value rather than an increase in the demand for specific productive skills.

For policy makers, however, the lessons are more complex. It seems clear that employers recognize only a limited number of familiar qualifications as reliable signals, either of specific skills or of general qualities. In fact, the evidence presented in Chapter 5 and here suggests that in the UK the plethora of vocational qualifications available in the UK are not only not recognized by most employers but furthermore have very little value in the labour market. One might argue that a major simplification of the vocational system of qualifications is needed if employers are ever to recognize the value of vocational qualifications and pay accordingly. In fact, the proliferation of qualifications appears to be continuing, and increases in formal certification have been especially marked in the areas of adult training, retraining and lifelong learning. It should also be noted that in many countries, and especially in the UK, education policy is tied increasingly closely to the acquisition of formal qualifications: a policy that imposes major assessment and certification costs.

The evidence reviewed in this chapter casts doubts on whether this emphasis on formal qualifications will have the expected results. If employers rely only on a limited number of familiar signals, then increasing the number of qualifications available will not help employers in their selection process. At least some of the money spent on certification and assessment might more usefully be redirected into less tightly regulated learning. Moreover, the regulatory frameworks within which employers now operate provide a clear example of how different parts of government policy may conflict. Many employers are reluctant to use qualifications as formal criteria for selection because of equal-opportunity concerns. While this is understandable, given recent legislation and tribunal decisions, it may also have perverse effects, since formal qualifications are a route by which some disadvantaged groups (notably immigrants) have traditionally gained access to the labour market.[14] Finally, the evidence presented here underlines the complexity and heterogeneity of the modern labour market. There is great variation across occupations and sectors

---

[14]The evidence on the GED from the US provides an example of this.

in the relative importance of those skills that are easily and reliably certificated by educational institutions. This too needs to be recognized: both by employers, in the demands they make of the education system, and by policy makers considering how to promote a fit between education and labour-market demands and how to help disadvantaged groups to improve their labour-market prospects.

Evidence on the Balance of Supply and Demand for Qualified Workers

By Steven McIntosh

9.1 Introduction

Education can yield many benefits. From the point of view of the individual it can be seen as an investment good or as a consumption good. The former view sees education as a costly activity that yields a future return. The analogy with investment in physical capital or financial products is then clear. The cost of this investment in education might involve the direct costs of studying, such as tuition fees and books, as well as the opportunity cost of the time spent in education, which is usually measured in terms of the wages foregone by choosing to study rather than work. The future benefits, or returns, will involve the possibility of access to higher-paying jobs. As a consumption good, however, the education itself is the end, rather than the means to the end, and the time spent studying itself yields benefits. Such benefits might include personal fulfilment and enrichment, as well as, thinking particularly of higher education for young people, enjoying new experiences such as living away from home, meeting new people and doing new things.

Thus, even if education played no other role, it would still be a desirable commodity to individuals. From the point of view of the labour market, however, education plays a role in supplying workers of different skill levels to this market. This role of education is the focus of this chapter, which examines how successful the education system is in supplying the skills that are desired by the labour market. The pertinent question is: do the skills produced by the education system match the skills demanded by the labour market?

9.2 Returns to Education

An obvious place to begin answering the question is to look at the returns to qualifications. These are the extra wages that individuals can expect to receive, on average, when they obtain a particular qualification, namely the future gains part of individuals' investment decisions described above.[1] In a competitive labour market, the size of these returns is likely to reflect the relative magnitude of the demand for and the supply of skills associated with that qualification. If there was an increase in demand for particular skills associated with a qualification, then, for a given supply, we would expect the return to that qualification to rise, and vice versa. Similarly, if there was an increase in the number of people holding a particular qualification, then, for a given demand, we would expect the relative return to that qualification to fall, and vice versa.

Table 9.1 looks at supply, showing the percentage of the UK adult population holding each particular qualification, using Labour Force Survey (LFS) data between 1993 and 2002. There is a discontinuity in that before 1996 respondents to the LFS were asked only to report their three highest qualifications, whereas since 1996 respondents have recorded *all* the qualifications that they hold.[2] Therefore, in the 1993 column, there is likely to be some underreporting of lower-level qualifications, which do not figure in respondents' top three achievements. The pattern in Table 9.1 is clear and illustrates an increasingly educated population, with growing proportions holding most qualifications, particularly academic qualifications. For example, the percentage of UK working-age adults holding a first postsecondary degree was 8.8% in 1993, but by 2002 this had risen to 12.5%. There has been a similarly large proportional increase in the percentage of adults holding GCE A level qualifications, from 17.3% in 1993 to 24.1% in 2002. On the vocational side, the largest increase has been in the relatively new National Vocational Qualifications (NVQs), although even here the numbers remain modest.

As for the other side of the market, there is a reasonable consensus that the demand for more educated and skilled labour is rising. The explanation most often given for this is technological change that is biased in favour of skilled labour. Evidence for the rising demand for skills can be found in the Skills Surveys undertaken in the UK in 1997 and 2001. These surveys show that between these dates, an increasing proportion of jobs required some qualifications, while an increase in required training times and an increase in the time taken to master jobs was also observed (Felstead *et al.* 2002).

---

[1] Thus the term "returns" refers just to the benefit side of the discussion in the opening paragraph of this chapter, and is estimated by wage differences between groups with and without a particular qualification. A full "rate of return" analysis would also take account of the costs of acquiring the qualification, analogous to the rate of return to any investment decision. Obtaining accurate information on *all* of the costs of acquiring a qualification, discussed in the opening paragraph, is, however, difficult, and this chapter follows the vast majority of the economics of education literature in simply discussing the returns to education (that is, the wage differences between those with and without a qualification) rather than the "rate of return" to education.

[2] Thus the categories are not mutually exclusive, and individuals appear in each category in which they hold qualifications.

Table 9.1. The percentage of working-age adults holding each qualification.

Qualification	1993[a]	1996[b]	1999	2002
Academic				
Higher postsecondary degree	2.0	1.8	2.4	2.7
First postsecondary degree	8.8	9.2	11.2	12.5
Other HE qualification	0.7	0.9	1.0	1.0
HE diploma	1.0	2.1	1.6	1.7
GCE A levels	17.3	20.7	22.6	24.1
2+ A levels	13.9	17.5	18.8	20.1
1 A level	3.4	3.2	3.0	3.7
A/S levels	0.3	0.3	0.4	1.3
GCSEs A*–C	41.5	52.2	54.8	57.2
5+ GCSEs A*–C	29.2	33.5	37.1	40.0
1–4 GCSEs A*–C	12.3	18.3	17.4	17.1
GCSEs D–F	7.0	4.7	4.8	4.4
Vocational				
Professional qualification	4.2	2.0	1.8	1.8
Teaching qualification	2.6	2.9	2.9	2.8
Nursing qualification	2.4	2.6	2.6	2.5
RSA higher	0.6	0.4	0.3	0.3
RSA lower	6.3	7.2	7.4	6.7
C&G Advanced Craft	2.4	2.9	3.9	4.3
C&G Craft	5.1	5.1	5.2	4.9
C&G other	4.6	9.2	7.2	7.0
HND/HNC	4.0	4.5	4.7	4.9
ONC/OND	4.0	4.0	4.2	4.2
BTEC diploma	1.0	1.1	0.9	0.8
NVQ3–NVQ5	0.3	1.4	2.7	4.1
NVQ2	0.5	2.2	3.4	4.5
NVQ1	0.2	0.7	1.2	1.5
Other	22.3	31.9	38.5	37.6
Apprenticeship (with no qualification associated)	2.0	1.2	1.0	1.0

Notes. Source: Labour Force Survey. [a]In 1993, the 5+ GCSEs A*–C and less than 5 GCSEs A*–C actually refer to 4+ and less than 4 GCSEs A*–C, respectively. [b]In 1996, the LFS changes from asking about the highest three qualifications held, to asking about all qualifications held.

Table 9.2 shows the average estimated wage returns, as defined above, to selected key qualifications, over the period 1993–2002, again using LFS data.[3] The figures in the table show the average percentage difference in the wages of individuals who hold each particular qualification and individuals who do not, after standardizing

---

[3]These returns are discussed in much more detail in McIntosh (2002).

for all other qualifications held and other characteristics (age, ethnicity, region, workplace size and sector of work).[4] Since the analysis considers all qualifications held, the returns should be viewed as cumulative. For example, from the upper half of the table, if a man holds five or more good GCSEs, two or more A levels and a first postsecondary degree, then he will earn on average 73% more than a man with none of these qualifications, holding constant other factors.

For our purposes, the most interesting aspect of Table 9.2 is how the returns have changed over time, in the light of the rising supply of and demand for the various qualifications described above. The fact is that the returns have changed surprisingly little over the previous 10 years. Consider the returns to a first postsecondary degree for men. Such a qualification raised wages by 30% in 1993 and by 29% a decade later in 2002. Similarly, for women the return was 26% in both 1996 and 2002.[5] Returns to the other academic qualifications are similarly very stable over the period considered. Although the returns to the various vocational qualifications display a slightly more erratic pattern over time, this may be due to random sampling variation, since cell sizes are smaller with fewer individuals holding particular vocational qualifications. We can say, at a minimum, that there is no evidence for systematic trends in the returns to vocational qualifications, either upwards or downwards, over the last 10 years.

The conclusion of this brief summary of the returns to qualifications is, therefore, that the demand for and the supply of skills in the UK labour market seem to have been moving harmoniously with each other over the last decade, resulting in fairly stable relative wages. Both sides of the market for qualifications and skills are increasing, but apparently at a similar rate, so the result has been that there have been no big shocks to relative wages over the last decade. So far, therefore, it seems that the education system is supplying the skills required by the labour market. The remainder of this chapter will now examine to what extent this is true. We shall see that particular areas of research suggest that, below the surface of these stable returns to education, mismatches between the demand for and supply of skills in the UK do occur.

9.3 OVEREDUCATION AND UNDEREDUCATION

The first literature concerned with skills mismatch that we will examine is the so-called overeducation and undereducation literature. Individuals are said to be

---

[4]The estimates are derived from OLS regressions of the log of hourly earnings against all qualifications and the control variables listed.

[5]The female return to a postsecondary degree is higher in 1993, although this may be due to the discontinuity in the data described above, with the return to a postsecondary degree being conflated with the returns to lower-level qualifications not mentioned amongst the top three qualifications of respondents.

Table 9.2. The returns to selected qualifications – all full-time employees.

Qualification	1993[a]	1996[b]	1999	2002
Men				
Academic				
First postsecondary degree	30	25	26	29
2+ A levels	18	17	16	15
5+ GCSEs A*–C	26	31	30	28
Vocational				
Professional Qualification	42	37	44	51
C&G Advanced Craft	10	4	5	4
C&G Craft	8	0	8	8
HND/HNC	21	14	15	14
ONC/OND	13	11	9	7
BTEC diploma	7	8	3	5
NVQ3–NVQ5	0	3	3	2
Women				
Academic				
First postsecondary degree	37	26	25	26
2+ A levels	16	14	15	15
5+ GCSEs A*–C	29	26	28	24
Vocational				
Professional qualification	46	43	46	47
RSA higher	12	1	9	5
RSA lower	6	3	1	1
HND/HNC	14	7	8	7
ONC/OND	11	12	5	5
BTEC diploma	5	6	6	7
NVQ3–NVQ5	2	1	3	2

Notes. The table shows the average percentage increase in wages when each qualification is obtained. Source: Labour Force Survey. For meaning of notes [a] and [b], see Table 9.1. Control variables are included for age and age^2, ethnicity, region, workplace size and (except in 1993) public sector.

overeducated if the qualifications that they hold are at a higher level than those needed to actually do their jobs, with the reverse being the case for the undereducated. Qualifications needed to do a job are measured in a number of different ways. Some are based on the objective views of work–study experts, who determine the skill needs of an individual's occupation (e.g. in the US Dictionary of Occupational Titles an assessment is made of the educational requirements of each job). An alternative, more subjective, approach is to use self-reports of the qualifications needed to do a job, on the basis of surveying individual job holders. A third method is to determine

Table 9.3. The incidence of overeducation and undereducation in the UK across time.

Survey	Year	Incidence of overeducation	Incidence of undereducation	Source
SCELI	1986	30%	21%	Green *et al.* (2002)
Employment in the UK	1992	31%	17%	Green *et al.* (2002)
Skills Survey	1997	33%	20%	Green *et al.* (2002)
Skills Survey	2001	37%	18%	Green and McIntosh (2002)

the required education needed to do a job by calculating the average actual education levels in the individual's occupation. Each measure has its strengths and weaknesses (see Groot and Maassen van den Brink (2000) for a more detailed discussion of measurement issues). There is a relatively high level of consistency in response between the objective method (asking work–study experts) and the subjective/self-report method. The majority of the literature uses self-report measures.

The available research suggests that overeducation (and also undereducation, though to a lesser extent) is a significant phenomenon. From the results of their meta-analysis, Groot and Maassen van den Brink (2000) report that the average incidence of overeducation across all studies considered is 23%, with 14% being the equivalent figure for undereducation. On average, therefore, about one in four workers are apparently overqualified for their jobs. There is variation around this average. For example, women are usually found to be more likely to be overeducated than men. Similarly, younger workers, individuals with children and those in part-time jobs are all usually found to have a greater risk of overeducation than the prime-aged, the childless and full-time workers, respectively. Overeducation therefore seems to be more prevalent in less secure forms of employment.

Focusing on the UK, an estimate of the extent of overeducation, using the most recent data (the 2001 Skills Survey), suggests that 37% of the UK workforce is overeducated, while 18% are undereducated (see Green and McIntosh 2002). It is clearly of some importance to know whether these proportions are changing over time, during a period that has seen a rapid expansion of actual education and qualification attainment. Such temporal comparisons are, however, difficult to make, given the different definitions of overeducation used in the literature, and the different groups considered in different studies. Table 9.3 does, however, show the results from various surveys from which broadly comparable measures of overeducation can be derived, culminating in the 2001 Skills Survey estimate described above. The tentative conclusion from this evidence is that the incidence of overeducation in the UK is increasing.

Table 9.4. The incidence of overeducation and undereducation across countries.

Country	Incidence of overeducation	Incidence of undereducation
Netherlands (1995)	24%	12%
Spain (1990)	28%	11%
Portugal (1992)	33%	38%
USA (1976)	33%	20%

Notes. Source: Hartog (2000).

Overeducation is by no means unique to the UK. Table 9.4 shows the most recent estimates of the extent of overeducation available in the literature, for a range of countries. These results are broadly similar to those of the UK, with somewhere between a quarter and a third of workers being overeducated, and a somewhat smaller proportion being undereducated.[6]

What impact does being overeducated or undereducated have on outcomes for the individuals affected? All studies consistently find that an overeducated individual earns more than someone with the appropriate level of education doing the same job as them, but less than a similarly educated person working in an appropriate job. In other words, if we imagine the wages of a graduate working in a graduate job, and an individual with A levels working in a job that requires A levels, then the wages of a graduate working in a job that only requires A levels will be somewhere between these two. In their meta-analysis of 25 studies of overeducation, Groot and Maassen van den Brink (2000) conclude that the return, as defined in the previous section, to required education is 7.8%, while the return to overeducation is 3.0% (i.e. the years of overeducation add less to wages since they are not being fully utilized). As for the undereducated, they earn less than an appropriately educated individual doing the same job as them, but more than someone at the same level of education as them who is performing an appropriate job for that education level. Again we can imagine the wages of an individual with GCSEs doing a job that requires GCSEs, and the wages of someone with no qualifications doing a job that does not require any. The wages of an undereducated individual with no qualifications working in a job that requires GCSEs will be between these two. Groot and Maassen van den Brink (2000) estimate that, on average, the return to undereducation is −1.5%.

Some researchers argue that overeducation could simply be a temporary phenomenon: for example, it may occur when individuals temporarily accept low-level

---

[6]The exception to this latter result is Portugal, where the incidence of undereductaion apparently exceeds that of overeducation. This seems likely to be an outcome of the different skills profile in Portugal, with a much higher proportion of workers having no qualifications than in the other countries.

jobs for which they are overqualified while they continue to search for more appropriate jobs, or when individuals temporarily work at a lower level while gaining experience and learning about the workplace, after which they will be promoted to a level commensurate with their skills. The fact, observed above, that young workers are more likely to be overeducated is consistent with such a possibility. In a sense, formal overeducation is compensating for a lack of experience in overall human capital. While such scenarios almost certainly exist, the limited evidence on the permanence or otherwise of overeducation does not seem to support the view that all overeducation is temporary. For example, Dolton and Vignoles (1997) show that, of those graduates who were overeducated in their first job following graduation, two-thirds are still overeducated six years later. Similarly, Battu et al. (1999) have longitudinal information on graduates at career points 1 year, 6 years and 11 years after graduation. Their results show that some 30% of the cohort is overeducated at *all* of the survey points. Finally, Sloane et al. (1999) find evidence against the theory that the overeducated are simply working in the first job that came along while continuing to search for a more appropriate job. The results of their study, using work history data, show that moving jobs did not typically result in an improved job match for overeducated workers. Overeducation therefore seems to be a permanent state for some workers, which has real consequences.

9.4 SKILLS SHORTAGES

One possible implication of the previous section, and the one that is often drawn from the overeducation literature, is that if some workers have to do jobs at a lower level than they themselves are educated, then there cannot be enough skilled jobs to go round. In other words, the implication seems to be that there is an imbalance in the labour market with the supply of skills exceeding the demand. However, if this was the case, then we would expect to see the returns to high-level qualifications falling relative to lower-level qualifications or no qualifications at all. As Table 9.2 and the discussion above made clear, however, there has been no evidence at all of such a fall in returns during the last 10 years (and indeed longer than this if Table 9.2 had considered earlier periods). It therefore seems very unlikely that there are simply too many educated and skilled workers in the UK. An alternative explanation for why some individuals are overeducated could be that, although they have the certificate to show their attainment, the skills they actually possess are not those currently demanded in the labour market, perhaps due to lower natural ability or simply following courses with little relevance to real jobs, and so they can only work in jobs apparently below their actual qualification level. In this scenario, then, rather than there being an excess supply of skills, the education system is actually failing to supply the skills demanded by firms in the labour market.[7]

In fact, this is often a claim made by firms. Although anecdotal evidence exists, more scientific evidence can be found in the answers given by employers to the Employers Skill Survey (ESS) (for details, see Hillage *et al.* 2002). The ESS has been conducted three times: in 1999, 2000 and 2002. It is representative of English firms with at least five employees. The results for 2002 reveal that 30% of firms reported that they had at least one vacancy in at least one occupation at the time of the survey. Just over half of these vacancies were proving hard to fill, with a skills shortage being cited as the reason for the difficulty in half of these cases. Thus 16% of all firms reported having a hard-to-fill vacancy, and 8% of all firms reported an external skills shortage, defined as a vacancy that is hard to fill because of a lack of available skills in the labour market. In addition, 23% of English workplaces reported having an internal skills shortage in 2002, defined as a significant proportion of their workforces being less than fully proficient.[8]

Which skills do firms report finding it difficult to obtain? Firstly, the survey evidence shows that vacancies particularly for associate-professional and skilled-trade occupations are proving hardest to fill for skills-shortage reasons. The skills most often reported as being unavailable to fill these vacancies are occupation-specific technical and practical skills, reported in 36% of skills-shortage vacancies. Following this, however, a number of more generic skills, such as communication (29%), customer handling (29%) and team working (25%) are reported. For internal skills shortages, the occupational group most likely to be reported as less than fully proficient are sales workers (24% of all internal skill gaps), followed by operatives, particularly in manufacturing (16% of all internal skill gaps), and administrative staff (15% of all internal skill gaps). Specific technical/practical skills, particularly for operatives, are again an important source of such skills shortages (mentioned in 43% of cases), although certain generic skills are also frequently mentioned, such as communication (61%), customer handling (51%), team working (48%) and problem solving (44%), particularly for the sales workers who are said to be less than proficient.

In summary, it seems to be in middle-level jobs, such as skilled manual occupations, and associate-professional jobs, such as technicians and engineers, that there is a shortage of specific technical and practical skills, as well as a lack of the more generic skills across the range of occupations. In terms of the former, technical,

---

[7] It might have been expected that such low natural ability or inappropriate skills amongst some of the highly educated would show up in falling relative wages to such people. Table 9.2 showed that this was not the case, however, with returns to most qualifications remaining stable.

[8] The workplaces suffering an external skills shortage were typically not the same workplaces that were suffering an internal skills shortage.

Table 9.5. Percentages at qualification levels 2+ and 3+ in
the UK, France and Germany, by type of qualification.

	Level 2+			Level 3+		
	UK	France	Germany	UK	France	Germany
16–64 year olds, general	27%	31%	25%	20%	25%	22%
16–64 year olds, vocational	27%	41%	58%	17%	12%	52%
25–28 year olds, general	33%	40%	33%	24%	36%	30%
25–28 year olds, vocational	28%	43%	52%	17%	18%	48%

Notes. Source: Steedman (1999). The data refer to 1998, except for Germany, which is for 1997. The German results refer to the old West Germany only.

skills, this ties in with what we know about qualification attainment in the UK. To show this, Table 9.5 takes information on qualification attainment similar to that in Table 9.1 and ranks it according to type (academic or vocational) and level. The resulting figures are then compared with equivalent figures for France and Germany, derived from a similar allocation of qualifications in those countries.[9] A similar analysis was conducted in Chapter 2 comparing the total proportions at each level in each country. Here, the focus is on the split between academic and vocational qualifications.

The results show that the UK is similar to Germany in terms of members of the working-age population holding academic qualifications at level 3 or above (20% versus 22%).[10] However, when we consider vocational qualifications, the picture changes dramatically. The proportion of the working-age population acquiring vocational qualifications at level 3 or above is over three times higher in Germany than in the UK (52% in Germany compared with just 17% in the UK). Clearly, therefore where the UK falls behind Germany in terms of the supply of qualifications is in the number of intermediate vocational qualifications.

Although the UK is similar to France at level 3, if we move down another level and consider the proportions reaching level 2[11] or above, then we see that the UK also trails France in terms of vocational qualifications at this level, as well as continuing to lag behind Germany. Thus, the UK can hold its own on the academic side, but it is in terms of vocational qualifications that it trails its European neighbours.

Perhaps it could be argued that the recent growth of qualification attainment amongst young labour-market entrants in the UK has not yet had a chance to influ-

---

[9]This allocation of qualifications in different countries to given levels was undertaken by Steedman (1999).

[10]Level 3 qualifications are A levels on the academic side and, for example, advanced GNVQ, NVQ3, City and Guilds Advanced Craft or ONC/OND qualifications on the vocational side.

[11]Level 2 qualifications include, among others, five or more GCSEs on the academic side and intermediate GNVQ, NVQ2 and City and Guilds Craft qualifications on the vocational side.

ence the figures for the whole working-age population. The bottom half of Table 9.5 therefore repeats the above analysis for 25–28 year olds, a group old enough for the process of qualification attainment to be complete for most, but young enough to be affected by the expansion of education participation in the UK. The results for this group, however, are no more encouraging than for the population as a whole. Although the proportions holding academic qualifications are higher for the younger cohort than for the whole population, there is no improvement in the vocational qualification acquisition rates when attention is focused on the young. Even amongst 25–28 year olds, the UK continues to trail Germany dramatically at level 3+ and both France and Germany at level 2+ in terms of the acquisition of vocational qualifications.

At the higher qualification levels, the ESS results suggest that there is a lack of science, mathematics and engineering degrees being obtained, leading to the technical skills shortages in associate professional jobs. Table 9.6 reports data from the Higher Education Statistics Agency (HESA), showing the number of first postsecondary degrees awarded in the UK by subject area, for 1995, 1998 and 2002. Amongst traditional academic subjects, the table shows a decline in the numbers graduating in humanities and physical sciences over this period, with little change in the small number of mathematics degrees being awarded. Amongst "traditional" vocational subjects, likely to be in demand by employers, there have been large falls, with the number of architecture and building degrees awarded falling by 11% in the period 1995–1998, and a further 15% in the following four years. As for engineering and technology degrees, despite a small rise between 1995 and 1998, the number awarded fell by 12% between 1998 and 2002. The table makes clear that expansion in HE is being delivered through "new" vocational subjects, such as business studies, computer science[12] and creative arts and design, which have all seen huge, continuous increases in the number of postsecondary degrees awarded over this period. The number of business-studies and creative-arts/design degrees awarded dominates the number awarded in the academic and traditional vocational sub-groups.

We can now return to the proposal made at the beginning of this section, which was that perhaps the overeducated are not supplying the skills that are in demand. The evidence so far suggests that employers continue to demand qualifications in subjects such as mathematics, science and engineering; however, there are increasing numbers of individuals graduating in the "new" vocational subjects, for which insufficient graduate level jobs exist. This is therefore a possible explanation for the simultaneous presence of employers reporting skills shortages and an apparent

---

[12]It should be acknowledged that the growth in the number of computing-science graduates may compensate for the stagnation in the numbers of mathematics and physical science graduates, as far as the needs of some employers are concerned.

Table 9.6. Subject area of first postsecondary degrees awarded in the UK.

	1995	1998	2002	% change 1995–1998	% change 1998–2002
Academic subjects					
Humanities	9 773	10 001	9 420	2	−6
Mathematics	4 033	3 904	4 075	−3	4
Physical science	12 833	12 876	11 975	0	−7
"Traditional" vocational subjects					
Architecture/building	6 717	6 008	5 115	−11	−15
Engineering/technology	20 511	21 010	18 425	2	−12
"New" vocational subjects					
Business studies	24 207	26 963	30 340	11	13
Computer science	7 789	9 334	13 055	20	40
Creative arts/design	14 337	18 987	22 740	32	20

Notes. Source: Higher Education Statistics Agency.

surplus of individuals holding high-level qualifications. Further evidence in favour of this proposal would be if the non-science, mathematics and engineering students were more likely to be overeducated.

In fact, this is exactly what is observed. Green and McIntosh (2002) find that, after controlling for background factors, graduates with computing or physical-science degrees are the least likely to be overeducated. In addition, there seems to be a role to be played by qualifications in mathematics, with those individuals whose highest mathematics qualification is either an A level or a postsecondary degree being significantly less likely to work in a job for which they are overeducated, compared with those with lower-level mathematics qualifications or none at all. Similarly, Dolton and Vignoles (2000a) observe that graduates with engineering, technical or science degrees are less likely to be overeducated than graduates in social sciences, arts and languages, with over half of arts graduates being overeducated in their first job following graduation.

9.5 Does Supply Determine Demand?

Summarizing the previous section, the evidence suggests that skill mismatch does exist in the UK labour market, and, in particular, in the supply of middle-level vocational qualifications and higher-level mathematics and science qualifications not matching the demand for these skills from firms. However, this is not quite the end of the story. If skill demand exceeds supply in these areas, then competition for scarce resources should be bidding up relative prices, which in this case are represented by wages. Thus, we should observe rising relative wages to mathematics and science degrees and in middle-level manual occupations where vocational qualifications are most in demand. Tables 9.7 and 9.8 investigate whether this is indeed the case.

Table 9.7 returns to the LFS data used earlier in Tables 9.1 and 9.2, and estimates returns to postsecondary degrees in various subject areas.[13] Due to small cell sizes for some of the degree subjects, data on men and women are pooled together. In order to clarify the results, it was decided to simply include only those with two or more A levels and/or a postsecondary degree in the analysis, rather than include all individuals and all qualifications as in Table 9.2. The A level group forms the reference category. Thus the interpretation of each coefficient is slightly different to earlier, this time indicating the estimated average *mark-up* in wages from acquiring a postsecondary degree in a particular field compared with remaining on two or more A levels. As before, the analysis holds constant across this comparison age, ethnicity, region, workplace size and sector of work.

In 1993, the postsecondary degree subjects with the highest returns (32–33%) were business/finance (including accounting) and law. These are obviously voca-tionally orientated postsecondary degrees leading to well-paid professions, so these results are not a surprise. The next batch of subjects in terms of returns are the ones that we are interested in, namely physical science, mathematics, computing and engineering, which in 1993 all had returns in the range 22–28%.[14] What we want to know is whether the returns to these latter degrees increased over the next decade, because of an excess demand for them. The results are mixed. For engineering, there does seem to be evidence of an increase in returns. In fact, engineering is the only subject group in Table 9.7 for which the returns rise continuously over the period, from 25% in 1993 to 33% in 2002. The latter figure represents the highest return to any of the subjects in 2002. The returns to computing degrees also seemed to rise over time, from 28% in 1993 up to 35% in 1999, although they have fallen back to 30% by 2002. This pattern may reflect a build-up of demand for highly skilled computer-literate workers leading up to the end of the last millennium and the antic-ipated "millennium bug", and a fall in demand after the year 2000. The returns to physical science and mathematics degrees have not changed significantly over the previous 10 years: the returns to the former falling from 22% to 19% between 1993 and 2002, and the returns to the latter rising from 25% to 27% over the same period. A final point worth noting in Table 9.7 is the apparent removal of any returns to arts and humanities degrees. These were a small but statistically significant 8% in 1993, since when they have been essentially zero. This is consistent with the finding of

---

[13] Returns to postsecondary degrees by subject group were considered in Chapter 5, when considering the possibility of variable fees for degree courses. There, the results were presented for a single, grouped, cross-section of data. Here, the focus is on changes over time.

[14] The returns to medical degrees also fell within this range.

Table 9.7. The returns to postsecondary degree subjects relative to holding 2+ A levels.

	1993	1996	1999	2002
Medicine	24	22	27	29
Biological science	9	9	7	11
Agricultural science	15	12	7	2
Physical science	18	12	14	16
Mathematics	23	25	26	25
Computing	24	21	29	24
Engineering	19	20	23	26
Architecture	16	8	10	10
Social science	10	15	11	13
Law	32	24	39	31
Business	31	22	22	25
Librarian	0	0	0	0
Languages	18	13	8	8
Arts and Humanities	9	0	0	0
Education	24	20	18	17

Notes. Source: Labour Force Survey. Control variables are included for gender, age and age^2, ethnicity, region, workplace size and (except in 1993) public sector.

Dolton and Vignoles (2000*a*) described above, i.e. that arts graduates in particular are finding it difficult to obtain graduate-level jobs.

Table 9.8 considers wages in occupations that we would expect to employ workers with middle- to high-level vocational qualifications. Since we are merely considering wages by occupation here rather than by qualifications as above, we can use data from the New Earnings Survey (NES), which has no education information but has earnings information that can be traced further back than with the LFS. We want to know whether wages in the chosen occupations are rising faster than some average. If we just used the simple mean, however, then this could be affected by fast wage growth at the very top of the wage distribution, so that earnings in our chosen occupations could be falling relative to the mean, and yet still rising faster than in most occupations. We therefore derived an indicator that made full use of the whole distribution of earnings, rather than simply comparing with the mean. This involved, for each individual in one of our occupations, seeing at which percentile of the full wage distribution his wages were located.[15] These figures were then averaged across all individuals in the occupation to give us an average percentile position in the wage distribution for that occupation. When this is done in successive time periods, we can then easily see whether an occupation is moving up or down the wage distribution. The analysis was performed for men only, since they dominate the occupations that

[15]Wages are weekly wages for full-time workers whose pay was unaffected by absence in the survey week.

Table 9.8. Average percentile position in the wage distribution for
selected occupations, men aged 30–39.

	1976–80	1981–85	1986–90	1991–95	1996–2000
Engineering technician	62	67	64	61	63
Electrician	54	53	53	50	53
Plumber	49	45	42	50	50
Laboratory technician	48	50	45	49	48
Sheet-metal worker	47	38	43	41	45
Metal maintenance/fitter	46	41	46	51	53
Carpenter	42	36	33	31	37
Bricklayer	41	34	32	28	35
Mechanic	41	35	36	37	37

Notes. Source: New Earnings Survey.

we are considering, and in particular for men in their thirties only. This was to control
for any changes in the age composition of the occupations' workforces over time.
Since the cell sizes were becoming small, we merged successive years of data, and
considered five-year windows rather than single years.

The occupations in Table 9.8 are ranked according to their average position in the
wage distribution in 1976–1980, with engineering technicians at the top at the 62nd
percentile, and mechanics at the bottom at the 41st percentile. As we move across
the columns, there is very little change in this ranking or the percentile positions. In
fact, most of the percentile positions remain remarkably constant, given that we are
considering a long time-frame of 25 years. The exception is the movement up the
pay distribution of "metal-working maintenance and fitting", which moves from an
average percentile position of 46th in 1976–1980 up to 53rd in 1996–2000, and this
despite an initial fall to 41st in 1981–1985. Carpenters and bricklayers also move
position, this time down the wage distribution, although they make a partial recovery
in the final period.

What are we to make of this evidence suggesting little change in the relative wages
of mid-ranking, skilled-manual or associate-professional non-manual occupations,
as well as the limited changes in the returns to science and mathematics degrees?
If there are skills shortages in these areas, then conventional wisdom would suggest that their relative wages will rise, to attract workers. If this has not happened
(i.e. the supply of qualifications and skills has not changed to meet demand), then
an alternative method of equating demand and supply of skills in the labour market
would be for demand to change until it equalled supply. The evidence on the supply
of qualifications above suggested that the UK did well at achieving qualifications
at the top level, but failed to get significant numbers completing qualifications at
levels 2 and 3, therefore leaving a longer tail of low achievers than in other Euro-

pean countries. If skill demand was to change to reflect this skill supply, then we would expect employment growth amongst the best, highest-skill jobs and amongst the worst, lowest-skill jobs, with employment contracting in the "middling" jobs. Recent research by Goos and Manning (2003) shows exactly this happening over the last 20–25 years in the UK, with employment growth occurring in high-skill managerial and professional jobs, but also in low-skill service-sector jobs. Thus, perhaps if wage relativities are sticky across jobs, equilibrium is reached via skill demand reacting to available supply, and the types of job on offer match the types of worker to be found in the economy.[16] In this way, it is possible for an economy to get stuck in a low-skill, low-productivity trap, as has been suggested in the theoretical literature (see, for example, Snower 1996; Acemoglu 1997, 1998). In other words, we have just argued that perhaps low-skill jobs are being offered in preference to middle-skill jobs because of the amount of available labour in the former category. It is not worth firms creating middle-skill jobs because of the excessive search costs that would be incurred finding a suitable worker. Given this situation, however, it is not worth the low skilled improving their skills, given the lack of suitable work at the higher level. Therefore, the low skilled remain low skilled, and so it is not worth firms opening middle-skill jobs, and so on, in a vicious circle.

9.6 THE IMPACT OF SKILLS SHORTAGES

Finally we ask: if skill mismatches exist, does it matter? It would be interesting to know what impact skills shortages have at the national level – on the growth rate of the economy, for example – but no work has been done in this area. Of course, there is much research linking education itself to economic growth. In the theoretical literature, the endogenous growth models that have recently been developed predict there to be an important role for the level of human capital in an economy for generating growth. An absence of skilled labour in sufficient numbers can reduce the incentive to engage in research and development or invest in physical capital, and vice versa. Thus, education and investment are complements in driving economic growth, and the absence of an appropriately skilled workforce can lead a country into a low-skill trap equilibrium, similar to that discussed above. Empirical evidence using macro-level cross-country data, summarized for example in Temple (2001), suggests that education, both in levels and in changes, can have important effects on economic growth, although the size of the effect is difficult to pin down and

---

[16] It should be noted that this is not the explanation offered by Goos and Manning for the polarization of employment. Rather than argue that it is supply driven by available skills, they argue that it is demand driven, and adapt the skill-biased technological-change arguments to say that such technological change replaces middling jobs (such as routine manual production and clerical jobs), while high-skill jobs requiring decision-making and low-skill service-sector jobs requiring human input are not replaceable by computers and continue to grow.

the estimates are not robust to changes in, for example, the definition of education adopted or the sample of countries included. To the extent that an expansion of education reduces skills shortages, these results are suggestive of the impact of such shortages on economic growth, although, of course, as the above discussion of overeducation suggested, the growth in education must be associated with the supply of appropriate skills. A more direct estimate of the impact of skills shortages on economic growth would certainly be of interest.

One direct study that has been undertaken, by Nickell and Nicolitsas (2000), examines the link between skills shortages and investment, suggested in the endogenous growth literature. Their results, using a panel of UK companies, show that the presence of skills shortages seems to reduce the incentive to invest in physical capital, with obvious implications for economic growth. The estimates suggest that a permanent 10 percentage point increase in the number of firms reporting skilled-labour shortages in a firm's industry will lead to a permanent 10% reduction in its fixed capital investment and a temporary 4% reduction in its research-and-development expenditure. Skills shortages therefore seem to have real implications for economic growth.

9.7 Summary and Conclusions

This chapter has examined the extent to which the supply of skills in the UK matches the demand. The evidence on returns to qualifications, which shows stable returns over the last decade, would seem to suggest that the supply and demand of skills, which are both increasing, are increasing at similar rates, leaving relative wages largely unaffected. However, further research suggests that things are not quite as ideal as this statement suggests.

On one side, data show that significant numbers of individuals report being overqualified for the job that they do. On the other side, significant numbers of employers report not being able to find the skills that they require, either amongst their existing staff or amongst potential recruits. One way to reconcile these findings is to recognize that the qualifications reported by individuals are not a perfect measure of the skills actually provided. Thus, although certain individuals may have the formal certificate for a qualification, the skills that they have – either their natural ability or the skills they learnt during their course – may not be what employers are looking for. Such individuals therefore end up working at a job level lower than their actual qualification, and so appear to be overeducated. Evidence in favour of this interpretation can be found in the observation made above that the returns to qualifications are not falling, which we would expect if overeducation was being caused by a simple excess supply of qualifications.

In addition, data from the Employers Skill Survey, as well as information on qualification-attainment rates, suggest that it is high-level science, mathematics and engineering skills/qualifications and intermediate-level vocational skills/qualifications that are in shortest supply (as well as a range of generic skills such as communication, customer handling, team working and problem solving). Given that individuals with such qualifications are the least likely to be overeducated, a state which is concentrated more on arts/humanities graduates and those with non-vocational intermediate qualifications, this is also consistent with our proposed theory for why some workers are overeducated, since they lack the skills and qualifications most demanded. It seems, however, that the relative wages on offer for mathematics and science degrees and in occupations requiring intermediate and advanced vocational qualifications are not rising and therefore are not likely to induce supply increases in these areas so as to eradicate the shortage. Instead, there is some evidence that the demand for skills is simply mirroring the supply, with the biggest growth in employment being in occupations from the very bottom, as well as from the very top, of the skills distribution.

Does this all matter? The final section of the chapter suggested that skills shortages can hinder economic growth. In addition, it has been suggested that if the desired skills are not supplied, then firms will continue opening jobs in low-wage areas of the service sector, where a good supply of labour is available, both from those with no or low qualifications, and from those with higher qualifications but unwanted skills (i.e. the apparently overeducated that we have discussed above). If such a low-skill trap exists with demand following supply, and further research is needed in addition to the anecdotal evidence above to prove that it does, it is necessary for the supply of desired skills to be stimulated in some way.

Regarding subject choice at postsecondary degree level, the choice of the new vocational subjects over traditional subjects seems to be demand led by students rather than supply led by institutions, which means that the solution is not as simple as supplying more courses and places, but requires a change of attitudes. Greater variation in the returns to different postsecondary degree subjects, such as the rise in the returns to engineering degrees noted above, may lead to such a shift in attitudes. More scope for change is presented at the intermediate level, where we have seen that the UK is lacking in vocational qualifications. While this is also partly a result of student choice, with the academic route apparently remaining more popular than the vocational one amongst a majority of students, this is turn may partly be a result of vocational qualifications being viewed as low quality or lacking significant economic benefits. Improvements in the provision, quality, certification and consistency of vocational qualifications may therefore have positive effects on the numbers acquiring such qualifications, with a resulting impact on employer skills shortages in trade occupations. Hopefully this would then stimulate firms to open more intermediate-level jobs than is currently the case.

Finally, there are the generic skills, which are also reported by employers to be in short supply. It is debatable how easy or desirable it is for such skills to be taught within general education, and it may be that firms have to take more responsibility in providing training in these skills. At present, although the UK fares well in international comparisons of training incidence, when type of training is studied, there seems to be more focus on induction or health-and-safety issues rather than training that directly leads to improved performance. Thus, improved training, availability and take-up of quality vocational qualifications and perhaps more employer involvement in university syllabi appear the most likely routes for reducing skills shortages and mismatch.

PART 4
What Can Education Policy Do?

Economic Evaluation of Education Initiatives

By Carl Emmerson, Sandra McNally and Costas Meghir[1]

10.1 INTRODUCTION: THE EVALUATION PROBLEM

By making appropriate investments in capital, both physical and human, productivity and hence economic performance can be improved. A key challenge for policy makers is to identify when a government intervention can improve the allocation of resources. In general, policy makers will want to know which interventions are the most attractive in terms of the net benefits they can deliver. Accurate assessment of the benefits and costs of each potential intervention are crucial, particularly when public funds, which have an obvious opportunity cost, need to be committed.

In this chapter, we describe some of the key issues in programme evaluation before providing details of different techniques that can be used. This section is necessarily technical and some readers may prefer to go straight to the assessment of the empirical results from two large innovative UK education initiatives (Section 10.5). The first, Excellence in Cities (EiC), is a programme aimed at improving the ability of schoolchildren so that they can achieve better education and labour-market outcomes. The second, the Education Maintenance Allowance (EMA), offers a financial incentive to young adults from lower-income families to continue into further education.

In terms of education initiatives, full evaluation requires two stages of analysis, neither of which is trivial. First, what would be the precise impact on certain outcomes of the policy intervention? For example, if class sizes are reduced what will be the impact in terms of improved ability of school leavers? Second, what would be the value of any improved outcome? For example, if there were a 5% increase in the percentage of school leavers attaining a given level of achievement, what would this be worth in terms of improved employment and earnings potential?

Estimating the current or future impact of a new education initiative requires assumptions to be made. This is regardless of whether a scheme is yet to be imple-

[1]We are grateful to colleagues who have worked on the evaluation of the Education Maintenance Allowance and the Excellence in Cities programmes, in particular Gavan Conlon, Lorraine Dearden, Christine Frayne and Stephen Machin.

mented, has been implemented nationwide, or has been piloted. The key is in estimating a counterfactual – namely, what would have happened in the absence of, or alternatively the presence of, the policy intervention. In many cases, piloting a scheme will make this possible with more reasonable assumptions than those required if a scheme is yet to be introduced or if it has already been implemented nationwide. Piloting a scheme also has the advantage of limiting the cost to the taxpayer (and potentially to the politician) of implementing a scheme that turns out to offer poor value for money. Finally, a well-designed evaluation, while weeding out ineffective policies, vastly strengthens the political case for preserving successful policies. The absence of evaluation, on the other hand, allows potentially valuable interventions to be eliminated with criteria other than their actual effectiveness.

This chapter describes a number of ways in which an evaluation can be designed in order to assess the impact of a programme, and highlights the importance of clarity over what impact is actually being identified. Many of the ideas discussed can be found in Heckman *et al.* (1999). Often the parameter of most interest to the policy maker might not be precisely the same as the parameter that the evaluator can estimate. In practice, evaluations cannot be simply lifted of the shelf, but instead need to be carefully designed with respect to the specific problems that arise with a particular programme that is to be evaluated. Hence we describe two specific evaluations of education initiatives that have been conducted in the UK. These pose different issues in terms of the information available to the evaluator and hence employ two different techniques.

This chapter begins by describing in more detail the issues that arise when trying to assess the impact of a programme. It then goes on, in Section 10.3 to describe different techniques potentially available to the evaluator. Section 10.4 explains why the impact of a specific programme might be expected to change if it is extended nationwide. Sections 10.5 and 10.7 describe two recent evaluations of English education initiates: the Excellence in Cities programme and the Education Maintenance Allowance scheme, respectively. Section 10.8 concludes.

10.2 THE EVALUATION PROBLEM

10.2.1 *Definition of the Problem*

There is a long history of evaluating educational interventions. The key development in the 1990s was the way in which many of these ideas were made systematic in terms of formal econometric models and the effort to link the assumptions made in each case to economic theory. In this section we lay out the evaluation problem as first conceived by Roy (1951) and then further discussed and used by Willis and Rosen (1979). Its identification is discussed in Heckman and Honoré (1990).

Finally, Heckman and Robb (1985a) offer a comprehensive analysis of the evaluation problem and methods to deal with it.

The Roy model is one of comparative advantage, where individuals face a different return, specific to themselves, depending on which sector they decide to work in. Thus, for example, one individual may do better in sector A relative to sector B, while a different person may be better matched to sector B than sector A. This idea of course carries over to practically any situation where individuals can choose different sectors, treatments, policies, etc. The idea can be formalized in the following simple model:

$$Y_i^1 = a + b + \varepsilon_i + u_i,$$
$$Y_i^0 = a + u_i,$$

where Y_i^1 is the outcome in sector 1 (say, with treatment), while Y_i^0 is the outcome in sector 0 (no treatment). The return to treatment for the ith individual is $Y_i^1 - Y_i^0 = b + \varepsilon_i$. The term u_i reflects the overall ability of the individual in each of the two circumstances, while ε_i reflects the relative benefit (over and above the average) of a particular individual joining sector i. We normalize this relative benefit to have mean zero. So individuals with negative ε_i perform worse than the average individual in sector 1, while those with a positive value perform better than average. Ultimately, it is possible that while on average the effect of being in sector 1 may be positive ($b > 0$) for some individuals, the overall effect ($b + \varepsilon_i$) may be negative.

The key evaluation issue is that the individual effect of a policy ($b + \varepsilon_i$) is not and cannot ever be observed, because the same individual cannot be in and out of treatment at the same point in time. The response of the evaluation literature has been to identify different parameters of interest that could perhaps be estimated under different evaluation designs and/or assumptions. These parameters of interest relate to different aspects of the distribution of ($b + \varepsilon_i$).

An obvious parameter of interest is the average treatment effect, which is b in the notation above. This is the expected effect of the policy for a random individual. However, this may not necessarily be the parameter of interest in all circumstances, or even a parameter that can inform us about the desirability of a policy.

In many situations individuals self-select into treatment or are selected in by some observable and unobservable criteria. In this case a parameter of interest may be the impact of treatment on those who are treated. To define this, we first need to define an assignment rule to the policy. Suppose that we can write

$$D_i = P(X_i) + v_i,$$

where D is equal to one for those assigned to the policy and zero otherwise, X is a set of observable individual specific characteristics, and we define

$$v_i \equiv D_i - E(D_i \mid X_i) = D_i - P(X_i).$$

The part of the assignment rule that depends on X defines the aspects of selection that can be explained by observables. These may in some cases define eligibility rules or just propensity to self-select on the basis of preferences. The residual v relates to unexplained assignment. This may reflect unobserved preferences or pure randomness. The assignment rule may derive from an individual's economic decision, made on the basis of a calculation comparing present values on the stream of outcome if they did participate in the programme relative to if they did not participate. It may also reflect constraints or a mixture of individual decisions and circumstances external to the individual. For example, a treatment may be made available only to individuals who live in a certain area. The way that individual unobservables relate to the unobserved components in the outcome equations (u_i and ε_i) is crucial for defining the correct identification strategy needed to estimate the effect of the treatment.

Returning to the parameters of interest, the effect of the treatment on the treated (TT) is defined as

$$\mathrm{TT} = b + E(\varepsilon_i \mid D_i = 1).$$

Thus TT is the effect of a treatment/policy on those who were selected by the assignment rule to receive it. This is often considered to be one of the most relevant parameters of interest, since it describes how a policy is likely to affect those actually participating in the treatment. Nevertheless, this preference may be misleading. While under certain circumstances the average treatment effect may be thought of as a structural parameter (see the discussion below on general-equilibrium effects), TT is not. The TT effect is highly dependent on how the selection into the treatment takes place. Thus if the selection mechanism is very different between evaluation and implementation, the effects of the policy may turn out to be very different from the ones predicted by the evaluation.

Other aspects of interest in the evaluation can of course be the entire distribution of returns $b+\varepsilon_i$, which may be very difficult to obtain, or perhaps impacts for subgroups of the population defined by particular values of the vector X. For example, it might be of interest to know if a treatment has a different impact on men than it does on women – an example of this is provided in Section 10.7.5. Heckman *et al.* (1997*b*) offer a discussion of how the relevant parameters of interest depend on the particular social welfare function or decision problem we may be interested in.

10.2.2 *A Simple Assignment Rule and Implications for Identification*

Suppose individuals compare the outcomes in two different states to decide whether they wish to participate in a programme. Moreover, suppose that participants have to overcome costs $(F(X_i) - r_i)$ to be admitted. Then a simple assignment rule can be written as

$$D = 1(b + \varepsilon_i - F(X_i) + r_i > 0).$$

In this equation two unobservables are relevant. First the unobserved individual return, and second an additional unobservable r which may reflect overall preference for being in the programme or luck in getting a place. The key point though is that $\varepsilon_i + r_i$ is likely to be correlated with the individual benefits from a particular activity, as denoted by u and ε in the Roy model of counterfactual outcomes. Thus a comparison of average outcomes between treated and non-treated individuals will provide an effect that is subject to selection bias, i.e.

$$E(Y_i^1 \mid D_i = 1) - E(Y_i^0 \mid D_i = 0)$$
$$= b + E(\varepsilon_i \mid D_i = 1) + [E(u_i \mid D_i = 1) - E(u_i \mid D_i = 0)].$$

While the first two terms on the right-hand side are the effect of treatment on the treated, the last two terms, in square brackets, reflect composition or selection bias.

Estimation of TT requires a way of eliminating the selection bias. Estimation of the average treatment effect will usually require additional assumptions. We now turn to a brief description of evaluation methods followed by the approach we rely on for the evaluation of a number of educational and labour-market interventions.

10.3 METHODS OF EVALUATION

10.3.1 *Random Assignment*

One way to resolve selection bias and estimate the average treatment effect, or in some cases the effect of the treatment on the treated, is to use random assignment to the policy. If random assignment is successful, the distribution of characteristics between the treatment and control group (i.e. those randomly excluded from the policy) will be approximately the same (identical in infinite samples). This means that $E(u_i \mid D_i = 1) = E(u_i \mid D_i = 0)$ and $E(\varepsilon_i \mid D_i = 1) = E(\varepsilon_i \mid D_i = 0)$, which directly implies that a comparison of mean outcomes between the treated and the non-treated will identify the average treatment effect in the population participating in the experiment. Sometimes the population participating in the experiment is self-selected by their willingness to receive treatment (e.g. Job Training Partnership Act (JTPA) experiments analysed in Heckman *et al.* (1997a)). In this case the effect identified can be interpreted as the effect of the treatment on the treated. However, it should be pointed out that participation in the experiment may be affected by the fact that treatment is subject to randomization, implying that the TT identified in this case may be different from the TT under other circumstances.

Finally, well-designed and well-implemented experiments have the great advantage of ensuring that the policy will be evaluated on types of individuals who would otherwise never be treated or who would otherwise always be treated (thus depriving us of a comparable treatment or control group, respectively). In other words, experiments solve what is known as the "lack of common support" problem to which we return later in the context of matching.

Often, randomizations are considered difficult to implement for political reasons; this is particularly the case because many of the policies considered, even when they do not achieve their stated aim, represent a pure transfer to the target population with no obvious negative effects on their direct welfare. The interests of those paying are usually ignored in this argument. Once this is recognized, randomization can be very appealing from an evaluation perspective and in many cases it can be designed in a way that is seen to be both fair and desirable. Thus, once it is accepted that the taxpayer is only willing to pay for programmes that achieve a well-specified aim, and that programmes have an opportunity cost, evaluation becomes a *sine qua non* for policy implementation. Participants randomized out can be presented with the argument that in the absence of the experiment the policy would not be available anyway. This is certainly the case in the long run where policies that are considered unsuccessful are always under pressure to be cut (and rightly so).

Thus, randomization has the great appeal of solving the selection-bias problem and is potentially a very important political tool for preserving successful policies. However, it would be wrong to think that this approach is without its problems. First, individuals who were randomized out may seek treatment, thus contaminating the experimental design. Similarly, those randomized in may also not comply and may avoid treatment. In this case we can carry out an "intention-to-treat" analysis whereby we compare those randomly assigned to the treatment with others, in the knowledge that this does not represent a comparison of a treated and an untreated population, but a population with a higher proportion of treated individuals compared with one with fewer treated individuals. Now suppose we assume that all those who would have received treatment in the absence of the policy did so in the presence of the policy as well.[2] Then rescaling the "intention-to-treat" parameter by the differential proportion of treated individuals in the two populations will identify the effect of treatment on those who obtained treatment because they were randomized in and who otherwise would not have obtained it.[3] In practice, compliance problems can be very serious and can blunt the results of an experiment. Keeping track of the original randomization and not relying on the actual assignments of treatment is of course key to an unbiased evaluation, even if this means identifying an intention-to-treat effect and ultimately a different parameter from the one we set out to measure.

---

[2]This is the monotonicity assumption (see Imbens and Angrist 1994). The assumption places strong restrictions on the model assigning individuals to treatment (see Vytlacil 2002).

[3]The Local Average Treatment Effect parameter of Imbens and Angrist (1994).

In the US, randomized experiments are becoming the accepted norm for large-scale evaluations, such as the Job Training Partnership Act (JTPA) and the Tennessee Student/Teacher Achievement Ratio (STAR) experiment on class size. Outside the US, randomized experiments have been rare but are now becoming more prevalent. Examples are the PROGRESA programme in Mexico, Travajar in Argentina and the forthcoming evaluation in the UK of training programmes for the longer-term unemployed (ERAD). Nevertheless, for a number of reasons, more standard observational methods will continue to form an important part of the toolkit for evaluation and it is important to understand the assumptions that underlie these.

Finally, one has to recognize that randomized experiments are typically designed to answer one particular question and usually cannot go much beyond that. For example, an area-based randomization where a treatment is available to all eligible individuals living within a certain area will not be informative about the impact of varying intensity of treatment (higher or lower subsidies, for example) and how this may affect ineligible individuals. In addition, it will not be able to account for the impact of the policy on outcomes observed on a selected group of individuals (for example, wage returns of the policy for those who end up working). It is of course possible to design more-elaborate experiments to answer virtually any question, mapping out the effects of different types and intensities of treatment on different subgroups of the population. However desirable we may view this as social scientists, governments are likely to be less than enthusiastic in practice. Thus, despite the obvious elegance and usefulness of randomized experiments, it is more than likely that they will need to be complemented by observational methods coupled with more structural modelling approaches.

10.3.2 *Differences-in-Differences*

One of the most popular evaluation methods using non-experimental data is differences-in-differences. The method is based on the Wald estimator and has been described and used in a number of early papers including Ashenfelter (1978) and Heckman and Robb (1985a). The key idea is that we can split up the population into two groups: one is exposed to a policy/treatment and the other one is not. Alternatively, one is more likely to obtain treatment and the other is less likely. The key assumption is that the *change* in the outcome variable is the same between the two groups in the absence of this exposure. The "effect" is then estimated as the difference in the growth of the outcome variables over time for the two groups, divided by the difference in the proportion of those exposed to the policy in the two groups. However, what effect is estimated and how to interpret it will very much depend on the model. Consider first a simplified Roy-type model for the actual outcome Y, where the impact is assumed homogeneous:

$$Y_i = a + bD_i + u_i.$$

Consider a variable Z which is equal to 1 if an individual belongs to group 1 and 0 otherwise. The group could be defined by geographical location or demographic/age group. Define a variable t which is 0 in the pre-policy period and 1 post policy. Then, under the differences-in-differences assumptions we get that

$$E(Y_i \mid z, t) = a + bE(D \mid Z, t) + m(t) + g(Z).$$

We can then identify the common treatment effect by

$$b = \frac{\begin{aligned}&[E(Y_i \mid Z_i = 1,\ t = 1) - E(Y_i \mid Z_i = 1,\ t = 0)]\\&-[E(Y_i \mid Z_i = 0,\ t = 1) - E(Y_i \mid Z_i = 0,\ t = 0)]\end{aligned}}{\begin{aligned}&[E(D_i \mid Z_i = 1,\ t = 1) - E(D_i \mid Z_i = 1,\ t = 0)]\\&-[E(D_i \mid Z_i = 0,\ t = 1) - E(D_i \mid Z_i = 0,\ t = 0)]\end{aligned}}.$$

This is a standard instrumental variables estimator, where the instruments are the group identity (Z) and the time period. The excluded instruments are the interaction between the two, which reflects the assumption that in the absence of the policy there is no differential growth between the two groups. Thus all differential growth is attributed to the policy.

If the impact of the policy is in fact heterogeneous, as in the original model, the interpretation of the estimated effect is no longer straightforward. In this case, if we assume that the policy caused some individuals to have more treatment and none to have less (monotonicity), then the estimate we obtain is the Local Average Treatment Effect (LATE) defined by Imbens and Angrist (1994). It estimates the effect on those who obtained treatment as a result of the policy inducement. However, the effect may be specific to the policy in question and may not relate to other types of inducements that may convince different types of individuals (with different returns) to have treatment.

We discuss further the relative merits of differences-in-differences vis-à-vis matching. However, we need to point out that the assumption of no differential trends is not innocuous: "Ashenfelter's dip" is an important counter-example. Here individuals eligible for training are compared with otherwise similar persons not eligible for training. However, eligibility for training may be induced by a negative (but transitory) shock to earnings. Since transitory shocks (by definition) revert to the mean, the earnings of trainees will grow faster on average following the determination of their eligibility than the earnings of non-trainees, even without any training. Thus the assumption underlying the use of differences-in-differences has to be scrutinized in each case and the underlying economics of the problem must be thought through carefully.

10.3.3 *Matching*

An alternative approach to evaluation is that of matching. In the matching framework it is recognized that selection of individuals into treatment is not random but that selection takes place based on observable variables plus random factors unrelated to outcomes. The basic evaluation problem is that we do not observe the average outcome that the treated group would have had if they did not obtain the treatment.[4] Formally we are missing data on $E(Y_i^0 \mid D_i = 1)$ as well as on $E(Y_i^1 \mid D_i = 0)$. As shown above, a simple comparison of outcomes between treated and untreated individuals generally leads to selection bias. The issue then is to construct such a counterfactual. To identify the impact of treatment on the treated, matching relies on the Conditional Mean Independence Assumption (CMIA): given a set of observable characteristics, the counterfactual outcome is independent of whether the individual was assigned to the treatment or not; formally

$$\text{CMIA}: E(Y_i^0 \mid D_i = 1, X) = E(Y_i^0 \mid D_i = 0, X).$$

We also assume that the probability of assignment to the treatment given any value of the vector of observables X is less than 1 and greater than 0, i.e. for any given X there is a treatment and a comparison group. Thus we assume

$$0 < \Pr(D_i = 1 \mid X) < 1 \; \forall X.$$

Another way of understanding this restriction is to say that the treatment can only be evaluated for individuals where X is such that there are both treated and control individuals.

Whether the assumption is credible or not will depend on the nature of the problem and on the available data. Sometimes, matching on some Xs can in fact make the problem worse, as in the case of training programmes where eligibility is driven by an unobserved shock to earnings. In that case, the more similar the treatments are to the controls the more likely it is that those who became eligible for training suffered a big negative transitory shock, and hence there will be larger post-training growth as a result of mean reversion. In addition, we rarely have a guide about which variables we should be matching on. Formally, the CMIA assumption may be valid for a specific set of Xs but not for others. Too many matching variables can be as bad as too few. Thus matching has to be used carefully and has to be well justified.

Implementing matching on the basis of a potentially large dimensional vector X may not be practical. However, the theorem by Rosenbaum and Rubin (1983) allows us to match only on one variable, i.e. the propensity score, which is simply the probability of being assigned to treatment given characteristics X

---

[4]We also do not observe the average outcome for the untreated group had they received treatment.

$(P(X) = \Pr(D_i = 1 \mid X_i))$. According to this theorem, if the distribution of characteristics for the treatment group is $F^1(X)$ and for the comparison group is $F^0(X)$, then $F^1(X \mid P(X) = p) = F^0(X \mid P(X) = p)$. Thus, conditioning on the propensity score balances the observable characteristics in the treatment and comparison samples. The effect of treatment on the treated can then be calculated as

$$\text{TT} = E(Y_i^1 \mid D_i = 1) - E_{F^1(P(X))}E(Y_i^0 \mid D_i = 0, P(X)),$$

where $E_{F^1(P(X))}$ is an average using as weights the distribution of the propensity score in the treatment population.

Several estimators have been proposed for the above. Heckman *et al.* (1997a) show that a kernel-based estimator smoothing out the counterfactual performs better than one-to-one (nearest-neighbour) matching.

Estimation of the average treatment effect requires an additional assumption that

$$\text{CMIA}_1 : E(Y_i^1 \mid D_i = 0, X) = E(Y_i^1 \mid D_i = 1, X).$$

This implies that there is no selection on the basis of unobserved returns.

10.3.4 *Combining Differences-in-Differences with Matching*

The matching approach allows for an arbitrary dependence of the programme effect on characteristics X. The simple differences-in-differences approach presented here does not. If the effect does differ with observed characteristics, the differences-in-differences approach will estimate some weighted average of the effects, but will not necessarily use the right weights to produce the estimate of TT defined above (to do so the weights would need to be the characteristics of the treated population). In addition it may be that the underlying assumption in the differences-in-differences estimator may be valid conditional on a suitable set of Xs (which may be time varying or have time-varying effects), but may not be valid unconditionally. Thus the question is whether the two approaches may be combined.

The differences-in-differences estimator compares average outcomes in four cells: before and after a policy exposure and treatment versus control group. Suppose that we have at our disposal a panel of individuals or schools or other well-defined treatment units (such as areas) and suppose that the relevant characteristics affecting outcomes do not change over time. Then we can construct a differences-in-differences estimator that is completely analogous to matching as described before. In this case the outcome variable Y is the *growth* of whatever we are measuring, e.g. the growth in test scores or the growth in wages. Matching can then be applied between the two groups based on the relevant characteristics X. This approach combines the advantages of differences-in-differences by eliminating unobserved group effects in levels and ensures that comparisons are made across comparable groups, thus taking full account of heterogeneous treatment effects.

The problem is more complicated when each of the four cells includes separate samples from the same population, as in the case of repeated cross-sections. In this case we need to balance the distribution of characteristics in all four cells and we cannot reduce the problem to a simple matching exercise between two groups as in the case when there are panel data with constant characteristics over time.

The key assumption here is that, conditional on fixed values of the characteristics X, growth in the treated group in the absence of the treatment would have equalled growth in the comparison group. Formally this may be written as

$$E(Y_i^0 \mid Z_i = 1, \, t = 1, X) - E(Y_i^0 \mid Z_i = 1, \, t = 0, X)$$
$$= E(Y_i^0 \mid Z_i = 0, \, t = 1, X) - E(Y_i^0 \mid Z_i = 0, \, t = 0, X).$$

Thus, the comparison is performed for a population with equal values of the characteristics X in all cells. This approach was used by Blundell *et al.* (2004). There is an analogy to propensity score matching here, where instead of matching on X we can match on a pair of propensity scores. Define a probability of being observed in period $t = 1$ as $P_t(X) = \Pr(t = 1 \mid X)$ and a probability of belonging to group $Z = 1$ as $P_Z(X) = \Pr(Z_i = 1 \mid X)$. Then the distribution of the characteristics in the four cells can be balanced by conditioning on these two propensity scores. Hence, under the differences-in-differences matching assumption it will also be true that

$$E(Y_i^0 \mid Z_i = 1, \, t = 1, P_t(X), P_Z(X)) - E(Y_i^0 \mid Z_i = 1, \, t = 0, P_t(X), P_Z(X))$$
$$= E(Y_i^0 \mid Z_i = 0, \, t = 1, P_t(X), P_Z(X)) - E(Y_i^0 \mid Z_i = 0, \, t = 0, P_t(X), P_Z(X)).$$

This approach can be very useful when there may be differential trends by characteristics and when we suspect that the support in the four cells may not be common, as well as when the treatment effects are heterogeneous.

Note that we have defined the treatment group by the variable Z. This could be an indicator for treatment itself, in which case $Z_i \equiv D_i$, or it could be an indicator for a group that is more likely to be treated. In this case, the treatment effect would be estimated by rescaling the reduced form effect obtained by matching. This is achieved by dividing by the effect of Z and t on treatment, as with instrumental variables. To the extent that the treatment effect depends on unobservables and making a suitable monotonicity assumption, the effect would have a LATE interpretation as before.

Implementing the matched differences-in-differences estimator involves estimating the conditional means and then averaging using the distribution of the two propensity scores in the cell defined by $t = $ "policy period" and $Z = $

"treatment group" after eliminating individuals who are not in the common support across all *four* cells.

10.4 GENERAL EQUILIBRIUM AND PEER EFFECTS

All evaluation methods discussed so far make the implicit assumption that treatment does not affect the comparison group either directly or indirectly. For example, a school intervention reducing class size for one group of pupils is assumed to have no implications for the group not directly targeted. Effects on the comparison group, however, can come from a number of sources. First, it is possible that there are peer effects. If the treatment group performs better as a result of the policy, this may induce individuals among the controls to put in more effort. Alternatively, an intervention that increases school attendance by lower-achieving groups may have negative effects on the group that would have attended anyway. A policy increasing the supply of education may change the wage structure for other groups, thus affecting their decisions by impacting on the returns to education. Finally, a number of labour-market programmes designed to increase the employment of a target group may in fact displace workers in other groups. The methods described above are not well designed to deal with these issues. It is sometimes possible to find different comparison groups that would allow an evaluation of the importance of general-equilibrium effects (as in Blundell *et al.* 2004). However, generally this is not easy to achieve. Ideally one needs to find isolated but similar comparison groups to identify the treatment effects. But even this may address too narrow a question because it does not explicitly deal with the effects of the policy on untargeted groups, which may have equally important welfare consequences (e.g. worker substitution in active labour-market programmes). In general, one would need to model the behavioural responses and treatment impacts of all groups under a particular policy to gain an understanding of possible spillover effects. To quantify them one generally needs a general-equilibrium modelling framework, which in practice will involve much more structure than the one *explicitly* involved in the type of evaluations discussed above. However, one needs to appreciate that the assumptions often implicit in evaluations may in fact be as strong as any involved in the specification of a general-equilibrium model.

From a discussion of the methodologies that may be used in an evaluation context, we now turn to examine how they have been applied to evaluate education policies in the UK. EiC and the EMA programme are two of the programmes that have been introduced by the Labour government to improve education opportunities for disadvantaged groups. EiC consists of a number of schemes to improve education opportunities for those of pre-compulsory school age, whereas EMA is aimed at improving access to education for young adults once they finish compulsory schooling. We discuss the evaluation of each initiative in turn.

10.5 EVALUATION IN PRACTICE. I. EXCELLENCE IN CITIES

10.5.1 *Description of Programme*

Excellence in Cities has been described as Tony Blair's flagship policy for transforming standards in inner-city schools. The programme includes a number of different strands, aimed at extending learning opportunities and tackling barriers to learning. The main focus of the programme is on secondary schools, although it has quickly been extended to cover both primary and post-compulsory phases of education. To date, most progress has been made in evaluating the effect of the policy in secondary schools. Hence, we discuss the programme in this context. For the most part, EiC has been broadly targeted to cover all state secondary schools within designated Local Education Authorities (LEAs). These LEAs have been selected in the light of their relative disadvantage (measured as the percentage of students eligible for free school meals) and urban location. Each LEA and its state secondary schools form a "partnership" in which they plan how to spend resources that have been allocated as a result of EiC. Much of the funding is allocated to schools on the basis of pupil numbers and the degree of disadvantage in the school (also indicated by the percentage of pupils eligible for free school meals). However, some components of EiC will not necessarily involve all schools in the partnership and this has funding implications.

EiC resources must be used in the context of a number of different strands. There are three core strands that should affect all schools in the partnership: Learning Mentors; Learning Support Units; and a Gifted and Talented Programme. The Learning Mentor strand involves the appointment of assistants who help students to overcome educational or behavioural problems. Learning Support Units are there to provide intensive teaching and support for students who need some time out of mainstream teaching, with the aim of integrating students back into the classroom as quickly as possible. The Gifted and Talented Programme is targeted at the 5–10% of pupils in each school who are expected to benefit from extra help and support. This strand is expected to involve a distinct in-school teaching and learning programme and an extensive programme of out-of-hours study support through local networks. Hence, the three core strands of EiC are designed to improve the performance of pupils in the entire distribution of ability. However, the resources are quite limited: the school mean allocation per pupil in the first year of the scheme was £50 for Learning Mentors; £26 for Learning Support Units; and £22 for the Gifted and Talented

Programme (Noden *et al.* 2002).[5] In fact this brings up a key issue in evaluation. Although evaluating impacts is of key importance, ultimately a policy should be judged while accounting for the costs of achieving the results.

The whole package of measures in EiC has been rolled out in various phases, so that by now about a third of all LEA-maintained secondary schools in England are involved in the programme (i.e. over 1000 schools). The first phase, involving 24 partnerships, began in September 1999. This was followed by the designation of 23 "phase 2" partnerships in September 2000. Then, in September 2001, the policy commenced for the most recent entrants – the 10 partnerships involved in phase 3 and schools involved in "excellence clusters". The latter designation is designed to bring the three core strands of the EiC programme to smaller towns (and does not necessarily involve all schools within a particular LEA).

Potentially, there are many components of the EiC programme that could be evaluated. A comprehensive cost–benefit analysis of the policy would involve enumerating all the benefits arising from the policy (as well as its component parts) and comparing this with the relevant costs. Ultimately, we are interested in outcomes that lead to economic or standard-of-living benefits – in this context, through enhanced labour-market performance (as reflected in wages or employment) and/or a reduction in crime. Although school-level measures may well have a direct effect on youth crime, any effect of the policy on labour-market outcomes will be indirect, through increasing participation in education (i.e. reducing pupil absences from schools) and improving pupil attainment. Of course, such educational outcomes of the policy may be thought of as valuable in their own right, although ultimately they should be justifiable by improvements in living standards. They are certainly of policy interest given that the government has set targets both in relation to exam attainment and absences. In the short term, relating educational outcomes to their likely impact in the labour market involves predicting how the estimated educational effects of the policy will affect these outcomes. In the longer term, a better approach would be to obtain information on the actual labour-market outcomes of people involved in the evaluation. However, the first step involves estimating the effect of the policy on initial outcomes. Since the EiC evaluation is still ongoing[6], we focus here on

---

[5]These strands do not directly affect all students in EiC schools. So the resource allocation per affected pupil will be considerably higher. Strands that don't directly affect all schools include the designation of "specialist" schools (i.e. in particular subjects) and "beacon" schools (chosen for their exemplary characteristics). Such schools receive additional funding and are expected to disseminate good practice throughout the partnership. Similarly, schools that are chosen as sites for City Learning Centres (to provide information and communication technology facilities) and schools involved in Education Action Zones are expected to share resources and disseminate good practice.

[6]This is being conducted by a consortium involving groups at the National Foundation for Educational Research, the Institute for Fiscal Studies and the London School of Economics. The final report is due in 2005. Results cited here are based on preliminary work by Stephen Machin, Sandra McNally and Costas Meghir.

the overall effect of the policy on measures of educational attainment at age 14. We show some preliminary results for the effect of the policy on attainment in mathematics. Before discussing the methodology, we briefly outline how the exam system operates in England.

10.5.2 *Educational Outcomes in English Schools*

Since 1988 there has been a National Curriculum in England. This sets out what pupils should study and the standards that should be achieved. There are four "key stages" and ten statutory subjects. Key Stages 1 and 2 refer to a student's primary-school education and apply to the phases of education when the student is 5–7 years old and 7–11 years old, respectively. Key Stages 3 and 4 constitute the secondary stage of education, and relate to pupils aged 11–14 and 14–16, respectively. Students are tested at the end of these stages of education. English, mathematics and science are the three core subjects. Due to data availability, it is attainment at the age of 14 (i.e. at Key Stage 3) that has been the main focus of attention in the EiC evaluation to date, although our current work also involves analysis of the effect of EiC on attainment at the end of students' compulsory education (i.e. at Key Stage 4).

Students take a number of tests in each subject. A score is assigned to each test. For each subject, scores from the various tests are aggregated and assigned to the relevant "level" (where the levels are on a scale of 1–9 for Key Stage 3). There are various complications such as the fact that not all students sit the same exam. In mathematics, where there are four different possible "tiers" of entry, the higher the tier of entry (and more difficult the exam), the higher the "level" the student may attain. Hence, we need to be concerned not only with the effect of the EiC policy on exam attainment, but also on whether it has an effect on other relevant choices made by the student or teacher (e.g. what tier to enter).

10.5.3 *Methodology*

As discussed in Section 10.3.1, if treatment status were randomly assigned to schools, and in the absence of compliance problems, it would be straightforward to evaluate the effect of a programme on outcomes. However, schools are selected into EiC based on an indicator of the average disadvantage of schools in the LEA (i.e. the percentage of students entitled to free school meals) and the urban status of the LEA. Although randomization would certainly have been possible as well as desirable within that group, it was not carried out. The choice of control schools is non-random and, hence, there will be variables correlated with treatment status and educational outcomes. Failure to account for such factors will make it impossible to distinguish their effect on educational outcomes from that of the EiC policy.

In an attempt to overcome this problem, we combine differences-in-differences and matching approaches to estimate the effect of EiC on educational outcomes in treated schools (i.e. the effect of the treatment on the treated). Ideally we would like to implement the matching differences-in-differences estimator described earlier. However, matching on the basis of two propensity scores with very large samples can be very time-consuming. We thus estimate the effect by using a two-stage approach: first we choose a set of control schools and treatment schools matching on pre-policy school characteristics, thus ensuring that the treatment and comparison groups are comparable in relevant observable dimensions. Having determined the set of schools in the treatment and comparison groups we then proceed to use differences-in-differences controlling linearly for characteristics at the individual and school level.[7]

In the EiC evaluation to date, we have drawn comparison schools from three different sets: all non-EiC state schools; a sample of schools based on the proportion of students eligible for free school meals, chosen to replicate the distribution within EiC schools (the "survey comparison" group)[8]; and schools in phase 3 of the EiC policy. The latter is possible since, up until recently, we have been evaluating the effect of EiC on outcomes in 2001, which was before phase 3 schools were entered into the policy. Schools in phase 3 might be a good comparison group given that similar criteria are used for selection to the policy in different time periods.

Since there are timing differences in when schools were entered into the EiC programme, we estimate separate effects for phase 1 (P1) and phase 2 (P2) schools. We then estimate a joint effect.

Given the treatment and comparison group, we run the following pupil-level regression:

$$P_{ist} = \alpha_o + \beta_1 \text{EiC P1}_{is} \times \text{P1 policy-on} + \beta_1 \text{EiC P2}_{is} \times \text{P2 policy-on}$$
$$+ \gamma_1 \text{EiC P1}_s + \gamma_2 \text{EiC P2}_s + \delta T\tau + \zeta X_{ist} + \eta Z_{st} + \theta P^*_{ist-1} + \varepsilon_{ist},$$

(10.1)

where P represents pupil attainment, for pupil i in secondary school s in a particular time period t; EiC is a school-level dummy variable indicating whether the school is in the "treatment group"; X denotes pupil characteristics; Z is a set of school characteristics; T is a set of year dummies, included to capture year-on-year differences in pupil attainment; and ε reflects unobserved determinants of achievement. The model includes a prior achievement measure for these pupils (P_{ist-1}). In other words, we are matching on the pre-policy performance of pupils in a different type

---

[7] One has to take this pre-selection into account when constructing standard errors for the effects.

[8] This "survey comparison" group consists of schools that were selected to participate in a series of interviews as part of the EiC evaluation. We do not use data from these surveys here since no information is available for the comparison group of students who sat Key Stage 3 exams in the pre-policy period.

of test, as well as controlling for the pre-policy aggregate school performance on the test being evaluated.

The parameters of interest are the βs, which capture an average effect of being in each of the EiC phases. The fact that we have more than one time period allows us to control for the systematic effect of being an EiC school (α) in each time period. This is useful to the extent that we do not observe all relevant factors that are correlated with treatment status and the outcome of interest. In fact, we can do better than this by controlling for school-specific dummy variables (which we do in some specifications).

The fact that we implement a linear differences-in-differences model is potentially more restrictive than the method we presented before, where we were combining differences-in-differences with non-parametric matching. First, the approach we use imposes the assumption that the growth rate in the outcome P_{ist} is the same for all groups defined by X; however, we only require common trends *within* each group defined by characteristics X. Second, the linear model provides an average effect of the policy with weights that may differ from the ones implied by the distribution of characteristics in the treated population. However, we followed this more-restrictive approach mainly for computational reasons, given the size of our sample.

Finally, one may have conducted the evaluation at the aggregate school level. However, in doing this we would not control for pupil-level differences in the distribution of characteristics. In computing standard errors, however, we do take account of clustering at the school level. This may have very large impacts on the standard errors, depending on the level of correlation of the unobservables between subjects within a treatment unit (in this case within a school) (see Moulton 1986).

10.5.4 *Data Sources*

The empirical analysis is based upon administrative records of pupil-level attainment and school-level data. The former consists of matched data on all students who were in year 9 in either 2001 or 1999 (i.e. the Key Stage 3 exam year), together with their Key Stage 2 exam results (taken in primary school, three years previously).[9] These anonymous data also contain a record of the student's gender, date of birth and codes for the primary and secondary school attended. School-level variables were matched up with these school codes using the school-performance tables and information available in the LEA and School Information Service (LEASIS). Only "non-special" schools that are LEA maintained are included in the analysis.

---

[9]We thank Mike Treadaway of the Fischer Trust for provision of these pupil-level datasets and much helpful advice.

Table 10.1. Average mathematics attainment: Key Stage 3 level.

	EiC phase 1	EiC phase 2	EiC phase 3	Comparison group	All schools not in EiC phase 1 or EiC phase 2
Sample size	132 505	97 351	54 697	42 281	775 531
Number of schools	456	308	159	147	2444
2001	4.91	5.01	5.04	4.93	5.35
	(1.41)	(1.37)	(1.37)	(1.37)	(1.36)
1999	4.72	4.81	4.90	4.79	5.18
	(1.35)	(1.32)	(1.33)	(1.31)	(1.30)

Notes. Calculated from pupil-level administrative data on Key Stage 3 examination results. Sample standard deviation in parentheses. Source: Machin *et al.* (2004).

10.6 A SUMMARY OF RESULTS

Table 10.1 shows summary statistics for Key Stage 3 mathematics for each group of schools: EiC phase 1, phase 2, phase 3, the "survey comparison" group, and all schools not in phase 1 or phase 2 of EiC. The outcome variable is discrete and takes nine values corresponding to each level of achievement possible (9 being highest). The average level in each subject is shown for 2001 and 1999, as well as the change between the two years.

Table 10.2 reports a selection of results from the EiC evaluation. First we report a model with separate phase 1 and phase 2 effects, starting in column (1) with no controls (but matching on pre-policy school characteristics) then including more controls in columns (2) and (3). The specification in column (4) imposes a single EiC effect for the most detailed column (3) model, which incorporates school fixed effects. This specification is reported for boys and girls separately in columns (5) and (6). An intuitive way to interpret the coefficient reflecting the impact of the policy is as the increase in the proportion of those attaining one level higher as a result of the reform.

A clear pattern emerges, with a significant, positive EiC effect, though it is small in magnitude. Column (1) shows pupils in EiC phase 1 schools to have levels 0.029 higher and pupils in EiC phase 2 schools to have levels 0.041 higher than in the comparison group. Column (2) shows results after controlling for a full set of school variables (both primary and secondary), plus pupil Key Stage 2 performance. The EiC effects tend to fall a little and the gap between phase 1 and phase 2 widens. Not much changes once school fixed effects are added in column (3). In column (4), the phase 1 and phase 2 effects are aggregated into a single EiC effect. This specification shows there to be a statistically significant improvement in mathematics for pupils in

Table 10.2. Mathematics Key Stage 3: levels of attainment.

	(1) Only EiC and year variables	(2) Includes KS2, gender and all school variables	(3) Includes KS2, gender and all school variables and KS3 school fixed effects	(4) Includes KS2, gender and all school variables and KS3 school fixed effects	(5) As column 4 but with boys only	(6) As column 4 but with girls only
EiC *year = 2001	—	—	—	0.029 (0.007)	0.037 (0.008)	0.019 (0.008)
EiC P1 *year = 2001	0.029 (0.012)	0.016 (0.009)	0.019 (0.009)	—	—	—
EiC P2 *year = 2001	0.041 (0.014)	0.041 (0.01)	0.041 (0.01)	—	—	—
EiC P1	−0.465 (0.03)	−0.019 (0.01)	—	—	—	—
EiC P2	−0.376 (0.03)	−0.041 (0.011)	—	—	—	—
Year = 2001	0.162 (0.004)	0.245 (0.005)	0.246 (0.005)	0.246 (0.005)	0.193 (0.005)	0.300 (0.006)
Sample size	1 005 387	1 005 387	1 005 387	1 005 387	508 621	496 766
R squared	0.02	0.73	0.74	0.74	0.75	0.74
P value, P1 *year = 2001 versus P2 *year = 2001	0.50	0.06	0.08	0.08	0.96	0.00

Notes. Sample: EiC Phase 1 schools (456); EiC Phase 2 schools (308); all other schools (2444). Coefficients reported, robust standard errors in parentheses (clustered on secondary schools). Columns (2)–(6) include a range of variables relevant to the pupil's secondary school and primary school (at the time when he/she attended that school). A range of variables reflecting the pupil's attainment in primary school (i.e. Key Stage 2, at age 11) are also included, as well as gender. Full details of the variables are reported in the appendix. Source: Machin *et al.* (2004).

EiC schools, with the estimated impact being 0.029 levels of Key Stage 3 (or, more intuitively, increasing the number of pupils moving up a level by 2.9% on average). When broken down by gender (in columns (5) and (6)), the average impact of EiC is shown to be higher for boys (0.037 levels of Key Stage 3). For boys, the EiC impact is not significantly different across the two EiC phases. All the difference in the effect of phase 1 and phase 2 is concentrated among girls, where the programme only seems to be effective (on average) for schools in the latter group.

10.7 EVALUATION IN PRACTICE. II. EDUCATION MAINTENANCE ALLOWANCE

10.7.1 Policy Background

Recent years have seen increases in participation rates in post-compulsory education in the UK. Despite this increase there are still concerns that participation rates are too low. These concerns stem from a belief that either some young adults might not be making informed education choices, or alternatively that they might be constrained from doing so. The evidence on the relatively high returns to education (see, for example, Chapter 8 in this book) has also lent support to this argument. Policy makers in the UK have expressed particular concern that it is among lower socioeconomic groups that inappropriate or constrained education choices are more likely to occur. In 1989 just 48% of 16 year olds stayed on in post-compulsory education in England and Wales. By 2000 this had increased to 72%. This increase occurred across all parental occupational groups, with larger percentage point increases occurring among those from lower socioeconomic groups. Despite these increases, participation in post-compulsory education among those whose parents were unskilled manual workers in 2002 was just 59%, compared with 82% among those whose parents were in managerial or professional occupations. (Further details of participation rates in both further and higher education can be found in Chapter 5).

There is little direct evidence on the importance or otherwise of liquidity constraints, and this is not completely clear-cut (see Cameron and Heckman 1998; Cameron and Taber 2000; Dale and Krueger 1999). Moreover, there is certainly no evidence in the UK on this issue. Given this, and the desire to increase the lower participation rates in post-compulsory education of those from lower socioeconomic groups, the UK government decided to pilot the EMA in a number of local authorities across England. The next section describes the EMA policy.

10.7.2 Description of Programme

The Education Maintenance Allowance (EMA) is a policy aimed at improving participation, retention and achievement among young adults from lower-income families in full-time post-compulsory education. It has been piloted in a number of areas in England since the autumn of 1999 and is to be rolled out nationwide from the autumn of 2004.[10] The EMA consists of a weekly payment during term time and bonuses for retention and achievement. Eligibility for the payment depends on a young person's parental income.

In each of the pilot areas subject to a full quantitative evaluation young people were eligible for the full weekly EMA award if their parental taxable income in the previous financial year was £13 000 or below. In most areas the maximum award was worth £30 a week during term time, although in some areas the maximum award was £40 per week. Entitlement was tapered away with parental income, with young people whose parental income was £30 000 eligible for the minimum weekly award of £5 a week. Those whose parental income was above £30 000 were not eligible for the EMA. All individuals qualifying for the weekly payment could, subject to certain attendance and achievement criteria being met, also qualify for retention and achievement bonuses.[11] We now turn to discuss how the evaluation of the EMA was carried out.

10.7.3 *Methodology*

Given that individuals are selected into the policy on the basis of whether they live in a pilot or a control area, there is not a clean randomized experiment that can be exploited. Furthermore, the absence of detailed individual-level data from before the reform was in place means that it is not possible to use a differences-in-differences methodology. Hence a matching framework was adopted, as described in Section 10.3.3. This makes the assumption that the selection of individuals into the treatment, conditional on the information available to us, is not related to the outcomes of interest.

The government defined the areas in which the programme was to be piloted (the treatment areas). A set of control areas were chosen on the basis of being similar in terms of the level of, and trends in, participation in post-compulsory education. The choice of control areas was also aided through the use of micro-data from the

---

[10]The EMA was initially introduced in 12 LEAs across England, 10 of which were subject to a large-scale quantitative evaluation. The March 2000 Budget announced the extension of the EMA to more areas in England from September 2001 (HM Treasury 2000, para. 5.36). As a result the scheme was available in 56 LEAs in England, covering a total of 30% of young adults (up from the 7% covered previously). The July 2002 Spending Review announced that the scheme was to be made available across all of England from September 2004 (HM Treasury 2002, para. 6.17). Finance has also been made available to the Scottish Parliament, Welsh Assembly and Northern Ireland Assembly so that the EMA can also be introduced there, though the decision over how to use those funds will be made by these devolved legislatures.

[11]The national scheme has a maximum award of £30 per week during term time paid to the young person. For more details see the DfES website at http://www.dfes.gov.uk/ema/.

Youth Cohort Survey, so that, as far as was possible, areas were selected that had similar trends in participation in post-compulsory education *after* controlling for a set of observable characteristics.

The data, briefly described below, were designed to include a wealth of individual and background characteristics ranging from information on the childhood of the subject to parental background and local-area characteristics.

We used propensity score matching to balance the distribution of observable characteristics in the treatment and control samples. The population consists of individuals whose parental income was £30 000 per year or less, i.e. individuals who would be eligible for an EMA award if they lived in a pilot area and they decided to remain in full-time education. This sample was split into four separate groups: urban women, rural women, urban men and rural men. A propensity score was estimated using a probit model separately for each of these groups. A very rich set of explanatory variables were included as independent variables, including parental characteristics, other household demographics, whether they have an older sibling who continued in education, early childhood experiences and year-11 educational achievement of the young person, in addition to the ward and nearest school information. Estimating the model across each of the four groups separately allows more flexibility in the model estimating the propensity score, and also allowed the impact of the EMA to be estimated separately across each of these four key groups.

The impact of the EMA was estimated using matching combined with kernel smoothing of the counterfactual since this has been shown to perform better than nearest-neighbour matching (Heckman *et al*. 1997a). Standard errors were estimated by bootstrapping (see Horowitz 2001). We now turn to the data used in the analysis.

10.7.4 *Data Sources*

A random sample of young adults in the 10 EMA pilot areas who had just completed compulsory education was drawn from child-benefit records. Eleven control areas were selected, and a random sample of young adults was drawn from these areas, again using the child-benefit records as a sample frame. Two cohorts of young adults were interviewed. The first cohort left compulsory education in the spring of 1999 and the second in the spring of 2000. The first-wave interview was conducted in the autumn after they finished compulsory education and consisted of a face-to-face interview with both the young adult and their parents. Both cohorts were followed up with a telephone interview one, two and three years later. Further waves of interviews are possible.

The information from the first-wave survey contained very detailed information on parental income. This was to enable accurate assessment of which young adults in the pilot and the control areas would be eligible for the EMA were it to be introduced in the area that they lived (i.e. whether their parental income was £30 000 or less in the last tax year). In addition, further background information was collected. For example, the age, education, work status and occupation of the young person's parents, the young person's GCSE results at year 11, whether they had any siblings, and, in the case of those with older siblings, whether those siblings had stayed on in full-time education past the compulsory school-leaving age. The first wave, and the subsequent telephone interviews, all collected detailed information on the young person's activity both at the time of interview and at various points over the previous 12 months.

Information on the respondent's postcode was used to map in ward-level indicators of deprivation, including the participation rates in further and higher education estimated at the ward level in 1998 (i.e. before the EMA policy was in place). In addition, the information on postcodes was used to map in the individual's nearest education providers. This allowed us to control for not only the distance to their nearest year-12 education provider, but also indicators of the quality of their nearest year-11 school (which for the majority of the sample will be the actual school that they attended). This school-level information came from both the performance tables and LEASIS data. We now turn to the results.

10.7.5 *Results*

The overall impact of the EMA on destinations after finishing compulsory education is contained in Table 10.3. This pools together all individuals who would be eligible for the EMA on grounds of family income across both cohorts (for further details of the analysis see Ashworth *et al.* (2002)). Overall in the pilot areas the participation rate in post-compulsory education was 71.0%, compared with 66.3% in the control areas – a difference of 4.7 percentage points. However, it is also known that, on average, the pilot areas are actually slightly more deprived than the control areas.[12] This suggests that this crude difference in education participation rates is likely to be an underestimate of the impact of the policy.

Once propensity score matching is used to control for observable differences and to re-weight to the characteristics of those in the pilot areas, the impact of the EMA on participation in full-time education is actually estimated to be 5.9 percentage points. This is significant at conventional statistical levels (standard error of 1.1 percentage points). The table also shows that those individuals who were drawn into education were split reasonably equally between those who would have entered work (with or without training) and those who would not have been in education or

---

[12]This is unsurprising since the pilot areas were not selected randomly by the government, but instead were chosen on the basis of being areas with relatively low education rates.

Table 10.3. Impact of the EMA on year-12 destination: all eligible young people from cohort 1 and cohort 2 (pilot weights).

	Unmatched sample		Matched sample		
	Pilot	Control	Pilot	Control	Increase
Total					
Full-time education	71.0	66.3	71.3	65.5	5.9
(S.E.)	(0.5)	(0.6)			(1.1)
Work/training	13.8	15.9	13.7	17.1	−3.4
(S.E.)	(0.4)	(0.5)			(0.9)
Other	15.3	17.8	15.0	17.4	−2.4
(S.E.)	(0.4)	(0.5)			(0.9)
Sample size	9 342	5 543			8 923
Population size	54 301	56 484			54 301

Notes. Source: Ashworth *et al.* (2002). Bootstrapped standard errors are reported based on 1000 replications.

work. This is also encouraging since it suggests that the EMA is not only having a positive impact on participation in full-time education, and that it is not exclusively drawing individuals away from work.

A breakdown of the impact of the EMA on participation in full-time education at year 12 by gender and whether the young person resides in an urban or a rural area shows that the impact of the EMA is very similar in both urban and rural areas. This is despite the fact that participation rates in rural areas are, on average, considerably higher than those in urban areas. The results also show that the EMA is, on average, having a larger impact on young men than on young women. For example, in urban areas the EMA is estimated to have increased participation rates in education among young women by 4.8 percentage points compared with 6.9 percentage points among young men. Given that young men have lower participation rates in education to start with, this suggests that the EMA is narrowing this gender gap.

The results presented here have focused on participation rates at year 12, and whether the impact of the EMA is the same for young men and young women and in urban and rural areas. The evaluation has also looked at the impact of the EMA on participation in year 13 (i.e. retention as well as participation) and has found that, if anything, the EMA seems to be having a larger impact at year 13 than at year 12 (although the results are not statistically different). Further analysis will go on to look at educational achievement, participation in HE and some early measures of labour-market outcomes.

10.8 Conclusions

Impact and cost–benefit evaluation of public policy programmes should take a central role in the design of public policy. This is the only way to ensure that scarce public funds are used effectively and for the purpose(s) that they were allocated. It is also the only way of ensuring that in the long run we will accurately learn what works and what does not, allowing governments to offer more beneficial and cost-effective interventions. Evaluation also has the major advantage that it places the public policy debate on scientific rather than ideological grounds; this makes it more likely that effective policies will be preserved while ineffective ones will not continue to be a burden on the public purse.

There are many evaluation methods and not all are suited to every circumstance. Simple randomized experiments may be particularly suitable in some cases where a well-specified question needs to be answered. In the absence of randomization, observational methods such as matching or instrumental variables may often usefully have a role to play. It also possible, however, that for more complex policies we will have to rely on detailed economic modelling of the numerous interactions that will occur as a result of a major policy initiative. This chapter has reviewed some of these issues.

As illustrations of evaluation of important policy initiatives, we briefly describe our approach to the evaluation of two major policy initiatives, Excellence in Cities and the Education Maintenance Allowance. In both cases we find significant impacts of the reform in the desired direction. However, we have not presented here a cost–benefit ratio for either of the policies. Ultimately, the success of an initiative will have to weigh up the benefits *and* the costs. Finally, it should be pointed out that in both these policies there was the opportunity to carry out randomized experiments. In these contexts, this would have been most appropriate and would have strengthened the credibility of the results even more without any ethical implications: in both cases individuals were excluded from the policy at the pilot phase. Excluding individuals randomly is arguably more impartial and fair than relying on the choices of specific individuals. The success of these evaluations should encourage the government to continue on this track and give an even more central role to evaluation by *integrating* the evaluation with the design of the policy itself. This can lead to even more credible evaluation with robust results and a long-lasting influence on policy-making, as well as being of serious scientific value.

Education Policy and the Evidence

By Stephen Machin and Anna Vignoles

11.1 Introduction

The material in this book addresses many of the policy-relevant questions of the day in the economics of education field. The previous chapter illustrated how economists can inform policy makers on the impact and efficacy of specific policy interventions. The evaluation of specific policies in this rigorous manner is still, unfortunately, relatively unusual. This is mainly because the design of policy interventions is often such that it is not amenable to rigorous economic evaluation. Therefore the bulk of the research in the economics of education is concerned with evaluating the production of education and its impact in a natural setting. In these circumstances it is, however, not straightforward to make direct links between empirical findings and the policy process. This concluding chapter discusses the key conclusions from the empirical analysis in the book and how they translate over to the role of education in the public policy debate. The focus is very much on highlighting what one can view as robust findings that are pertinent to policy discussions, as compared with those that are less persuasive or relevant in their applicability to policy.

A lot of discussion on the efficacy (or otherwise) of education policy concentrates on how one might best spend money on different policies. In other words, how one might spend on the margins to generate the largest benefits. There is an increased tendency in the policy world (encouraged by some academics) to argue very strongly that intervention in the early years is the only thing that matters. It is very hard to see that the research field has accumulated enough knowledge on what does and does not work to reach this position. Because of this, the aim in this chapter is more to try and say what we know about what raises performance at different stages of the education process and how the economics of education as a research area can best be used to establish that such conclusions are to be reached.

In Chapter 1, we reviewed the illustrious history of the economics of education, starting with Adam Smith (1776), and moving on through the key texts of Becker (1964), Mincer (1974), Spence (1974), Arrow (1973), Blaug (1976) and others. The reader will note that most of these definitive works date from the 1960s and 1970s.

There have been remarkably few key texts in the economics of education field since that time, with of course notable exceptions. An additional purpose of this chapter is therefore to assess how far the economics of education field has moved on as a research field in the intervening period, highlighting where it has made substantial inroads into key policy issues, and equally identifying where there are still major gaps in our knowledge and understanding.

As with the rest of the book this chapter considers different aspects of the education sequence in turn, beginning with compulsory schooling, turning next to further and higher education, and finally considering what role education plays when children reach adulthood and enter the labour market.

11.2 COMPULSORY SCHOOLING

In the area of compulsory schooling it seems that two main questions and issues dominate. The first, perhaps rather naive, question to the "man in the street" is, do schools matter for pupil attainment? This is the subject addressed in the now voluminous school-effectiveness literature, reviewed briefly in Chapter 3. The answer that emerges is schools do matter, in that a significant proportion of the variance of pupil attainment can be accounted for by school and teacher effects. However, even here, the story is not so simple. Parental influences are very important factors in terms of simple associations between attainment and its possible determinants, although in the best work in this area (what is referred to in Chapter 3 as the "comprehensive" model of school effectiveness) one still identifies a significant contribution from school attended over and above other factors. So schools do matter, but one needs to be careful to place findings into their appropriate context, especially if one wants to make links with policy.

The second key question, given that the school you attend does matter, is how can education policy be best designed to enhance student performance? The answer to this depends on a number of issues. First, as the theoretical literature on public-sector service delivery (Dixit 2002; Besley and Ghatak 2003) makes very clear, one needs to think carefully about what the objectives of decision makers in schools actually are. Schools are not like private-sector firms, where the dominant mode of thinking amongst economists is that the objective is to maximize profits and where clearly defined principal–agent relationships exist. Rather, in the case of schools, there are multiple principals and agents with often conflicting objectives. Of course, there are also multiple outputs from the education system, ranging from improving test scores to engendering a love of learning. Thus, as Besley and Ghatak (2003) state, the critical issue facing policy is to work out the best means by which competition, incentives and accountability can be brought together to enhance educational outcomes in the broadest sense. This leads straight to the second point, namely that evidence (mainly from the US (e.g. Hoxby 2000*b*, 2003*a*, *b*)) shows that increased competition among schools and moves to decentralize school finance can enhance attainment, but can raise inequality because richer parents are better able to take advantage. This, of course, has a productivity cost associated with it, in that more-able pupils from poor economic and social backgrounds fall behind. This is particularly important in the UK context where there is a tail of poor achievers. However, as Chapter 10 showed in the context of discussing economic evaluation methods, the UK situation is not so bleak here because, despite the moves to set up quasi-markets in schooling (Chapter 3), the current government has been introducing initiatives to raise attainment at the bottom end of the education distribution, and these do seem to be working in the desired direction.

From a practical policy perspective the work on school resources, and their potential impact on pupil attainment, is an important area. Distinguishing between what works and what does not is difficult, and again the lines are somewhat hazy here since it is hard to compare the efficacy of different policies. It is more feasible to state what does seem to raise pupil attainment. The literature on school resources is a controversial one, especially the large research area on the effects of class-size reductions. The vast majority of studies on class size find any positive pupil achievement effects to be of small, and often statistically insignificant, magnitudes (and sometimes counter-intuitive negative effects) associated with class-size reductions. However, this can be misleading. The best, although rather context-specific, studies, which adopt a more rigorous experimental approach to evaluating the impact of class-size reductions (Angrist and Lavy 1999; Krueger 1999; Krueger and Whitmore 2001), do find important effects on pupil attainment. Nonetheless, such reductions only offer a "one-off change", the effects do not persist and the changes that do seem to impact on attainment involve relatively large decreases in class size, and so are costly. Moreover, some studies using similar methods do not reach the same conclusions (like Hoxby's (2000*b*) paper based on US data, which finds no class-size effects).

From an anecdotal perspective one can find many statements about how teachers, and the way that teaching is organized, matter for pupil attainment. Whilst some UK evidence exists on this, the US evidence showing important links between year- and grade-specific variations in test-score gains and teacher characteristics (Rivkin *et al.* 2002) does establish that some teachers achieve consistently better achievement scores from the children they teach than do others. As Chapter 4 showed in some detail, there are currently severe problems in attracting high-ability, highly qualified students into teaching. One important policy angle seems to be to try and re-establish teaching as an important and well-respected profession. This requires policy makers to think seriously about improving the total compensation package for teachers, including, of course, their pay relative to other well-respected professions, as well as their non-pecuniary conditions of work. As to the content of teaching, there is again little quantitative evaluation work on this issue in the UK setting. However, Machin and McNally's (2003a) work on the literacy hour shows that improving the way in which teaching is delivered – in their case through the well-structured literacy hour – can provide a cost-effective means of raising pupil attainment.

Of course, knowing what works in education is not sufficient to inform policy. We need to know what works and at what cost, relative to alternative policy options. Yet there remains a deficiency of good cost–benefit evaluations in the field of education. Perhaps the best example of a properly designed evaluation in the UK is the Educational Maintenance Allowance evaluation discussed in Chapter 10, but even this does not include a full cost–benefit analysis and there are relatively few examples in the field as a whole. Simple comparisons of the magnitude of intervention effects (ignoring costs) are more common. Some good examples are in Hoxby's recent book on the impact of greater school choice (Hoxby 2003a, b). For example, in Chapter 1 of that book, Hanushek and Rivkin conclude that greater school competition increases teacher quality, or more specifically reduces the variance in teacher quality. They then attempt a direct comparison of this school competition effect with the class-size impacts arising from the now infamous Tennessee class-size experiment. They suggest that a one standard deviation reduction in class size has an effect on pupil attainment that is of the order of 20–25% as large as a one standard deviation increase in the impact of greater school competition and higher teacher quality. Whilst one might dispute the generalizability of the Hanushek and Rivkin findings, what is clear is the importance of at least being able to compare the magnitude of any intervention impacts that can be found. Only when this is done to a much greater extent in the economics of education will researchers be able to give stronger advice to policy makers as to where they should be spending the marginal dollar or pound of taxpayers' money.

In the 1960s and 1970s, much of the focus in the economics of education was on the interaction between schooling and the labour market (e.g. Becker 1964; Spence 1974). Researchers attempted to explain the relationship between outputs from schooling (skills, qualifications and other attributes) and performance in the labour market (employment, earnings, occupational success). The process of schooling itself was viewed rather as a black box into which inputs were fed (teachers, resources) and outputs emerged (cognitive skills, qualifications). Although there was great concern at that time about whether education actually increased productivity or merely provided an elaborate means of signalling innate ability (Spence 1974; Arrow 1973), what went on in schools was not of paramount interest to economists in the field. In recent decades, however, there has been a distinct shift in the economics of education, with much more emphasis on the education production process itself. As Hoxby (2003a) argues, the analysis of schools and the production of education and learning certainly benefit from the application of economic principles and econometric techniques, and this shift in emphasis in the economics of education is to be welcomed. Certainly, an important contribution of this book has been to review this area of research and present new evidence on the impact of schools (Chapter 3) and teachers (Chapter 4) on pupil performance. Nonetheless, we are left with the conclusion that still more research is needed to enhance our understanding of the interactions between school resourcing levels, incentives, competition and performance. Only then will we be better able to understand why increasing school resourcing levels at the margin does not generally seem to lead to better pupil outcomes. This would seem to be one of the major gaps in our knowledge and understanding that needs to be addressed by researchers working in the economics of education over the next few decades.

11.3 Post-Compulsory Education

The size of the post-compulsory sector of education has changed dramatically in many countries in recent years (see Chapter 2). So has the socioeconomic mix of students. Contrary to what many believed before the expansion of HE, the expansion has actually acted to increase educational inequalities, so that a greater share of HE participants are from well-off backgrounds (see Chapter 6). This means that although poorer students are more likely to go on to HE than they were in the past, the likelihood of them doing so relative to their richer peers is lower than was the case in earlier decades. This is one of the key policy challenges facing many governments, and certainly that of the UK. This matters if, as appears to be the case, one is in a situation where more-able children from less advantageous economic backgrounds are missing out. Moreover, there are longer-term inter-generational consequences: Chapter 6 showed that one consequence of rising educational inequality in the UK is less cross-generation mobility in economic status, driven by the fact that educational outcomes are becoming more closely tied to parental resources than before.

Thus, simply expanding the UK HE system in the 1980s and 1990s did not narrow the socioeconomic gap (Blanden and Machin 2004), a point that should be borne in mind when considering future expansion of the system, especially in the light of government targets aimed at getting 50% of all young people to attend university by 2010. Going beyond the issue of socioeconomic inequality in education, there are two main questions concerning the expansion of HE. First, one needs to address the question of whether more graduates are needed and whether, in the face of an increased supply of graduates, the investment in postsecondary degree acquisition remains one that yields a significant return. This question was considered in Part III of the book, where robust evidence was presented that suggests that the demand for graduates still outstrips the supply and so there is still a significant payoff for possessing HE qualifications. The second policy question is, in the face of continually rising student numbers, where are resources to fund universities to come from? The issue of charging student fees to attend UK universities is an important policy question since many people think students should pay (especially if they are to earn a future payoff), whilst others believe university should be a free good. On this second issue the empirical evidence is much weaker, partly because tuition fees were introduced in the UK in a manner that has prevented any robust evaluation of their impact on student participation. From an economic perspective, the extensive and robust empirical evidence of persistent high private returns to a postsecondary degree would appear to provide justification for greater student contributions in the form of higher fees. However, the critical point here seems to return to the issue of the socioeconomic mix of students who attend university. If fees are charged (that may in future move in the direction of the situation in the US, where there are (often-sizable) differential fees by subject and/or university), then it is absolutely vital that this does not act to reinforce the inequalities already present. We know that the demand for education is generally quite inelastic: increasing the price will not depress demand substantially. However, to the extent that the demand from poorer students is more elastic, fees will provide yet another barrier preventing wider access to HE. Providing proper financial support for highly able students from poor backgrounds has to be built in, even if it is costly. The 2003 proposals, which include exemption for poorer students and an income-contingent loan system to cover fees, do go some way towards this.

The other aspect of post-compulsory education that is highly policy relevant is the issue of academic versus vocational qualifications (Chapter 5). The "problem" of vocational education appears to be a recurring theme the world over. Many countries, like the UK, are concerned with the evident lack of parity between vocational and academic education, as measured by the lower economic returns to vocational qualifications (discussed in Chapters 5 and 7). This is to miss the point. A major reason that employers hold vocational qualifications in lower esteem is because less academically able students choose to go down the vocational route, as discussed in Chapter 5. Education acts at least partially as a screening device, and we have presented evidence that in the UK opting to take the vocational route generally signals less cognitive ability than does taking the academic one. However, there are additional problems within the vocational education system itself, at least in the UK. The proliferation of vocational qualifications in the UK has led to a system little understood by employers, as was discussed extensively in Chapter 8. If employers are not even sure what a person has learned as a result of taking a particular vocational qualification, it is unsurprising that some vocational qualifications have very little or nil economic value. Continuing to develop new vocational qualifications in the fruitless struggle for parity with academic qualifications may actually exacerbate the problem.

Post-compulsory education is generally one of the most researched areas in the economics of education. As discussed in the next section, the field has developed increasingly robust methods to evaluate the impact of post-compulsory education on labour-market participation and performance (Card 1999), and has in recent years focused much more on the important question of who gets what type of education. Allowing for the fact that education is a choice, and that students of differing abilities and inclinations make different schooling decisions, has been one of the major methodological developments in the economics of education field in the last 20 years. Using some of these methodological tools, in this book we have been able to present robust empirical evidence on schooling choices (Chapter 5), socioeconomic inequalities in education (Chapter 6), and the interaction between post-compulsory schooling and the labour market (Chapters 7–9). Nonetheless, there remain gaps in our knowledge. There remain large, and in the recent period of rising income inequality we suggest increasing, gaps in attainment between rich and poor children. There is extensive evidence on factors that may contribute to this gap at various stages of children's lives. Nonetheless, we are still some way from being able to show empirically which intervention and what time of intervention could reduce this gap most cost effectively. For example, we may know that HE benefits students enormously in the labour market, yielding a high private rate of return that may justify (on equity grounds) tuition fees for this type of post-compulsory education. We also know that the socioeconomic gap in HE participation is large and has been growing in the UK. However, we cannot say for sure whether introducing tuition fees is going to exacerbate this already large socioeconomic gap, or whether the barriers faced by poorer children, and the choices they make as a result, occur much earlier in the education system.

11.4 EDUCATION AND THE LABOUR MARKET

The focus so far has been on policy discussion about people currently in, or who in future will enter, the education system. What of people who have left the system? Or who may return at a later age? As Chapters 8 and 9 made clear, the critical issue here is how well does the education system meet the needs of the labour market and, from a policy angle, what can be done if it does not meet labour-market needs.

As has already been noted, what is evident from changes over time is that employer demand for graduates is not letting up. Despite rapid increases in the supply of graduates, facilitated by the expansion of the HE system, wage differentials between graduates and non-graduates have not fallen through time (Chapter 9). This implies that skill demand continues to rise. The other side of this is that, in rapidly evolving modern workplaces, there are fewer places for those without educational qualifications.

This is one of the key policy issues of our time. It is compounded in some countries (notably the UK and US), where the education and skill distribution has a significant proportion (as many as one in five) of adults with basic skills problems (Chapter 2). Add to this the fact that lifelong learning has very little directly measurable labour-market value (at least in the UK labour market (Chapter 7)) and it would appear that "getting it right" in the compulsory schooling phase is critically important. We also know that less able UK students who go down the vocational route at age 16 often end up with qualifications that do not benefit them in the labour market (Chapter 7). Whilst improving the content and marketability of these vocational qualifications is one strategy, as is improving the ability to switch between vocational and academic qualification routes, the underlying message for policy makers is that as many as possible of our 16 year olds should have attained good basic skills and the cognitive ability to pursue a high-value qualification by the age of 16. If we continue to let students leave the education system at age 16 with very poor basic skills, these individuals will be disadvantaged for life. Going back and trying to repair the damage in mid-career is unlikely to help them, at least from an economic perspective.

The interaction between education and the labour market lies at the heart of the field of the economics of education. As noted in our introductory comments, our understanding of these interactions, at least from a theoretical perspective, continues to be based largely on the theory of human capital (Becker 1964). For instance, in this book the analysis in Chapter 7 on the rate of return to different types of schooling is rooted in human-capital theory. Certainly other theoretical perspectives may help us understand some of the problems in this area. For example, the work of Spence (1974) on the signalling value of education can help us understand why lower-level vocational qualifications do not substantially enhance workers' earnings, given the perception by firms that they are largely taken by lower-ability individuals. Nonetheless, human-capital theory has proved remarkably robust as a framework within which to evaluate the interaction between education and the labour market. Add to this the fact that there have been substantial developments in the empirical techniques used to analyse the labour-market value of schooling (Card 2001), and we would argue that this is the area with the fewest gaps in our understanding and knowledge. This does not mean that further work in this area is not needed. In particular, we need much more empirical evidence on the social rates of return to schooling, as distinct from the private rates or return, particularly given that some of the costs of post-compulsory schooling are being shifted from the state to the individual.

11.5 CLOSING REMARKS

This book aims to paint a contemporary picture of research in the economics of education and education policy. It is evident from the contents of the chapters above that this is a thriving research field, which looks at policy-relevant questions that matter for people in society. The approach taken by researchers who have contributed to this book, all of whom are members of the Centre for the Economics of Education, is that one needs to take first-order principles from the economics of education and confront them with data using a rigorous and thorough methodological approach. The book highlights where progress in the field has been most rapid, e.g. in the development of methods of analysing the interactions between education and the labour market, and where much more remains to be done, such as in improved cost–benefit analyses of policies designed to improve the production of education. The fact that developments on the cost–benefit front have been markedly slow in this field is not due to the laziness of researchers, however. Unlike in other fields, such as health economics, data on educational and labour-market outcomes have been far more readily available than data on the myriad inputs that go into the education process, such as teachers, books, infrastructure, peer groups and parenting. This is slowly being rectified in the UK at least, with the construction of superior datasets. Therefore, in the next 5–10 years, this is where one would expect to see the most progress being made, in terms of empirical analysis.

Another area where there is much more work to do is in terms of our theoretical understanding in the economics of education. Certainly we are some way from being able to fully understand and model the education production process, for example. As we have noted elsewhere in the book, much of the progress in the economics of education field in the last few decades has been in terms of the tools needed to undertake robust empirical analyses, rather than the development of new theories. The economics of education has certainly borrowed liberally a range of theoretical concepts and ideas from other fields of research, including education, psychology and industrial relations. Theoretical modelling on certain issues is also proceeding apace. For example, the theoretical work on the impact of school choice (Hoxby 2003a) or the relationship between education and inequality (Benabou 2000; Fernández and Rogerson 1996, 1998). Nonetheless, the next decades should see better application of economic thinking and economic modelling to a range of educational issues, particularly perhaps in the area of education production.

So how do we assess the economics of education research field as a whole, in terms of its usefulness for policy-making? Chapter 10 illustrates what can be done, detailing as it does effective and robust evaluations of particular education policies. For example, the evaluation of the Educational Maintenance Allowance (EMA) scheme ("paying children to stay on at school"), whilst by no means perfect, certainly provides a standard to aim for, in terms of robust and policy-applicable analysis. The reason that the EMA evaluation was so effective, however, is twofold. The first reason for its success is that in this particular policy area economists already had the necessary tools with which to undertake the analysis. The more important reason, however, was that policy makers specifically designed the EMA intervention in such a way as to make it amenable to rigorous quantitative evaluation. For example, it was not rolled out nationally and a serious attempt was made to obtain proper control groups. This would seem to be the future of effective policy-making in education. Policies need to be drawn up in such a way that robust quantitative evaluation is possible, with much emphasis on the need to construct a proper control, and to fully document the inputs and outputs associated with the policy intervention. In the right circumstances, randomization can be an attractive, and conceptually appealing, possibility here and one that government should be more open to pursue. However, we would not go as far as some in the US who have argued that we require random experiments to be conducted to test any educational policy that is to be introduced. There are instances where random experiments are neither feasible nor ethical. Nonetheless, if one wishes to see a step improvement in the quality of education policy-making, much more attention must be directed towards the design of such policies and their potential to be accurately and precisely evaluated. Those working in the field of the economics of education have, of course, an important role to play in this process.

References

Aaronson, D., L. Barrow and W. Sander. 2002. Teacher and student achievement in the Chicago public high schools. Federal Reserve Bank of Chicago, Working Paper 2002-28.

Acemoglu, D. 1997. Technology, unemployment and efficiency. *European Economic Review* 41:525–533.

Acemoglu, D. 1998. Why do new technologies complement skills? Directed technical change and wage inequality. *Quarterly Journal of Economics* 113:1055–1089.

Acemoglu, D. and J. D. Angrist. 2000. How large are the social returns to education? Evidence from compulsory schooling laws. In *NBER Macroeconomics Annual.*

Adnett, N. and P. Davies. 2002. *Markets for Schooling.* London: Routledge.

Andrews, M. and S. Bradley. 1997. Modelling the transition from school and the demand for training in the United Kingdom. *Economica* 64:387–413.

Angrist, J. and A. Krueger. 1999. Empirical strategies in labor economics. In *The handbook of labor economics* (ed. O. Ashenfelter and D. Card), Chapter 23. Amsterdam: Elsevier Science.

Angrist, J. and V. Lavy. 1999. Using Maimonides' rule to estimate the effect of class size on scholastic achievement. *Quarterly Journal of Economics* 114:533–575.

Arrow, K. 1973. Higher education as a filter. *Journal of Public Economics* 2:193–216.

Ashenfelter, O. 1978. Estimating the effect of training programs on earnings. *Review of Economics and Statistics* 60:47–57.

Ashton, D., F. Green, D. James and J. Sung. 1999. *Education and training for development in East Asia. The political economy of skill formation in East Asian newly industrialised economies.* London: Routledge.

Ashworth, J. 1988. A waste of resources? Social rates of return to higher education in the 1990s. *Education Economics* 6:27–44.

Ashworth, K., J. Hardman, Y. Hartfree, S. Maguire, S. Middleton, D. Smith, L. Dearden, C. Emmerson, C. Frayne and C. Meghir. 2002. *Education maintenance allowance: the first two years a quantitative evaluation.* Department for Education and Skills, Research Report 352. London: DfES.

Atkins, M., J. Beattie and W. Dockrell. 1993. Assessment issues in higher education. Employment Department Report, Sheffield.

Atkinson, J., L. Giles and N. Meager. 1996. Employers, recruitment and the unemployed. Institute for Employment Studies, Report 325.

Barlett, W. 1993. Quasi-markets and education reform. In *Quasi-markets and social policy* (ed. J. LeGrand, W. Barlett and W. McMilland), Chapter 6. London: Macmillan.

Barro, R. and J. Lee. 1993. International comparisons of educational attainment. National Bureau of Economic Research, Working Paper 4349.

Barro, R. and J. Lee. 2001. International data on educational attainment: updates and implications. *Oxford Economic Papers* 53:541–563.

Battu, H., C. Belfield and P. Sloane. 1999. Overeducation among graduates: a cohort view. *Education Economics* 7:21–38.

Bauer, T., P. Dross and J. Haisken-DeNew. 2002. Sheepskin effects in Japan. Centre for Economic Policy Research, Discussion Paper 3609.

Becker, G. 1964. *Human capital: a theoretical analysis with special reference to education.* New York: Columbia University Press.

Becker. G. 1967. *Human capital and the personal distribution of income.* Ann Arbor, MI: University of Michigan Press.

Becker, G. and N. Tomes. 1986. Human capital and the rise and fall of families. *Journal of Labor Economics* 107:123–150.

Bee, M. and P. Dolton. 1985. Educational production in independent secondary schools. *Bulletin of Economic Research* 37:27–40.

Belman, D. and J. Heywood. 1991. Sheepskin effects in the returns to education: an examination of women and minorities. *Review of Economics and Statistics* 73(4):720–728.

Benabou, R. 2000. Unequal societies: income distribution and the social contract. *American Economic Review* 90(1):96–129.

Bennell, P. 1996. Using and abusing rates of return: a critique of the World Bank's 1995 education review. *International Journal of Education Development* 16:235–248.

Ben-Porath, Y. 1967. The production of human capital and the life-cycle of earnings. *Journal of Political Economy* 75:352–356.

Besley, T. and M. Ghatak. 2003. Incentives, choice, and accountability in the provision of public services. *Oxford Review of Economic Policy* 19:235–249.

Besley, T. and M. Ghatak. Forthcoming. Incentives and organisational design for motivated agents. *American Economic Review.*

Betts, J. 1996. What do students know about wages? Evidence from a survey of undergraduates. *Journal of Human Resources* 31:27–56.

Black, S. 1999. Do better schools matter? Parental valuation of elementary education. *Quarterly Journal of Economics* 114:578–599.

Blacklock, W. 2003. The regulation of qualifications. Unpublished EdD thesis, Institute of Education, London.

Blanden, J. and S. Machin. 2004. Educational inequality and the expansion of UK higher education. *Scottish Journal of Political Economy* (Special Issue on the Economics of Education) 54:230–249.

Blanden, J., A. Goodman, P. Gregg and S. Machin. 2004. Changes in intergenerational mobility in Britain. In *Generational income mobility in North America and Europe* (ed. M. Corak). Cambridge University Press.

Blanden, J., P. Gregg and S. Machin. Forthcoming. Changes in educational inequality. Centre for the Economics of Education, Discussion Paper.

Blatchford, P., H. Goldstein, C. Martin and W. Browne. 2002. A study of class size effects in English school reception year classes. *British Educational Research Journal* 28:171–187.

Blaug, M. 1972. *An introduction to the economics of education.* Harmondsworth: Penguin.

Blaug, M. 1976. The empirical status of human capital theory: a slightly jaundiced survey. *Journal of Economic Literature* 14:827–855.

Blundell, R. and J. Powell. 2003. Endogeneity in nonparametric and semiparametric regression models. In *Advances in economics and econometrics* (ed. M. Dewatripont, L. Hansen and S. Turnovsky). Cambridge University Press.

Blundell, R., L. Dearden, A. Goodman and H. Reed. 2000. The returns to higher education in Britain: evidence from a British cohort. *The Economic Journal* 110:F82–F99.

Blundell, R., L. Dearden and B. Sianesi. Forthcoming. Estimating the returns to education: models, methods and results. *Journal of the Royal Statistical Society* A.

Blundell, R., M. Dias, C. Meghir and J. Van Reenen. 2004. Evaluating the employment impact of a mandatory job search program. *Journal of the European Economic Association* 2:569–606.

Bowles, S. and H. Gintis. 1976. *Schooling in capitalist America: educational reform and the contradictions of economic life*. New York: Basic Books.

Bradley, S. and J. Taylor. 1998. The effect of school size on exam performance in secondary schools. *Oxford Bulletin of Economics and Statistics* 60:291–325.

Bradley, S. and J. Taylor. 2002. The effect of the quasi-market on the efficiency–equity trade-off in the secondary school sector. *Bulletin of Economic Research* 54:295–314.

Bradley, S., G. Johnes and J. Millington. 2001. School choice, competition and the efficiency of secondary schools in England. *European Journal of Operational Research* 135:527–544.

Callender, C. 2003. Attitudes to debt: school leavers' and further education students' attitudes to debt and their impact on participation in higher education. Report commissioned by Universities UK and the Higher Education Funding Council.

Cameron, S. and J. Heckman. 1998. Life cycle schooling and dynamic selection bias: models and evidence for five cohorts of American males. *Journal of Political Economy* 106:262–333.

Cameron, S. and C. Taber. 2000. Borrowing constraints and the returns to schooling. National Bureau of Economic Research, Working Paper 7761.

Card, D. 1999. The causal effect of education on earnings. In *Handbook of labor economics* (ed. O. Ashenfelter and D. Card), Volume 3. Amsterdam: North-Holland.

Card, D. 2001. Estimating the returns to schooling: progress on some persistent econometric problems. *Econometrica* 69:1127–1160.

Card, D. and T. Lemieux. 2001. Can falling supply explain the rising return to college for younger men? A cohort-based analysis. *Quarterly Journal of Economics* 116:705–746.

Carneiro, P., K. Hansen and J. Heckman. 2003. Estimating distributions of treatment effects with an application to the returns to schooling and measurement of the effects of uncertainty on college choice. National Bureau of Economic Research, Working Paper 9546.

Chevalier, A. 2003. Class size effects in English test achievement: evidence from PISA. Institute for the Study of Social Change, University College Dublin, mimeo.

Chevalier, A. and G. Conlon. 2003. Does it pay to attend a prestigious university? Centre for the Economics of Education, Discussion Paper 33. (Also: IZA, Discussion Paper 848.)

Chevalier, A., P. Dolton and S. McIntosh. 2001. Recruiting and retaining teachers in the UK: an analysis of graduate occupation choice from the 1960s to the 1990s. Centre for the Economics of Education, London School of Economics mimeo.

Chevalier, A., P. Dolton and S. McIntosh. 2002. The job satisfaction of UK teachers. Centre for the Economics of Education, London School of Economics mimeo.

Chevalier, A., C. Harmon, I. Walker and Y. Zhu. 2004. Does education raise productivity, or just reflect it? *The Economic Journal* 114:F499–F517.

Chubb, J. and T. Moe. 1990. *Politics, markets and America's schools.* Washington, DC: The Brookings Institution.

Ciccone, A. and G. Peri. 2000. Human capital and externalities in cities. Centre for Economic Policy Research, Discussion Paper 2599.

CIPD. 1999, 2001. *Recruitment survey.* London: Chartered Institute of Personnel and Development.

Clark, D. 2002. The impact of local labour market conditions on participation in further education in England. IZA (Institute for the Study of Labor), Discussion Paper 550.

Clark, M. and D. Jaeger. 2002. Natives, the foreign-born and high school equivalents: new evidence on the returns to the GED. IZA, Discussion Paper 477.

Cohn, E. and J. T. Addison. 1998. The economic returns to lifelong learning. *Education Economics* 6:309–346.

Confederation of British Industry (CBI). 1989. *Towards a skills revolution.* London: CBI.

Confederation of British Industry (CBI). 1994. *Quality assessed: the CBI review of NVQs and SVQs.* London: CBI.

Conlon, G. 2001. The differential in the rate of return to academic and vocational qualifications in the United Kingdom. Centre for the Economics of Education, Discussion Paper 11.

Coopers and Lybrand. 1998. Reducing the bureaucratic burden on teachers. Department for Education and Employment, Research Report 41.

Corcoran, S., W. Evans and R. Schwab. 2004. Women, the labor market, and the declining relative quality of teachers. *Journal of Policy Analysis and Management* 23:449–470.

Court, G., S. Morris, B. Reilly and M. Williams. 1995. Teachers: recruitment and the labour market. Institute for Employment Studies, Report 292.

Croll, P. and N. Hastings. 1996. Teachers matter. In *Effective primary teaching: research based classroom strategies* (ed. P. Croll and N. Hastings). London: David Fulton.

Croll, P. and D. Moses. 1985. *One in five: the assessment and incidence of special educational needs.* London: Routledge and Kegan Paul.

Cronbach, L. 1990. *Essentials of psychological testing.* New York: Harper and Row.

Dale, S. and A. Krueger. 1999. Estimating the payoff to attending a more selective college: an application of selection on observables and unobservables. National Bureau of Economic Research, Working Paper 7322.

Dearden, L. 1999*a*. The effects of families and ability on men's education and earnings in Britain. *Labour Economics* 6:551–567.

Dearden, L. 1999*b*. Qualifications and earnings in Britain: how reliable are conventional OLS estimates of the returns to education? Institute for Fiscal Studies, Working Paper 99/7.

Dearden, L., S. Mcintosh, M. Myck and A. Vignoles. 2002*a*. The returns to academic and vocational qualifications in Britain. *Bulletin of Economic Research* 54:249–274.

Dearden, L., J. Ferri and C. Meghir. 2002*b*. The effect of school quality on educational attainment and wages. *The Review of Economics and Statistics* 84:1–20.

Dearden, L., E. Fitzsimmons and A. Goodman. 2004. An analysis of the higher education reforms. Institute for Fiscal Studies, Briefing Note 45.

de la Fuente, A. 2003. Human capital in a global and knowledge-based economy. Phase II: assessment at the EU country level. Report of the European Commission – Employment and Social Affairs DG, Brussels.

Denny, K., C. Harmon and S. Redmond. 2000. Functional literacy, educational attainment and earnings: evidence from the International Adult Literacy Survey. Institute for Fiscal Studies, Working Paper 00/09.

Denny, K., C. Harmon and V. O'Sullivan. 2003. Functional literacy, educational attainment and earnings: a multi-country comparison. University College Dublin, Working Paper WP03/19.

Department for Education and Employment (DfEE). 2000. *Research into teacher effectiveness*. DfEE: London.

Department for Education and Skills (DfES). 2001. Education maintenance allowance: the first two years. A quantitative evaluation. DfES Research Report 352.

Dickerson, A. P. and F. Green. 2004. The growth and valuation of computing and other generic skills. *Oxford Economic Papers* 56(3):371–406.

DiNardo, J. and J. Tobias. 2001. Nonparametric density and regression estimation. *Journal of Economic Perspectives* 15 (Fall):11–28.

Dixit, A. 1997. Power of incentives in public versus private organisations. *American Economic Review, Papers and Proceedings* 87:378–382.

Dixit, A. 2002. Incentives and organizations in the public sector. *Journal of Human Resources* 37:696–727.

Dolton, P. 1990. The economics of UK teacher supply: the graduate's decision. *The Economic Journal* 100:91–104.

Dolton, P. 2002. Improving educational quality: how best to evaluate our schools? A discussion. In *Education in the 21st Century, 47th Economic Conference, Boston Federal Reserve Bank*.

Dolton, P. and G. Makepeace. 1993. Female labour force participation and the choice of occupation: the supply of teachers. *European Economic Review* 37:1393–1411.

Dolton, P. and D. Newson. 2003. The relationship between teacher turnover and school performance. *London Review of Education* 1(2):132–140.

Dolton, P. and W. van der Klaauw. 1995. Leaving teaching in the UK: a duration analysis. *The Economic Journal* 105:431–444.

Dolton, P. and A. Vignoles. 1997. Overeducation duration: how long did graduates in the 1980s take to get a graduate job? University of Newcastle upon Tyne, Working Paper.

Dolton, P. and A. Vignoles. 2000a. The incidence and effects of overeducation in the UK graduate labour market. *Economics of Education Review* 19:179–198.

Dolton, P. and A. Vignoles. 2000b. The pay-off to mathematics A level. In *The maths we need now: demands deficits and remedies* (ed. C. Tikly and A. Wolf). London: Institute of Education.

Dolton, P., G. Makepeace and W. van der Klaauw. 1989. Occupational choice and earnings determination: the role of sample selection and non-pecuniary factors. *Oxford Economic Papers* 41:573–594.

Dolton, P., S. McIntosh and A. Chevalier. 2003a. *Teacher pay and performance: a review of the literature*. Bedford Way Papers. London: Institute of Education.

Dolton, P., A. Tremayne and T.-P. Chung. 2003b. Teacher supply and the economic cycle. Report to the OECD.

Dominitz, J. and C. Manski. 1996. Eliciting student expectations of the returns to schooling. *Journal of Human Resources* 31:1–26.

Dore, R. 1997. *The diploma disease: education, qualification and development*, 2nd edn. London: Institute of Education.

Dustmann, C., N. Rajah and A. van Soest. 2003. Class size, education and wages. *The Economic Journal* 113:F99–F120.

Erikson, R. and J. Goldthorpe. 1992. *The constant flux: a study of class mobility in industrial societies.* Oxford University Press.

Eurydice. 2002. *The teaching profession in Europe: supply and demand.* Brussels: Eurydice Network.

Feinstein, L. 2003. Inequality in the early cognitive development of British children in the 1970 cohort. *Economica* 70:73–97.

Feinstein, L. and J. Symons. 1999. Attainment in secondary schools. *Oxford Economic Papers* 51:300–321.

Felstead, A., D. Gallie and F. Green. 2002. *Work skills in Britain 1986–2001.* London: Department for Education and Skills.

Fernandez, R. and R. Rogerson. 1995. On the political economy of education subsidies. *Review of Economic Studies* 62:249–262.

Fernandez, R. and R. Rogerson. 1996. Income distribution, communities, and the quality of public education. *The Quarterly Journal of Economics* 111(1):135–164.

Fernandez, R. and R. Rogerson. 1998. Public education and income distribution: a dynamic quantitative evaluation of education-finance reform. *The American Economic Review* 88(4):813–833.

Figlio, D. 1997. Teacher salaries and teacher quality. *Economics Letters* 55:267–271.

Fitzgibbon, C. 1991. Multilevel modelling in an indicator system. In *Schools, classrooms and pupils: international studies from a multilevel perspective* (ed. S. Raudenbush and J. Willms). Academic Press.

Freeman, R. 1976. *The overeducated American.* Academic Press.

Galindo-Rueda, F. and A. Vignoles. 2003. Class-ridden or meritocratic? An economic analysis of recent changes in Britain. Centre for the Economics of Education (CEE), Discussion Paper 32.

Galindo-Rueda, F. and A. Vignoles. Forthcoming. The declining relative importance of ability in predicting educational attainment. *Journal of Human Resources.*

Galton, F. 1886. Regression towards mediocrity in hereditary stature. *Journal of the Anthropological Institute of Great Britain and Ireland* 15:246–263.

Galton, M. and B. Simon. 1980. *Progress and performance in the primary classroom.* London: Routledge and Kegan Paul.

Garen, J. 1984. The returns to schooling: a selectivity bias approach with a continuous choice variable. *Econometrica* 52:1199–1218.

Gibbons, S. 2002. Geography, resources and primary school performance. Centre for the Economics of Education, Discussion Paper 25.

Gibbons, S. and S. Machin. 2003. Valuing English primary schools. *Journal of Urban Economics* 53:197–219.

Gibbons, S. and S. Machin. 2004. Paying for primary schools: supply constraints, school popularity or congestion? Centre for the Economics of Education, Discussion Paper 42.

Gifford, B. (ed.). 1989. *Test policy and the politics of opportunity allocation: the workplace and the law.* Kluwer.

Gipps, C. and G. Stobart. 1997. *Assessment: a teacher's guide to the issues.* London: Hodder and Stoughton.

Glennerster, H. 1991. Quasi-markets for education? *The Economic Journal* 101:1268–1276.

Glennerster, H. 2002. United Kingdom education 1997–2001. *Oxford Review of Economic Policy* 18(2):120–136.

Goldstein, H. 1997*a*. Value added tables: the less than holy grail. *Managing Schools Today* 6:18–19.

Goldstein, H. 1997*b*. Methods in school effectiveness research. *School Effectiveness and School Improvement* 8:369–395.

Goos, M. and A. Manning. 2003. Lousy and lovely jobs: the rising polarisation of work in Britain. Centre for Economic Performance, Discussion Paper 604.

Gorard, S., G. Rees and J. Salisbury. 2001. Investigating the patterns of differential attainment of boys and girls at school. *British Educational Research Journal* 27:125–139.

Gosling, A., S. Machin and C. Meghir. 2000. The changing distribution of male wages. *Review of Economic Studies* 67:635–66.

Gospel, H., P. Ryan and H. Steedman. 1998. Apprenticeship: a strategy for growth. Centre for Economic Performance, LSE, Special Report 11.

Graddy, K. and M. Stevens. 2003. The impact of school inputs on students performance: an empirical study of private schools in the UK. University of Oxford, Discussion Paper in Economics 146.

Grawe, N. 2003. Lifecycle bias in the estimation of intergenerational income mobility. Statistics Canada Analytical Studies Working Paper Series, no. 207.

Green, F. 2003. The problem of British education policy as economic policy. In *Industrial and labour market policy and performance* (ed. D. Coffey and C. Thornley). London: Routledge.

Green, F. and S. McIntosh. 2002. Is there a genuine underutilisation of skills amongst the over-qualified? SKOPE, Discussion Paper 30.

Green, F., S. McIntosh and A. Vignoles. 2002. The utilisation of education and skills: evidence from Britain. *The Manchester School* 70:792–811.

Greenaway, D. and M. Haynes. 2003. Funding higher education in the UK: the role of fees and loans. *The Economic Journal* 113:F150–F167.

Gregg, P., S. Harkness and S. Machin. 1999. Poor kids: child poverty in Britain, 1966–96. *Fiscal Studies* 20:163–187.

Griliches, Z. 1977. Estimating the returns to schooling: some econometric problems. *Econometrica* 45:1–22.

Griliches, Z. 1979. Sibling models and data in economics: beginnings of a survey. *Journal of Political Economy* 87:S37–S65.

Groot, W. and H. Maassen van den Brink. 2000. Overeducation in the labor market: a meta-analysis. *Economics of Education Review* 19:149–158.

Hanushek, E. 2003. The failure of input-based schooling policies. *The Economic Journal* 103:F64–F98.

Hanushek, E. and D. Kimko. 2001. Schooling, labor-force quality and the growth of nations. *American Economic Review* 90:1184–1208.

Hanushek, E. and R. Pace. 1993. Who chooses to teach (and why)? *Economics of Education Review* 14:101–117.

Harmon, C. and I. Walker. 1995. Estimates of the economic return to schooling for the UK. *American Economic Review* 85:1278–1286.

Harmon, C. and I. Walker. 2000. The returns to the quantity and quality of education: evidence for men in England and Wales. *Economica* 67:19–35.

Harmon, C., I. Walker and N. Westergaard. 2001. Returns to education in Europe. In *Returns to education in Europe: a cross-country analysis of the returns to education* (ed. C. Harmon, I. Walker *et al.*), pp. 13–21. Edward Elgar.

Harmon, C., H. Oosterbeek and I. Walker. 2002. The returns to education: a review of evidence, issues and deficiencies in the literature. *Journal of Economic Surveys* 17:115–155.

Hartog, J. 2000. Overeducation and earnings: where are we, where should we go? *Economics of Education Review* 19:131–147.

Harvey, L. 1994. *Employer satisfaction*. Birmingham: Quality in Higher Education Project.

Haveman, R. and B. Wolfe. 1994. *Succeeding generations: on the effects of investments in children*. New York: Russell Sage Foundation.

Heckman, J. and B. Honoré. 1990. The empirical content of the Roy model. *Econometrica* 58:1121–1149.

Heckman, J. and R. Robb. 1985*a*. Alternative methods for evaluating the impact of interventions. In *Longitudinal analysis of labour market data*. New York: Wiley.

Heckman, J. and R. Robb. 1985*b*. Using longitudinal data to estimate age, period and cohort effects in earnings equations. In *Cohort analysis in social research beyond the identification problem* (ed. W. Mason and S. Feinberg). Springer.

Heckman, J., H. Ichimura and P. Todd. 1997*a*. Matching as an econometric evaluation estimator. *Review of Economic Studies* 65:261–294.

Heckman, J., J. Smith and N. Clements. 1997*b*. Making the most out of programme evaluations and social experiments: accounting for heterogeneity in programme impacts. *The Review of Economic Studies* (Special Issue: Evaluation of Training and Other Social Programmes) 64:487–535.

Heckman, J., R. LaLonde and J. Smith. 1999. The economics and econometrics of active labor market programs. In *Handbook of labor economics* (ed. O. Ashenfelter and D. Card), Vol. 3A. Amsterdam: North-Holland.

Heckman, J., L. Lochner and P. Todd. 2003. Fifty years of mincer earnings regressions. National Bureau of Economic Research, Working Paper w9732.

Higher Education Policy Institute. 2003. Graduate supply and demand: a consideration of the evidence. Report, available at http://www.hepi.ac.uk/.

Hillage, J., J. Regan, J. Dickson and K. Mcloughlin. 2002. Employers skill survey 2002. Department for Education and Skills, Research Report 372.

Hirschman, A. 1970. *Exit, voice and loyalty*. Cambridge, MA: Harvard University Press.

HM Treasury. 2000. *Financial statement and budget report: March 2000* (Hc346). London: The Stationery Office.

HM Treasury. 2002. *Spending review 2002: July 2002* (Cm5570). London: The Stationery Office.

Hodgson, A. and K. Spours. 2003. *Beyond A levels: curriculum 2000 and the reform of 14–19 qualifications*. London: Kogan Page.

Holmstrom, B. and P. Milgrom. 1991. Multi-tasking principal–agent analyses: linear contracts, asset ownership and job design. *Journal of Law, Economics and Organisation* 7:24–52.

Horowitz, J. 2001. The bootstrap. In *Handbook of econometrics* (ed. J. Heckman and E. Leamer), Chapter 52. Amsterdam: North-Holland.

Hoxby, C. 2000*a*. Does competition among public schools benefit students and taxpayers? *American Economic Review* 90:1209–1238.

Hoxby, C. 2000*b*. The effects of class size on student achievement: new evidence from population variation. *Quarterly Journal of Economics* 115:1239–1285.

Hoxby, C. 2003*a*. *The economics of school choice*. University of Chicago Press.

Hoxby, C. 2003*b*. School choice and school competition: evidence from the United States. *Swedish Economic Policy Review* 10:9–66.

Hoyles, C., A. Wolf, S. Molyneux and P. Kent. 2002. *Mathematical skills in the workplace.* London: Science, Technology and Mathematics Council.

Iacovou, M. 2002. Class size in the early years: is smaller really better. *Education Economics* 10:261–291.

Illich, I. 1971. *Deschooling society.* New York: Harper and Row.

Imbens, G. and J. Angrist. 1994. Identification and estimation of local average treatment effects. *Econometrica* 62:467–476.

Inner London Education Authority Research and Statistics Branch. 1986. *The junior school project. Part C: understanding school effectiveness.* London: ILEA.

Institute of Directors (IoD). 1994. *Performance and potential: education and training for a market economy.* London: IoD.

Institute of Directors (IoD). 2003. *The government's plans for the 14–19 phase of education: an assessment.* London: IoD.

Jackson, M., J. Goldthorpe and C. Mills. Forthcoming. Education, employers and class mobility. *Research in Social Stratification And Mobility.*

Jaeger, D. and M. Page. 1996. Degrees matter: new evidence on sheepskin effects in the returns to education. *Review of Economics and Statistics* 78:733–740.

Jenkins, A. 2001. Companies' use of psychometric testing and the changing demand for skills: a review of the literature. Centre for the Economics of Education, Discussion Paper 12.

Jenkins, A. and A. Wolf. 2002. Why do employers use selection tests? Evidence from British workplaces. Centre for the Economics of Education, Discussion Paper 27.

Jenkins, A., A. Vignoles, A. Wolf and F. Galindo-Rueda. 2003. Determinants and effects of lifelong learning. *Applied Economics* 35:1711–1721.

Jesson, D. 2000. The comparative evaluation of GCSE value-added performance by type of school and LEA. University of York, Discussion Paper 00/52.

Jesson, D. and J. Gray. 1991. Slants on slopes: using multilevel models to investigate differential school effectiveness and its impact on school examination results. *School Effectiveness and School Improvement* 2:230–271.

Kane, T. J. and D. O. Staiger. 2002. Volatility in school test scores: implications for test-based accountability systems. In *Brookings papers on education policy* (ed. D. Ravitch). Washington, DC: Brookings Institution.

Kingdon, M. and G. Stobart. 1998. *GCSE examined.* London: The Falmer Press.

Krueger, A. 1999. Experimental estimates of education production functions. *Quarterly Journal of Economics* 114:497–532.

Krueger, A. and D. Whitmore. 2001. The effect of attending a small class in the early grades on college-test taking and middle school test results: evidence from project star. *The Economic Journal* 111:34–63.

Lakdawalla, D. 2001. The declining quality of teachers. National Bureau of Economic Research, Working Paper 8263.

Lavy, V. 2002. Evaluating the effect of teacher's group performance incentives on pupil's achievements. *Journal of Political Economy* 110:1286–1317.

Layard, R. and G. Psacharopoulos. 1974. The screening hypothesis and the returns to education. *Journal of Political Economy* 82:985–998.

Lazear, E. 2001. Educational production. *Quarterly Journal of Economics* 116:777–804.

Lazear, E. 2003. Teacher incentives. *Swedish Economic Policy Review* 10:179–214.

Levacic, R. 2002. The effectiveness of specialist schools in England: rhetoric and reality. In *British Educational Research Association Annual Conference, University of Exeter.*

Little, A. (ed.). 1997. The diploma disease twenty years on. *Assessment in Education* (Special Issue) 4:5–22.

Luyten, H. 2003. The size of school effects compared to teacher effects: an overview of the research literature. *School Effectiveness and School Improvement* 14:31–52.

Machin, S. 1999. Wage inequality in the 1970s, 1980s and 1990s. In *The state of working Britain* (ed. P. Gregg and J. Wadsworth). Manchester University Press.

Machin, S. 2003. Wage inequality since 1975. In *The labour market under New Labour* (ed. R. Dickens, P. Gregg and J. Wadsworth). MacMillan.

Machin, S. and S. McNally. 2003*a*. The literacy hour. Centre for the Economics of Education mimeo.

Machin, S. and S. McNally. 2003*b*. Gender and educational attainment. Centre for the Economics of Education mimeo.

Machin, S. and J. Van Reenen. 1998. Technology and changes in skill structure: evidence from seven OECD countries. *Quarterly Journal of Economics* 113:1215–1244.

Machin, S. and A. Vignoles. 2001. The economic benefits of training to the individual, the firm and the economy: the key issues. Cabinet Office Report.

Machin, S. and A. Vignoles. 2004. Educational inequality: the widening socio-economic gap. *Fiscal Studies* 25:107–128.

Machin, S., S. McNally and C. Meghir. 2004. Improving pupil performance in English secondary schools: excellence in cities. *Journal of the European Economic Association* 2(2–3):396–405.

McIntosh, S. 2002. Further analysis of the returns to academic and vocational qualifications. Department for Education and Skills, Research Report 370.

Mackinnon, D. and J. Statham. 1999. *Education in the UK: facts and figures*, 3rd edn. London: Open University, Hodder and Stoughton.

McVicar, D. 2001. School quality and staying on: resources, peer groups and ethos. *Economic and Social Review* 32:131–151.

McVicar, D. and P. Rice. 2001. Participation in full-time further education in England and Wales: an analysis of post-war trends. *Oxford Economic Papers* 53:47–56.

Manski, C. 1987. Academic ability, earnings, and the decision to become a teacher: evidence from the national longitudinal study of the high school class of 1972. In *Public sector payrolls* (ed. D. Wide). University of Chicago Press.

Marsden, D. 2004. The role of performance-related pay in renegotiating the "effort bargain": the case of the British public service. *Industrial and Labor Relations Review* 57:350–370.

Micklewright, J. 1989. Choice at sixteen. *Economica* 56:25–39.

Milgrom, P. and J. Roberts. 1992. *Economics, organization and management.* Englewood Cliffs, NJ: Prentice Hall.

Mincer, J. 1974. *Schooling, experience and earnings.* New York: Columbia University Press (National Bureau of Economic Research).

Moretti, E. 2004. Estimating the social return to higher education: evidence from longitudinal and repeated cross-sectional data. *Journal of Econometrics* 121:175–212.

Mortimore, P. 1991. The nature and findings of school effectiveness research in the primary sector. In *School effectiveness research: its messages for school improvement* (ed. S. Riddell and S. Brown). London: HMSO.

Mortimore, P., P. Sammons, L. Stoll, D. Lewis and R. Ecob. 1988. *School matters: the junior years*. Wells: Open Books.

Moulton, B. 1986. Random group effects and the precision of regression estimates. *Journal of Econometrics* 32:385–397.

Muijs, D. and D. Reynolds. 2000. School effectiveness and teacher effectiveness in mathematics: some preliminary findings from an evaluation of the mathematics enhancement programme. *School Effectiveness and School Improvement* 11:273–304.

Muijs, D. and D. Reynolds. 2001. *Effective teaching: evidence and practice*. London: Paul Chapman.

Murnane, R. and D. Cohen. 1986. Merit pay and the evaluation problem: why most merit pay plans fail and a few survive. *Harvard Educational Review* 56:1–17.

Murnane, R., J. Willett and J. Tyler. 2000. Who benefits from obtaining a GED? Evidence from high school and beyond. *Review of Economics and Statistics* 82:23–37.

Murphy, J. 1993. A degree of waste. *Oxford Review of Education* 20:81–92.

Naylor, R., J. Smith and A. McKnight. 2002. Why is there a graduate earnings premium for students from independent schools? *Bulletin of Economic Research* 54:315–339.

Neuman, S. and A. Ziderman. 1999. Vocational education in Israel: wage effects of the VocEd–occupational match. *Journal of Human Resources* 34:407–420.

Neuman, S. and A. Ziderman. 2001. Vocational schooling, occupational matching and labor market earnings in Israel. *Journal of Human Resources* 26:256–281.

Nickell, S. and D. Nicolitsas. 2000. Human capital, investment and innovation: what are the connections? In *Productivity, innovation and economic performance* (ed. R. Barrell, G. Mason and M. O'Mahony). Cambridge University Press.

Nickell, S. and G. Quintini. 2002. The consequences of the decline in public sector pay in Britain: a little bit of evidence. *The Economic Journal* 112:F107–F118.

Noden, P., A. West and R. West. 2002. Mapping resources, assessing effects. Report to the Department for Education and Skills for the Excellence in Cities Evaluation, Report 06/2002.

Odden, A. and C. Kelley. 1997. *Paying teachers for what they know and do: new and smarter compensation strategies to improve schools*. Thousand Oaks, CA: Corwin Press.

OECD. 1999. *Education at a glance*, OECD Indicators 1999 edn. OECD.

OECD. 2001a. *Education at a glance*, OECD Indicators 2001 edn. OECD.

OECD. 2001b. *Knowledge and skills for life: first results from PISA 2000*. OECD

OECD. 2004. *Education at a glance*, OECD Indicators 2004 edn. OECD

Oliver, J. and J. Turton. 1982. Is there a shortage of skilled labour? *British Journal of Industrial Relations* 20:195–200.

Payne, J. 2001. Student success rates in post-16 qualifications: data from the England and Wales Youth Cohort Study. Policy Studies Institute (PSI) (London), mimeo.

Pissarides, C. 1981. Staying-on at school in England and Wales. *Economica* 48:345–363.

Pissarides, C. 1982. From school to university: the demand for post-compulsory education in Britain. *The Economic Journal* 92:654–667.

Pollard, A., P. Broadfoot, P. Croll, M. Osborn and D. Abbott. 1994. *Changing English primary schools: the impact of the Education Reform Act at Key Stage 1*. London: Cassell.

Psacharopoulos, G. 1973. *Returns to education: an international comparison*. Jossey-Bass, Elsevier.

Psacharopoulos, G. 1981. Returns to education: an updated international comparison. In *The economic value of education: studies in the economics of education* (ed. M. Blaug). International Library of Critical Writings in Economics, Vol. 17. Aldershot, UK: Edward Elgar.

Psacharopoulos, G. 1994. Returns to investment in education: a global update. *World Development* 22:1325–1343.

Psacharopoulos, G. and H. Patrinos. 2002. Returns to investment in education: a further update. World Bank Policy Research, Working Paper 2881 (September).

Reynolds, D., P. Sammons, L. Stoll, M. Barber and J. Hillman. 1996. School effectiveness and school improvement in the United Kingdom. *School Effectiveness and School Improvement* 7:133–158.

Rice, P. 1987. The demand for post-compulsory education in the UK and the effects of educational maintenance allowances. *Economica* 54:465–475.

Rice, P. 1999. The impact of local labour markets on investment in further education: evidence from the England and Wales Youth Cohort Studies. *Journal of Population Economics* 12:287–312.

Rivkin, S., E. Hanushek and J. Kain. 2002. Teachers, schools and academic achievement. National Bureau of Economic Research, revised version of Working Paper 6691 (available at http://edpro.stanford.edu/eah/eah.htm).

Robbins Report. 1963. *Committee on higher education. Report.* London: HMSO.

Robertson, I. and S. Downs. 1989. Work-sample tests of trainability: a meta-analysis. *Journal of Applied Psychology* 74:402–410.

Robinson, P. 1996. Rhetoric and reality: Britain's new vocational qualifications. Centre for Economic Performance, LSE, Special Report.

Robinson, P. 1997. Measure for measure: a critical note on the national targets for education and training and international comparisons of educational attainment. Centre for Economic Performance, LSE, Discussion Paper 355.

Rosen, S. 1977. Human capital: a survey of empirical research. In *Research in labor economics* (ed. R. G. Ehrenberg), Vol. 1. Greenwich, CT: JAI Press.

Rosenbaum, P. and D. Rubin. 1983. The central role of the propensity score in observational studies for causal effects. *Biometrika* 70:41–55.

Rosenthal, L. 2003. The value of secondary school quality. *Oxford Bulletin of Economics and Statistics* 65:329–355.

Roy, A. 1951. Some thoughts on the distribution of earnings. *Oxford Economic Papers* 3:135–146.

Rutter, M., B. Maughan, P. Mortimore and J. Ouston. 1979. *Fifteen thousand hours: secondary schools and their effects on children.* Shepton Mallet: Open Books.

Sammons, P. 1999. *School effectiveness: coming of age in the twenty first century.* Lisse, The Netherlands: Royal Swets & Zeitlinger.

Sammons, P., J. Hillman and P. Mortimore. 1995. *Key characteristics of effective schools: a review of school effectiveness research.* London University Institute of Education.

Schagen, S., D. Davies, P. Rudd and I. Schagen. 2002. *The impact of specialist and faith schools on performance.* Slough: NFER.

Schmitt, J. 1995. The changing structure of male earnings in Britain, 1974–88. In *Changes and differences in wage structures* (ed. R. Freeman and L. Katz). University of Chicago Press.

Schultz, T. 1961. Investment in human capital. *American Economic Review* 51:1–17.

Schultz, T. 1963. *The economic value of education*. New York: Columbia University Press.

Sianesi, B. 2003*a*. Comments on "Human capital in a global and knowledge-based economy. Part II. Assessment at the EU country level" by Angel de la Fuente. European Commission – Employment and Social Affairs DG, Brussels.

Sianesi, B. 2003*b*. Returns to education: a non-technical summary of CEE work and policy discussion. Institute for Fiscal Studies, mimeo.

Sianesi, B. and J. Van Reenen. 2003. The returns to education: macroeconomics. *Journal of Economic Surveys* 17:157–200.

Sloane, P., H. Battu and P. Seaman. 1999. Overeducation, undereducation and the British labour market. *Applied Economics* 31:1437–1453.

Smith, A. 1776. *An inquiry into the nature and causes of the wealth of nations*. London: Methuen.

Smith, D. and S. Tomlinson. 1989. *The school effect: a study of multiracial comprehensives*. London: Policy Studies Institute.

Smithers, A. and P. Robinson. 2003. Factors affecting teachers' decisions to leave the profession. Department for Education and Skills, Research Report 430.

Snower, D. 1996. The low-skill, bad-job trap. In *Acquiring skills: market failures, their symptoms and policy responses* (ed. A. Booth and D. Snower). Cambridge University Press.

Solon, G. 1992. Intergenerational income mobility in the United States. *American Economic Review* 82:393–408.

Solon, G. 1999. Intergenerational mobility in the labor market. In *Handbook of labor economics* (ed. O. Ashenfelter and D. Card), Vol. 3A. Amsterdam: Elsevier Science.

Solon, G. 2004. A model of intergenerational mobility variation over time and place. In *Generational income mobility in North America and Europe* (ed. M. Corak). Cambridge University Press.

Spence, M. 1973. Job market signalling. *Quarterly Journal of Economics* 87:355–374.

Spence, M. 1974. *Market signalling: informational transfer in hiring and related screening processes*. Cambridge, MA: Harvard University Press.

Spilsbury, D. 2002. Learning and training at work, 2001. Department for Education and Skills, Research Report 334.

Steedman, H. 1996. Measuring the quality of educational outputs: a note. Centre for Economic Performance, Discussion Paper 302.

Steedman, H. 1999. Report to the Department for Education and Employment: updating of skills audit data 1998. Centre for Economic Performance, LSE, Working Paper.

Steedman, H., S. McIntosh and A. Green. 2004. International comparisons of qualifications: Skills Audit update. Department for Trade and Industry, Research Report RR548.

Stiglitz, J. 1975. The theory of screening, education, and the distribution of income. *American Economic Review* 65:283–300.

Stinebrickner, T. 2001. A dynamic model of teacher labor supply. *Journal of Labor Economics* 19:196–230.

Teddlie, C. and D. Reynolds. 1999. *The international handbook of school effectiveness research*. London: RoutledgeFalmer.

Temple, J. 2001. Growth effects of education and social capital in the OECD countries. *OECD Economic Studies* 33:57–101.

Tsang, M. 1997. The cost of vocational training. *International Journal of Manpower* 18:63–89.

Turner, A. 2001. *Just capital: the liberal economy*. London: Macmillan.

Twist, L., M. Sainsbury, A. Woodthrope and C. Whetton. 2003. Reading all over the world: PIRLS national report for England. National Foundation for Educational Research.

Vignoles, A., F. Galindo-Rueda and L. Feinstein. 2004. The labour market impact of adult education and training: a cohort analysis. *Scottish Journal of Political Economy* (Special Issue on the Economics of Education) 51:266–280.

Vytlacil, E. 2002. Independence, monotonicity and latent index models: an equivalence result. *Econometrica* 70:331–341.

Walker, I. and Y. Zhu. 2001. The returns to education: evidence from the Labour Force Survey. Department for Education and Skills, Research Report 313.

Weiss, A. 1984. Determinants of quit behaviour. *Journal of Labor Economics* 2:371–387.

Weiss, A. 1995. Human capital versus screening explanation of wages. *Journal of Economic Perspectives* 9:133–154.

Wernimont, P. and J. Campbell. 1968. Signs samples and criteria. *Journal of Applied Psychology* 52:372–376.

West, A. and H. Pennell. 1999. School admissions: increasing equity, accountability and transparency. *British Journal of Education Studies* 46:188–200.

West, J. and H. Steedman. 2003. Finding our way: vocational education in England. Centre for Economic Performance, LSE, Occasional Paper.

Whitfield, K. and R. Wilson. 1991. Staying on in full-time education: the educational participation rate of 16 year olds. *Economica* 58:391–404.

Willis, R. 1986. Wage determinants: a survey and reinterpretation of human capital earnings functions. In *Handbook of labor economics* (ed. O. A. Ashenfelter and R. Layard). Amsterdam: North-Holland.

Willis, R. and S. Rosen. 1979. Education and self-selection. *Journal of Political Economy* 87:S1–S36.

Wills, J. (ed.). 1998. *Employers talk about building a school-to-work system: voices from the field*. American Youth Policy Forum and the Institute for Educational Leadership's Center for Workforce Development.

Wolf, A. 2002a. *Does education matter? Myths about education and economic growth*. London: Penguin.

Wolf, A. 2002b. Qualifications and assessment. In *A century of education* (ed. R. Aldrich). London: Falmer.

Wolf, A. and A. Jenkins. 2002. The growth of psychometric testing for selection: why has test use increased, will growth continue and what does this mean for education? Centre for the Economics of Education, Discussion Paper 29.

Wolf, A., A. Scharaschkin, H. Jones and J. Ghosh. 2000. *GNVQs 1993–97: a national survey report*. London: The Nuffield Foundation.

Zabalza, A., P. Turnbull and G. Williams. 1979. *The economics of teacher supply*. Cambridge University Press.

Zarkin, G. 1985. Occupational choice: an application to the market for public school teachers. *Quarterly Journal of Economics* 100:409–446.

Zimmerman, D. 1992. Regression toward mediocrity in economic stature. *American Economic Review* 82:409–429.

9 780691 117348